Christmas, 1999

To Baba —

From Scotland

to

Winnipeg

&

parts

between!

Enjoy

xx Heather.

THE DESIRE OF
EVERY LIVING THING

A Search for Home

DON GILLMOR

Random House Canada

Canadian Cataloguing in Publication Data

Gillmor, Don
    The desire of every living thing : a search for home

ISBN 0-679-30977-2

1. Gillmor, Don – Family.   2. Winnipeg (Man.) – Biography.
3. Winnipeg (Man.) – History.   I. Title.

PS8563.I59Z53 1999   C818'.5409   C99-931439-4
PR9199.3.G5425Z466 1999

Cover design: Spencer Francey Peters
Cover image: Jean and Georgina Ross at eleven,
    photograph courtesy of the Gillmor family
Text design: Gordon Robertson

Printed and bound in the United States of America

10 9 8 7 6 5 4 3 2 1

For my mother and father
and for Georgina Ivel Ross

The eyes of all look to thee,
and thou givest them their food in due season.
Thou openest thy hand,
thou satisfiest the desire of every living thing.

PSALM 145

God hath made man upright; but they have
sought out many inventions.

ECCLESIASTES 7:29

This is what history consists of. It's the sum total
of all the things they aren't telling us.

DON DELILLO, *Libra*

CONTENTS

Sunday   1

North of Eden   15

Lowland   37

The Imagined Hills   51

Fallen   67

Zetland   101

The Forty Years Agitation   131

Gateway to the West   161

Detroit   175

Depression   199

Flood   213

New Romans   237

Ascension   269

List of Illustrations   273

Acknowledgements   275

I

SUNDAY

FROM THE BACK of the Fort Garry
United Church that Sunday, my grandmother looked out on
rows of blond oak pews bolted to the floor and the unthreat-
ening backs of people's heads. A pale winter light was diffused
by beige translucent windows. There were hats still; it was
1962. Small dark hats that perched, hats with netting and
dried flowers and sombre ribbon. Furs were out at the first
opportunity, which in Winnipeg could be September. By December they were a fixture. One woman had a wrap with the
mink heads still attached. The jaw was hinged and the mouth
used as a clasp. The dead marble eyes stared across the congregation without rancour. The mink had its own fur in its

mouth, an act that seemed to imply loyalty, like a golden lab swimming to shore with a stick in its jaw.

Behind the varnished pulpit, his voice searching for the perfect monotone, Reverend Donald Ray read from Exodus, *And the Egyptians were urgent upon the people, that they might send them out of the land in haste; for they said, We be all dead men.* My grandmother sat with her hands folded around a small black cloth purse, her eyes widened in effort, blinking away sleep. Her Scottish brooch was pinned to her bosom and her hair curled in soft grey waves. Before the children of Israel were led by Moses, before God had drowned all the Egyptians *(And Israel saw the great work which the LORD did upon the Egyptians; and the people feared the LORD)*, my grandmother was asleep, her breathing occasionally hiccupping into a soft snore.

I sat beside her, eight years old, wearing a tan corduroy sports jacket that I was either growing into or out of, my father's tie dangling below my waist. My mouth was still bright with the flavour of eating Colgate toothpaste. *Damn shit shit piss.* These words went through my head involuntarily in galloping repetition. It was part of the reason I was in church; toothpaste hadn't banished them. My grandmother slept heavily beside me. We sat in the back pew with our separate sins.

My grandmother, Georgina Mainland, had been raised in the Free Presbyterian Church, which had taken its doctrine from Calvin, who believed that human beings were fundamentally corrupt and deserved to be damned. The Free Presbyterians disapproved of organ music and hymn singing and talking on Sunday. They disapproved of most things. It was a stark, wintry religion and was conducted in bleak brown churches, the antithesis of Rome's magnificent, frivolous cathedrals. As a child, my grandmother had lived on the northern coast of Scotland, at Fanagmore, a fishing village with only a few houses, the youngest of ten children. Her family came to Canada in 1905, when Georgina was six.

My grandmother now attended the United Church because it was handy and her friends went there. She was a soft, beneficent presence, her face unlined at sixty-two. But she held to certain Free Presbyterian ideas and felt personally at risk when my brother and I played Go Fish on Sunday at her house. Cards were the devil's tool.

The United Church didn't have the rigour and strict discipline of the Free Presbyterian Church. You didn't need to memorize anything or kneel or wear a hat. You didn't need to chant in Latin or confess or forsake your foreskin or shake hands with the person behind you or fall down speaking in tongues. And you didn't need a gift for music to sing the amelodious hymns. Formed in 1925, the United Church brought together Presbyterians, Methodists and Congregationalists. It wasn't a smooth transition and threatened to erupt into a minor Holy War, as it involved not only the division of faith but of property. If a majority of Presbyterians wanted to become United, then the church was turned over to them and the stalwart Presbyterians were left to build their own. Four decades after its inception, the United Church, in our sunny enclave at least, believed that a congregation could govern itself, without the tyranny of popes, bishops or kings. It was a convenient belief that in 1962 was given more to folk songs than to Hell, though there was some overlap. It was the ideal religion for an eight-year-old boy.

At least it was most of the time. The week before, the Sunday-school teacher, a tall, lank-haired man with an imposing

Easter Island face, had written on the blackboard, "Can God Decide the Outcome?" Beneath he had scrawled subheadings; Blue Bombers and Tiger-Cats. He listed the strengths of our fabled Winnipeg Blue Bombers football team. Kenny Ploen was the quarterback, a square-jawed hero. On football cards, he seemed to be looking not just downfield but into the future, the ball cocked behind his head. The mercurial Leo Lewis was in the backfield and the dependable Ernie Pitts at tight end. On the Ti-Cat side was Hamilton's lunchbucket defence, a feared, mauling crew led by the trash-talking Angelo Mosca. They were quarterbacked by Joe Zuger, whose very name was missile-shaped and threatening.

Football wasn't a regular topic. Most Sundays, I sat uncomfortably on the wooden stacking chairs in the church basement, checking the contents of my pockets, mouthing the words to hymns. Keeners stood up in their awkward dress clothes and rattled off the books of the Old Testament: Genesis, Exodus, Leviticus, Numbers, Deuteronomy, Joshua, Judges, Ruth. I whispered heresies and daydreamed.

But here the teacher was asking if we had done anything personally to jeopardize Winnipeg's chances in the Grey Cup. God would be watching the game, he said, but would He interfere? My teacher posed this theological conundrum and opened the floor to discussion. I twitched uncomfortably under his gaze and prayed for our defensive secondary. Would my sins pile up and thwart Kenny Ploen? Religion was in effect an accounting system: I could be punished for my sins, but a neighbourhood, a city or a football team could be punished as well, in the way an entire class was kept after school for one boy's mischief. My main hope came from our opponents. Surely people in that Dickensian, steel-producing city were more sinful than we were, their thoughts as polluted as the air. The Hamilton fans looked like a prison break, angry and threatening.

I was in church with my grandmother the day after the Grey Cup was played. At least most of it had been played. The game that year was in Toronto, at Exhibition Stadium near the shore of Lake Ontario. As we watched, a bewitching fog enveloped the field, a fog of such density that it was being discussed in church as divine intervention.

The game had begun in bright sunlight. Prime Minister John Diefenbaker had reluctantly and imperfectly performed the ceremonial kickoff, his wattled neck shivering in the early December air, stiff in his overcoat, his standard look of owlish peeve threatening to erupt. In the first quarter, the fog collected politely at the Hamilton end of the field, an innocent haze. But the warm air moving north over Lake Ontario formed a rolling fog that slowly engulfed the game, eclipsing the field by the third quarter. "Zuger's pass to Henley, I think, was incomplete, I think," the announcer said. "Tiger-Cats have second and ten on their own forty-five. Or forty, or thirty-five . . . The penalty is on Winnipeg, I think, for interference, I think. Correction, that's Winnipeg offside." On our black-and-white television, dull shapes loomed in dirty gauze.

By the third quarter none of the 32,655 fans at Exhibition Stadium could see the players, and most of them had left for home to listen to their radios. There was a forty car pile-up along the lakeshore. Eight people died in traffic that day. The Liquor Control Board of Ontario posted its largest weekend gross in history. Beneath the fog, at field level, the game was a bloody, mud-covered battle. By the fourth quarter, referee Paul Dojack couldn't see the ball.

Canadian Football League Commissioner G. Sydney Halter was left with a difficult decision. He had engineered a sale of the broadcast rights to a U.S. station, a historical event. It was the first time that Americans would see a Canadian football game on television. Now football fans in Detroit and Toledo and Albany were watching the muffled grey image, affirming that our game was inferior to the American game in every way, including weather. The day was lost, as far as Halter was concerned. Five minutes and thirty-one seconds into the fourth quarter, with the Bombers leading 28-27, Halter fulfilled the dismal foreordainment of his name and stopped the game. The remaining nine minutes and twenty-nine seconds were going to be played today.

The pending outcome sat in our church like a squirming child, distracting the fans, no one more than me. The best team from the East against the best in the West, divided by a single point with just under ten minutes to play. I tried to kill time by counting the lines in the grain of the oak pew in front of me, then counting the hats in the congregation, then the number of people in the choir. The country was conveniently linear and football divided it into blocs that were separated by the Manitoba/Ontario border. The Grey Cup carried with it the loose prejudice of geography, the arrogant, established East versus the brash, independent West. Winnipeg had played Hamilton for the championship three times in the last four years. Each time we were victorious.

Shitshitpissshit. I was in church now because I couldn't trust myself in Sunday school, where I thought these words would fly unbidden from my mouth. The order changed, the cadence quickened and the words stubbornly remained. I didn't know where they came from, the schoolyard or the devil, or why they stayed. God could have sent them, like a plague of locusts. In Sunday school I would be asked why the Bombers had gone with a two quarterback system (Kenny Ploen and Hal

Ledyard) or I would be asked to name the books of the New Testament in order and a string of obscenities would come out of my mouth like a tapeworm. Church with my grandmother was a safer bet. Church was passive; nothing would be asked of me except the twenty-five cents in the envelope in my pocket when the offering plate was passed.

The Reverend Ray conducted the service like a man hosting his first party, trying to attend to everyone's needs and wishing they would leave. He read his sermon without inflection and without looking up. God judged us but accepted us, the reverend said. God knew I was swearing, sometimes forty times a minute. He could look into my head as if the top had been cut away and the inside was a bowl of Scrabble tiles tumbling madly, spelling out every curse I'd ever heard.

The hymns for that day were posted on a small oak plaque at the front of the church, large black numbers arranged before the service started. Also listed was "Little Boxes," a song written by Malvina Reynolds and made popular by the folksinger Pete Seeger. The lyrics were mimeographed onto a white sheet and stuck inside the hymn books. After the sermon, the congregation rose, my grandmother awake now and among them, and we sang, "Little boxes on the hillside, little boxes made out of ticky-tacky. Little boxes, little boxes, little boxes all the same." We were led by the choir, which included my mother. The choir members all wore black gowns and my mother's bright red hair looked like the burning bush that had surprised Moses, on fire but not consumed.

Our house was made of ticky-tacky. We lived in Wildwood Park, an experimental development that used a series of U-shaped section roads built around a central park, separating pedestrian and vehicular traffic. It was possible to walk between any two houses without crossing a road. We were in contact with one another and isolated from the outside world, contained in a loop of the Red River and bordered by a private boy's school and a private golf course. For a child, it was a hermetic, enchanted world, though at eight, other thoughts were starting to encroach.

My paper route took me all over Wildwood, a uniform suburb of three essential designs and two subtle variations. Once every two weeks I collected the money from the customers and then sent it in to the *Free Press* who paid me in coupons that I could redeem for bicycles or record players. The previous week I had gone to a house the same design as ours and a woman came to the door in her bathrobe. Her hair was mussed and there were dots of perspiration on her upper lip. A man's voice came from upstairs, asking who was at the door. "It's the *Free Press*," she said, turning toward the voice, "collecting." When she turned, her robe opened slightly and I glimpsed her bare breast in profile, the shape of a pomegranate, sloping, perfect. She turned back to me.

"How much is it?" she asked.

"Two dollars." I stared into the box of cat litter on the landing.

"Oh, ah look, can you come back?"

"Okay."

The woman was in the congregation now, sitting straight as a stick, reaching for her hymn book and standing in one fluid, practised motion. She was wearing earrings with ivory cameos on them and a pastel-coloured dress. There were quite a few pastel dresses. The men in the congregation had dark suits, narrow ties and close-cropped Fred MacMurray haircuts, apparently interchangeable. Their white Arrow shirts arrived from Quinton's drycleaners folded in boxes with a paper band around them. The green Quinton's panel truck moved through the neighbourhood every Thursday making uniform deliveries to each home. Most were young parents, in their twenties and early thirties. Their children were below us, in Sunday school, singing "Onward Christian Soldiers" or handicapping the Grey Cup. I was one of the few among the adults. So we sang of little boxes made of ticky-tacky in our hats and mink wraps and stately green dresses and corduroy blazers from Eaton's; we sang of the forces that would bring change to our unblighted garden.

After the hymn, Reverend Ray talked briefly about people in other lands who were oppressed and hungry. In Sunday school we sometimes wrote to these people. ("Dear Friend, How is everything in Ethiopia? It's autumn here and the leaves are red.") Jesus was with us, he said. I hoped that if Jesus came to Winnipeg he would be preoccupied with the North End, where buildings were burning, the result, an uncle said, of Jewish lightning, a reference to landlords torching their unprofitable buildings for the insurance money. And where had the Children of Israel picked up this trick with the pillar of fire? It had worked with the Egyptians and it would work with the Great West Life Assurance Company. Gangs roamed the North End, but the food was good. This was the scuttlebutt; I had never been there.

Small shot glasses of Welch's grape juice were passed through the congregation on a tray and another tray was piled with pieces of Weston's enriched white bread. My grandmother didn't allow me to drink the grape juice because it represented wine, which in turn represented the blood of Jesus, a symbol itself of sacrifice. I chose a piece of bread, avoiding any with crusts. To keep from swearing, I used my tongue to probe my broken front tooth, the result of a bicycle accident. Along with swearing, it was a major preoccupation. Half the tooth was left and it had discoloured, making me look like a slow learner.

Trying to avoid a collision with another bicycle, I fell off my bike on the loose gravel of Manchester Boulevard. The road came up slowly, hitting my face, and I sat, dazed, with a shocking gap where my tooth had been. I had heard that you could reattach it if you got to a dentist within an hour. It took twenty minutes to find the missing piece of tooth in the gravel. It was cut diagonally and had growth spears pointing downward. I wrapped it in Kleenex and rode home weeping. My parents were out of town and my grandmother was waiting for me. She sat me on the couch and kneeled in front of me and looked up into my mouth. She was wearing a thin cotton dress with a floral pattern. The bustline sagged, revealing her generous bosom, a line disappearing into the fabric. It was slightly hypnotic. It was the first time that I imagined her to have been anything other than a grandmother.

Sitting beside me now in church, her view of the congregation was the inverse of Reverend Ray's. He saw hopeful faces glazing incrementally, where she saw the backs of stolid heads, whose posture and Sunday polish hid many things; sloth, envy, pride, perhaps even adultery. All of these were foreign to my grandmother. But she felt that the secret she carried inside was the greatest sin, the one closest to the Garden. It had a palpable weight, her sin, one that she had borne in silence for most of her life.

I didn't know anything of this though. I didn't know much about her life. She babysat me on occasion and was a comforting fixture. I had my own sins to worry about. In the dense woods between our house and the Red River, several acres of mystery, I had built a fort in the summer. It was ingeniously sited, almost invisible unless you wandered through the nettles.

The mud floor was covered with leaves. I had revelled in the forest solitude, reading books, inventing danger. One afternoon a girl from the neighbourhood had come to the fort with me. She was a year older. We took off all our clothes in increments in a hesitant ritual, standing finally in our underwear. Then, in a casual way, she stepped out of hers. Naked, she was both a revelation and a disappointment. I stared at her mysterious line, a quick slash of the pencil. Our bodies were identically white and thin and boyish and freckled. We both, I think, felt cheated by this coincidence. *Shitshitpissshit.*

The Benediction signalled the end of the service and collective relief. Men could soon return to their Black & Decker tools and to the game, those nine minutes and twenty-nine seconds that would dictate the extent of our civic pride for the next twelve months.

Outside the church the air still had the crispness of fall. Though it was the first week in December, it was above zero. The congregation mingled on the lawn, exchanging compliments and pleasantries, gently hawking insurance or gossip. Confetti from yesterday's wedding drifted along the sidewalk, the small pastel circles sparkling in the grass. I stared at the handsome calves revealed below conservative hemlines and wondered which brand of sin would be mine. My father the usher, my mother the choir member and my brother the heretic ("I don't want to be in God's army") exited late, joining my grandmother and me on the lawn.

"He was as good as gold," my grandmother said with a pat.

The nine minutes and twenty-nine seconds lasted an eternity. We were ahead by just a single point and our ranks had thinned from injury. In Toronto it was foggy today, too, a persistent blanket. Hamilton threatened to score on three occasions. Garney Henley shone for them. But Dick Thornton and Kenny Ploen held tough. We shut down Kuntz and Caleb and knocked Zuger out of the game. They tried desperately for a single point to tie, kicking for the end zone, but Kenny Ploen caught the ball on our two-yard line and knelt down as time expired. Even the Hamilton coach, Jim Trimble, complimented the western effort. "Those bastards played magnificently," he said. It was Winnipeg's fourth championship in five years. We were the centre of the world.

After the game we went to my grandmother's house for Sunday dinner. She bought odd cuts of meat that she roasted into asphalt and boiled vegetables for safety rather than flavour. She had the culinary esprit of her Scots heritage and a running feud with germs. Before church she made a bowl of lime Jell-O with a can of Del Monte fruit cocktail in it. She used Jell-O to preserve lesser foods, and like archaeologists we stumbled on celery, chicken, cabbage and marshmallows, stuck in that perfect, shivering translucence. After church she took lettuce, radishes and tomatoes and covered them with viscous orange Kraft French dressing and left them to compost in the rounded Viking refrigerator for three hours.

Her house was sepulchral, and seemed a separate universe. My brother and I killed the time before dinner throwing a tennis ball over the roof to one another. Down the street lived Mitchell Tulloch, the smartest kid in school. His head was heavy and his eyes bulged froggishly. He eventually went into physics and turned finally to religion, finding God in the ineluctable perfection of those equations.

My great-uncle, Jim Mainland, came for dinner too. He was my late grandfather's brother, a dapper man who was regularly compared to the late Prince of Wales for his ability to combine various checkered patterns. Jim had a spotless red Chrysler Imperial and went through red lights if there were no traffic because he didn't like to waste the gas required to stop and start. He once dropped my brother and me off without coming to a full stop. We spun onto the curb, falling over as Uncle Jim continued along the street. When he talked he stared straight ahead as if reciting something. A baseball fan, he would only listen to the National League on the radio because he believed the American League was riddled with Catholicism. It was thought that Jim had money. "It won't hurt to be nice to him," my grandmother told me. "Jewel your crown."

At the dinner table, we bowed our heads and my father said a solemn grace and we wrestled with a pot roast that had failed to escape the pillar of fire. *Pisspot shitpot shitpot piss.* The words ricocheted against the walls of my skull like grasshoppers in a jar. We shovelled our cinders and ate the vegetables that had been drowned in a boiling sea. And for what we were about to receive we were thankful.

2

NORTH

OF EDEN

WHEN TELEVISION was in black
and white and limited to two channels, when it still had a test
pattern and a lifespan like a fruit fly, dying each night and re-
born at breakfast, I believed that the commercials displaced
the programming for those two minutes that they were on.
They weren't interruptions; the drama continued, unseen,
while I watched the Aqua Velva ad. So the ads were especially
irritating, but they also gave the shows a sense of mystery they
wouldn't have had otherwise. What was Daniel Boone doing,
I wondered, while Kraft was demonstrating another alarming

recipe. The gaps were meaningful. They left room for speculation and debate.

The two sides of my maternal family, the Mainlands and Rosses, existed in a similar way. They were defined by the silences, the unseen drama. In the summer, when I was a child, there would be family gatherings at my grandmother's house. Great-aunts and great-uncles sat in wooden lawn chairs faded to pastel colours from the sun and sipped lemonade and ate devilled eggs and talked about politics and family. My brother and I went into the earthen-floored garage and played with my grandfather's First World War paraphernalia, gutting Germans and dodging bullets. When we tired of that game we sat in the garden, dipping rhubarb into a cup of white sugar, watching the adults as if they were theatre. The cadences of their conversation would rise in agreement and fall into conspiratorial tones when they talked of certain relatives. A second cousin by marriage, Max Chisvin, had once run a local scam where he persuaded cinema owners to raffle off a set of dishes where the take on the tickets would be split between the theatre owner and Max. His wife won the dishes each time and they took their routine to the next venue. Papoo, as my maternal grandfather's father had been called, also was cause for lowered voices. What was that about Papoo? Nothing. Eat your rhubarb.

Papoo was dead, though Gran, his wife, was still alive at ninety. She had spent twenty years sitting on the porch of their small bungalow, staring at the hedge, reciting Robbie Burns's poetry. "My heart's in the Highlands, My heart is no here. My heart's in the Highlands a-chasing the deer." Her final years were spent in the Nightingale nursing home, in the shadow of the Donald Street bridge, downtown. Occasionally my family would visit her there. In memory, the nursing home was dimly lit, cramped and labyrinthine, filled with despairing crones, though when I saw it many years later, converted to a home for unwed mothers, it was large and airy and reasonably bright. When we visited Gran, she was sitting in a wheelchair, under a plaid blanket, her skin stretched over her skull like a surgical glove. My mother coached my brother and me to go up and give her a kiss and we crossed the floor toward her like condemned men.

Gran had held on to her Highland heritage for her entire life, which wasn't unusual. Scottish immigrants who settled in Winnipeg after the turn of the century often described themselves as Scots, even though they had lived in Canada since they were children. The city had been founded by Highlanders. The T. Eaton Company carried Scottish papers and it employed several hundred Scots. The Scots community was insular and it recreated the idea of the Highlands in Canada, partly as a defence against the ideas of Russia, Poland and Scandinavia that competed around them. My homeland is bigger than your homeland. My grandmother retained this sense of Scotland, too, though she had left the country at the age of six.

She was born in 1899 and her life ascended with the century: a teenager during the Great War, dressed as a flapper in the Jazz Age, her sense of thrift hardened by the Depression, another war in the forties, then peace, only to be scandalized by the sixties. When the streets were laid out around the house my grandfather had built, the spaces were quickly filled with neat, optimistic boxes. My grandmother's twin sister Jean moved into one of them, on Windermere Avenue, a block away. Jean had married late and hadn't had children. She scoffed at Georgie's worries about germs, strangers and playing cards on the Sabbath.

It was Jean who took me to see *Pinocchio* on a Sunday, damning us both. We sat at the back of the Garry Cinema so she could smoke. She lit a Black Cat and I ate licorice whistles as we watched the lumbering Freudian lark: a boy made by his father. Sitting deep in the plush seat, engulfed by the vast luxury of that blackness, the Garry Cinema was the most comforting place I had ever been. The whale terrified me, and I feared for Pinocchio, in this, my first brush with commercial drama. Jean smoked and watched me watching the wooden boy. After the movie we walked the half block to her house and she made me a meatloaf sandwich and gave me a colouring book and some pencils. A vaguely anarchic presence, she told me not to worry about staying inside the lines.

My grandmother, on the other hand, took me downtown on the Point Road bus and made me practise getting up and offering my seat to women, even when there were other seats available. Crippled by embarrassment, I approached women who were almost seated, pointing to my seat like a mute, my face crimson. They gave me a sympathetic smile. Downtown, my grandmother and I took the elevator to the top floor of Eaton's and slowly worked our way to the basement. We looked at furniture, sportswear, porcelain figurines, umbrellas, paint and cheese. We examined rubber boots, flatware, skin cream and toasters. She surveyed the prices as a form of entertainment and rarely bought anything. We ended our tour in the dark wood-panelled Grill Room where I ate red Jell-O among the other victims.

Georgie and Jean bickered regularly but Jean held the upper hand; she had a quick tongue and a worldly veneer. Before she finally married Leslie Barratt, she had played the field. In photographs of her as a young woman she had a darting fox-like presence, a capricious air next to the responsible weight of Georgina. Jean had utterly rejected the strict Free Presbyterianism of the family. She smoked and flirted, dancing her way through a large, looser landscape, while my grandmother retained the narrow righteousness of Scotland.

When my grandmother babysat my brother and me and our baby sister, we tried to take advantage of her trusting disposition, claiming that we were allowed to sleep in the yard and eat my mother's baking chocolate. When her patience was exhausted, she chased my brother and me to the room we shared and whacked us with a wooden spoon. Spare the rod, she repeated as she flailed the shapes under the bedclothes, the spoon ineffective through the thick blankets.

When I was sixteen, my family moved to Calgary and I stayed in Winnipeg for the summer, working on a construction crew and living with my grandmother. Sometimes on weeknights, I went out with friends to bars on Pembina Highway to drink beer. The drinking age was twenty-one, but I was tall, a hair over six feet, and thickened slightly by construction work. Our fake IDs had come from a high school classmate who was born in the Yukon. His birth certificate was a simple piece of paper rather than the laminated card most of us had. We copied it, then used white out to erase the particulars. We made multiple copies of the blank form then typed in different names and birthdays. We folded them into wallet-sized squares and ironed the creases with a damp towel covering them. After soaking the fake certificates in tea to age them, we crumpled them into balls and put them into the dryer on the gentle cycle, then reironed them along the creases. That summer, the taverns along Pembina Highway were peopled by twenty-one-year-old boys from the Yukon with names like Ignatz Schitt and Jack Meoff.

We drank at the Montcalm and the Voyageur taverns, sipping our twenty-five-cent draft beer and listening to cover bands. It was an incomparably adult world. At the Voyageur Tavern a 300-pound stripper named U.C. Moore wrapped her awning-sized panties around the head of a friend, leaving us horrified and titillated.

My grandmother's house would be dark when I came home and I'd stand in the kitchen, eating the sandwiches she had prepared for the next day's lunch, drinking milk from the plastic gallon container in the refrigerator, holding it by the red plastic handle and slinging it over my forearm like a jug of moonshine. I'd eat the cookies she'd packed while feeling my way up the incredibly steep stairway, answering that it was me when my grandmother called out. She kept a majorette's baton in her dresser as a defence against burglars. She rose at 5 a.m. and did forty-five seconds of calisthenics, lying on her back and bicycling her legs in the air.

At 6 a.m., dreading work, the persistence of the jackhammer, I sat at the Formica table in the kitchen with my grandmother and listened to the morning man on CJOB. Idiots phoned in to explain civic politics in broad personal anecdotes. The sun was up, a red prairie sunrise, and the air was fresh before the heat. My grandmother made me another lunch and warned me that she would start hiding the sandwiches if I didn't quit eating them at night. Where would she hide them, I wondered. It was July and ninety degrees.

She also warned me not to trade lunches with the Galicians, a blanket term for any foreign-seeming people. They ate different parts of the animal than we did, she said, inexplicable parts. Her sandwiches were soggy, thin white bread and a single slice of processed cheese, or pale packaged cold cuts. The construction crew were mostly Italians who took out elaborate soups and roasted chickens and fruit and pizza from their lunch buckets. There weren't any offers to trade.

I waited for the bus on Pembina Highway, but rarely caught it. Usually someone from the crew driving down from the North End would see me and stop. I sat in the cluttered, dusty backseats of Dodge Darts or Chevrolet Malibus, not saying anything, enjoying those twenty minutes before work as much as any time I had known. The minutes were delicious, ending when my card received the staccato approval of the punch clock. We were building a new biology centre on the University of Manitoba campus. I cleaned the forms used to pour concrete and pulled nails from two-by-fours. Sometimes I helped pour concrete, shovelling it into the forms until my arms were numb. On my first day on the job, I was pouring concrete on the top floor, sweating in the July sun, parched. A man came by and said, "Coffee." I didn't understand. "Coffee," he said impatiently. He had a pencil and was writing on a small board. "I'm taking orders." Who drinks coffee when it's ninety degrees? I wondered. But it would be better than nothing. It would be wet at least. I could let it cool. "Coffee," I nodded. He scurried away. Half an hour later he came back with a wooden tray that was filled with cold Cokes and Seven-Ups and Pepsis, the condensation beaded up on the icy aluminum, and one coffee.

When I came home from work, I had a bath and scrubbed the cement dust from my arms. My grandmother stood outside the bathroom door, reminding me that cleanliness was next to godliness; though she thought I used too much hot water. "The King of England bathed in three inches of water during the war," she said. But who checked?

On those few occasions when we had guests for dinner, we ate in the dining room. When Uncle Jim came over, he and I sat taciturnly at the table while Georgie fussed in the kitchen. He wasn't one of those chatty uncles who asked you about school and teased about girlfriends and said my God you're about big enough to burn diesel. His silence was a bit unnerving. As my grandmother walked down the narrow corridor between the kitchen and the dining room, carrying a damp salad and a dark roast, Jim said to me, "She poisoned my brother, you know." Georgie set everything down and we said grace.

Jim would later go mad in an entertaining way. For those burdened with his care it wasn't entertaining, certainly, but from our remove, his eccentricity lent itself to anecdote. He felt that thieves had targeted him. He began hiding his money in his house, filling odd places with cash. Then he'd forget where he hid the money and was sure he had been robbed. He phoned the police, who came on occasion to help him look for the stolen money. His obsessions diminished, from cash, which he was no longer trusted with, to hiding the refill blades for his razor. But, in Georgie's dining room that summer, he was a dapper enigma.

After dinner the three of us sat on the sofa and watched television. The sofa was undersprung and we sank into the cushions, staring past our knees at the black-and-white image on the television. Georgie quickly fell asleep and Jim and I sat in silence, watching a plodding drama.

My immediate family was already in Calgary and I would be there in September. My school friends would be left behind and, though I felt a tinge of melancholy, I felt a sense of freedom too. My grandmother was at a generational remove; she never suspected that I was in the Voyageur Tavern, drinking draft beer, or playing pool for money at Garry Billiards or exploring Laurie Henning's panties on a basement couch. Those two months were spent in a warped version of adulthood. I worked at a job that was measured in slow, painful minutes and spent much of my money on room and board. I was largely self-sufficient. I was going to be moving on.

When we didn't have guests, which was most of the time, my grandmother and I had dinner at the kitchen table, the back door open to let in a breeze. We argued about French Canada and its position on conscription during the war, her with the resentment of the war generations, me with the certitude and ignorance of a teenager. My grandmother had a family photo album that we looked through on occasion, black-and-white Kodak snapshots of babies and young parents. There were older sepia pictures from the twenties as well. In one of them, my grandmother and grandfather were standing beside a Ford Model T. It was taken in Detroit, where they lived for six years. My grandmother is wearing a low-waisted flapper dress and my grandfather has an oversized straw hat set at a jaunty angle and a vanilla-coloured three-piece summer suit. They looked optimistic, I thought. My grandmother told me that she worked as an assistant buyer in the children's department of Hudson's, a department store. She had once gone on a buying trip to New York and had eaten at a famous Chinese restaurant. She remembered the bustle of New York. It had exhilarated her.

I couldn't imagine her in the newsreel world of America in the Roaring Twenties. She had been an installation in my own life, a reliable presence. Few things are less mysterious to a sixteen-year-old than his grandmother.

When she was eighty-four, Georgie collapsed in her bathroom and was unable to get up. The bulb of bone at the end of her femur had deteriorated to the point where it wouldn't support her weight. It had begun to dissolve years earlier, becoming porous, wearing away like a pothole in the rain. It had been uncomfortable at first, then in increments it became more painful, though she hadn't mentioned anything. Now she was lying on the cold tile, white, with a black border. An hour passed. She hadn't left the kettle on, thank goodness. The pain moved out from her hip, rising upward like a tide. The downstairs was clean, that was something. It was Thursday. On Sunday, Mrs. Mansell would come by and ring the bell to pick her up for church.

Was she numb? The pain gathered when she adjusted herself, a sudden glare, like a flashbulb going off, then subsided. What hymns would they sing on Sunday? Last week it had been, "Silence! Frenzied, Unclean Spirit." *Lord the demons still are thriving in the grey cells of the mind . . .* What was the next line? She couldn't remember. Her mind wandered. That boy who had chased her with the garter snake. He ran as if the snake were leading him, yelling, his tongue flicking like the snake's. A terrible boy. She was still afraid of snakes, seventy-five years later. The hardwood floors had been polished with Murphy soap on Monday. Cleanliness was next to godliness. And the basement had been painted in the spring. She had mixed together the remains of four cans of paint, oil-based and water-based, the colour like clay. No point in throwing it away.

Was this what God had planned for her? A curious end. Staring up at the light fixture, crumpled on the spotless, cold tile. Who can fathom His ways. Remember the Ingmansens, right across the street from Jean. The daughter was odd, Lois, that was her name. She used to ride the Point Road bus occasionally, huddled as if she was hiding from someone. Georgie saw her less often, then eventually not at all. A plain girl. The mother was mad as a hatter. Perhaps it was something in the blood. But Mr. Ingmansen seemed fine. One January night, their furnace went out and Mr. Ingmansen went down to the basement to see what the problem was and dropped dead of a heart attack right on the spot. Two days later the police forced the door of the house. The neighbours called when they noticed the walk hadn't been shovelled. Well, they found poor Mr. Ingmansen dead as a stone in the basement and not that old, not sixty. The house was colder than an icebox; it was minus thirty-five outside. Mrs. Ingmansen was up in her bed, frozen to death. Her eyes were wide open, they were that blue, like the spring sky. Her mouth was drawn back, as if she had one final curse to get out. Lois had gotten the oven working and was kneeling in front of it in her nightgown. Her fingernails were three inches long and her hair was as matted and dirty as an animal's. She didn't say a word when the police put old Mrs. Ingmansen's coat over her shoulders and led her out to the car. Poor thing, as wild as nature. You couldn't anticipate God's plan. Which was just as well.

The cold tiles were hard on her arthritis. She couldn't move now. There was a numbness. The Eaton's white sale was today. Percale sheets thirty per cent off. Not that she needed them but she liked to inspect the savings. She sang from "Rock of Ages." *Rock of Ages, cleft for me, let me hide myself in thee.* Her daughter thought she sang too loud in church. But she couldn't sing loud enough now. Maybe she would be heard. She may have slept for a few minutes, or was it an hour. She was colder. A horse had died of sunstroke on Pembina Highway. It was during the Depression and no rain, just that heat every day, but she couldn't imagine that heat now, lying on the cold tile.

She had lived with trouble, with a burden. But everyone did, she supposed. She thought about Pat Glover, who had lived next door. Her husband was the quiet type, a stock-broker. He called one day, the first time he had ever called. It was 1950 maybe, after the war anyway. His voice was heavy and panicked, as if suddenly he wished he hadn't been so quiet all his life. He asked Georgie to come over right away. Something awful had happened, he didn't know how but it had and could she just come over. When she went next door, Pat was lying on the floor and blood was everywhere. Georgie ran to get a towel and there in the kitchen sink was a butcher knife, covered in blood.

He said he never meant for it to be like this. Though what he'd meant was for it to be worse. He said he thought it would be peaceful. But it wasn't peaceful for Pat, having her husband stab her in the back with a butcher knife. Georgie phoned Winnie, Les Barratt's sister, who lived on the other side of Pat. She was a nurse, she'd know what to do. Goodness what a mess, like slaughtering cattle. Georgie did what she could for Pat, all the time wondering if her husband wouldn't suddenly try and finish the job. Winnie came and then the ambulance and they got Pat to the Misercordia in time and she wasn't the same exactly but it was the shock as much as anything.

What came out was her husband was the treasurer of the curling club and he had used the club's money to invest in the stock market. A sure thing. Of course it wasn't a sure thing and the annual audit was coming up and the money was gone and he thought the only solution was to kill his wife and then kill himself. Except when that knife went in, the flesh offering no more resistance than warm butter, he lost his nerve. He certainly wasn't going to stab himself. He could see that. It was just another poor decision. You made decisions every day, then you made the wrong one and you atoned. That was all that was left. You atoned every day.

Georgie hadn't made any bad decisions, but still she atoned, didn't she? That was what you'd have to call it. It was funny that the neighbourhood was so quiet. People kept themselves to themselves, but when you looked back you saw all these events. All that effort to keep things neat, to do the laundry, keep the house swept, every part of your life arranged in rows because sooner or later something would blow through that would leave a messy trail. All the right angles that had been so carefully laid would be reduced to a shambles. Bing, who owned the Chinese restaurant on the corner, and his son as smart as a whip. Bing was laying a bet down on a horse one day and collapsed. And that was that. She didn't eat there very often. You never knew with restaurants. They were always serving leftovers and calling it something else. And those colours; the food looked like a rainbow.

They had worried about the Great Flood in 1950. The Red River quietly rose up, each day gaining a little and they weren't that far away. But her husband Don had built on high ground. The water filled the government ditch that ran off the river but it didn't take the house; though it covered entire neighbourhoods. Every Sunday, the minister in the United Church talked about helping those whose lives were devastated. Georgie couldn't help but think that God was exercising His Judgment here.

From the floor she could see the plumbing under the sink. Water was condensing on the pipe and below it there was a yellow stain where the water had dripped over the years. You wouldn't be able to find a replacement tile now. Don had built the house fifty years ago. Never had a mortgage on it. They lived within their means. When they had company and she baked a pie, Don used to go down to the basement and come up with a saw to cut it. My how they'd laugh.

She thought of the trip she took to Scotland in 1977. There had been a piper at Ullapool. She went into a pub there, the first one she had ever been in. It wasn't what she had expected. There wasn't the sense of desperate sin that she held in her head. You didn't have to drink if you didn't want to and the people were pleasant and well-dressed. Inverness was pretty, though the Queensgate Hotel was expensive. They should have found somewhere cheaper. She never took her eyes off Loch Ness but the monster didn't appear. Culloden was so sad, reading those billboards on the battlefield. Men butchered where they lay.

They drove to Scourie on the north coast, and then to Fanagmore, where she had been born. She had left the house when she was six but she picked it out, a two-storey white house with a chimney at each end. It sat on the shore of Loch Laxford, which went out to the sea.

The roads were narrow and the hills a rich green. There were beaches, a surprise. Looking for traces of departed relatives, they had been invited into a variety of isolated homes by helpful locals. She remembered sherry and tea and warm scones and loneliness like a gaping wound. That woman asking if Georgie would send her a Christmas card, her hair like black wires, her eyes held open as if against a strong wind.

In the Free Presbyterian Church in Scourie, the service had been conducted by an elder; the minister had twisted his knee and couldn't come. It was the same church she had gone to as a child, a varnished wooden interior like the inside of a ship. And what a coincidence that the bed and breakfast she stayed in was the very house her family had stayed at in 1905 when they began their journey to Canada, ten of them sleeping in a hopeful pile. She felt like the prodigal child.

She heard Les at the front door. Jean's husband, he had his own key. A good man, patient as the day, but then you'd have to be. He called upstairs. She could hear his footsteps on the hardwood stairs. Her dress was clean. She was tired.

———————

At the hospital, she was told that the bone had deteriorated to a point that wouldn't allow her to walk again. In some cases, it was possible to graft a plastic bulb onto the bone, but her condition had advanced too far. She would have to sell the house and move to a nursing home. When my mother made arrangements to move her into West Park Manor out near the zoo, she noticed that the date on my grandmother's birth certificate wasn't the same date we celebrated as her birthday and she was a year younger than we thought. When my mother asked about this discrepancy, my grandmother told her a story. It came out in hesitant sentences, a secret that had been held in for eighty years. It emerged relatively intact. It hadn't been edited and polished, perhaps because it had never been told before; it was the original version.

Georgina told my mother that she wasn't the youngest child in a large family, she wasn't Jean's twin. She wasn't even Jean's sister, in fact. Jean was her aunt. Georgie was the illegitimate child of the oldest Ross daughter, Catherine, who had been working as a cook in Edinburgh when she met a Highland Rail worker named George Ivel. They had an affair, though Georgie didn't use that word. They had met, simply, and when Catherine discovered she was pregnant, she returned alone to the family in Fanagmore. She sat in the house and waited. When the baby was born, she named her Georgina Ivel Ross.

My grandmother's story proceeded in increments, and some of it was later filled in by a kind of familial triangulation. Catherine's reputation was ruined in that small town of Free

Presbyterians. When the baby was a year old, the mother was sent to South Africa to recapture her virginity. The family stayed for five more years and Georgie's secret spread past the church and percolated through the community. In 1905, Lachlan Ross gathered the clan and they walked the four miles to Scourie, trudging over the low hills, heads down against the wind, the older children helping the young ones. In Scourie, they stayed the night at the MacKay home, the future bed and breakfast of my grandmother's homecoming, then took a carriage to Ullapool and the train to Glasgow. From there they went to the New World to remake themselves.

On the boat over, a fellow passenger mistook Georgie and Jean for twins. They were a year apart in age, Georgie six and Jean seven. And so twins they became. This decision involved the collusion of the whole family, including the newly minted twins. At a pre-school age, they had embarked on a secret that would affect them all. The twinning offered a practical solution and it also granted a psychological respite from illegitimacy. As a twin, Georgie became a sort of immaculate conception. Her arrival, like those infants brought by storks or found under cabbage leaves, sidestepped sin.

The crossing was miserable and took longer than expected. The Atlantic was a mountainous grey landscape that seemed always to be moving toward the ship. They brought little with them.

—————

My family weren't the only ones, certainly, who had come to Canada to remake themselves. The Old World, all of the various Old Worlds, are littered with discarded names, crimes, families, identities, nationalities, religions. My grandmother's secret was easily concealed from the larger world but impossible to keep among the clannish Scots expatriates in Winnipeg. Although my relatives were sometimes ungenerous with this information, they guarded it from the next generation.

My family greeted the news of Georgina's illegitimacy with surprise, but regarded it as without moral significance. Catherine's sin was a crucial one in the Free Presbyterian Church and it reflected on Georgie. Perhaps she had moved to the United Church, a much diluted version of her family's faith, as a hedge. My parents attended the United Church until middle age, then quietly drifted. My siblings and I abandoned the church at the earliest opportunity. What had been of crushing consequence to my grandmother was a social commonplace to her grandchildren. But her sense of hidden sin shaped her and it shaped the family and it followed them through the featureless landscape they had chosen.

What surprised us about her admission was that she had a complicated history. To me, she had always been a comfy presence, uneventful and benign. Her Scots background spoke of solidity. When quizzed about my own heritage, I usually claimed Ireland, where my father's paternal line had come from. The Irish were romantic and literary, tragic and musical, all of these being attractive traits. I had been there and seen its lush, impaired history. I associated Scotland with porridge and thrift. My grandmother was always ready with Scottish maxims, "Waste not, want not." And now this new wrinkle, though there had been other, minor family scandals. Over the years there had been mumbled references to Papoo—Peter Mainland, Georgina's father-in-law and my great-grandfather. He might have liked a wee nip now and again. He had been a contractor, more or less. Not a rogue per se, a gentleman almost. When surveying a job site, he sometimes dressed formally, in tails, as if he were on his way to advise King Edward on etiquette. Peter was vaguely sketched, too distant really to be a black sheep. My grandmother's illegitimacy skewed the historical line, opening up a new line of inquiry.

―――――――

When my grandmother arrived in Winnipeg in 1905, the city was without any history in the European sense. There was almost a century of hardship surrounding it, but the city itself had only been incorporated in 1873, barely a generation earlier. The centuries of native history were discounted by the immigrants who weren't interested in the previous century or genocide. They'd had enough of that back home. The land was without myth too, partly the result of the empty geography. There was nowhere to hide a mythology, no forests or mountains. The plains shone in an unmysterious vista. My grandparents had come to a place that hadn't been invented yet, though it was busy trying.

As students in Oakenwald Elementary School, we had celebrated Winnipeg's status as the fourth-largest city in the country. The nearest of the three larger cities was more than 1,200 miles away; we existed in happy isolation, kingly on the expansive prairie. We studied the city's centrality. We didn't learn that at the turn of the century both Winnipeg and the surrounding farmland were advertised heavily to Americans, Ontarians and Europeans, using the language, emphasis and ethics of television pitchmen selling discount furniture. The city was inventing itself and both the Mainland and Ross families were doing the same thing, on a smaller scale.

My grandparents came to the plains from a place that had a surfeit of history and mythology. The Highland population had been decimated by the Clearances in the eighteenth and nineteenth centuries; farmers were forcibly removed from their land to make way for sheep. The Scottish bid for independence had been crushed in the failed Jacobite Rebellion of 1745, and there is nothing like proud defeat to create a romantic history. As with the American Confederacy, myth is the sustaining force of the Highlands. The landscape is ideal; the dramatic views and raw, violent weather seem like they're from another era. The Highlands have been emigrated from in large numbers, and those who left have recast it as either a romantic place or a source of eternal rectitude.

Three of my four grandparents came from the Scottish Highlands or islands. Evoked in nostalgic tones, the homeland came to resemble a landscape from a Grimm's fairy tale; mountainous, fierce, covered in mist, populated by monsters. This childish construct wasn't wholly inaccurate. In 1380, John of Fordham wrote that, "The Highlanders and people of the islands are a savage and untamed race, rude and independent, given to rapine, ease-loving, clever and quick to learn, comely in person and unsightly in dress, hostile to the English people and language and, owing to this diversity of speech, even to their own nation." The tribalism that formed the character of the Highlanders is often cited as a root cause for their eventual decline. In the end, they were their own most effective enemy, a trait the Highlanders share with many families.

Highland history seems to narrow to a point where leaving was inevitable. My ancestors survived the Clearances and the systematic destruction of the clan system; they left finally when the weight of their personal history was too much to bear. Georgina's husband, Donald Mainland, left the Shetland Islands at around the same time as my grandmother's family emigrated from the Highlands. But the Mainlands left for different, larcenous reasons. Don's father, Peter Mainland, had driven the family farm into bankruptcy and had left a trail of bad debt, legal actions and ill will. Both families came to Winnipeg at the turn of the century, which claimed to be the fastest growing city in North America. It was certainly one of the most optimistic. But that unbounded optimism dimmed after the First World War and the growth slowed. Eventually Winnipeg, too, became a city that people left, a place that lives vividly in nostalgia.

Winnipeg was drawn into perspective every summer when we left it to drive south to St. Paul, Minnesota, to visit my uncle—through Morris, Emerson, Oslo and Bagley and thousands of square miles of durum wheat. We made these trips south in a Chevrolet Corvair, a sporty, low-riding car with a sense of Californian panache. It had an air-cooled rear engine and a tiny lever on the dashboard that served as the stick shift. It was sleek and minimalist and would soon be identified as the unsafest car on the road by Ralph Nader. The front end was light and came off the pavement in strong crosswinds, offering no protection in the event of a head-on collision, and oil fumes leaked into the passenger compartment. But for a child of a certain age, there is no place that is safer, no place more lulling, than the back seat of your parents' car, driving down a highway at night. It is a dreamy, mobile cocoon. There was the rhythmic feel of the wheels hitting the small gaps in the highway that had been left to accommodate the contraction and expansion of the asphalt that came with our extreme climate. And there was the earnest hum of the radio. The back seat folded down to form a raised platform and it was on this platform that I lay with my siblings as we drove, staring out the window at the night sky, imagining my life on a larger scale, perhaps in the company of a famous actress.

It was an easy thing to imagine New York, or Paris, or Lilliput, but it was hard to imagine my own landscape, which was so burdened by reality. And it was hard to imagine myself within it. What accident of history and migration had delivered me to the back seat of the unsafest car on the road, flying past Ste-Agathe and Crookston and Mentor with the nascent, uneasy marriage of Calvinism and larceny sitting within me like two strangers on a train who are trying to avoid conversation. How did I come to the howling, blank prairie?

My grandparents embodied many of the qualities of the city as they all moved uncertainly through the century. The traits that personified my maternal family were diametric: the Rosses with their well-developed sense of hell and hesitant thoughts of heaven; the Mainlands and their more immediate fear of the policeman's knock at the door. Both had come to Winnipeg with the sense of renewal that propaganda encourages. Neither found salvation, but, against all probability, they found one another. In some ways I inherited their city, and with it, their yearning to leave.

My family, like most families, like most countries, is a daisy chain of anecdote, rumour and secrets that recedes into the dim past. Stories are retailed and embellished. Family members are revised, made more charitable or more colourful. On my mother's side, my grandmother is the still centre of the family history, the stationary object around which everything revolves. Her illegitimacy was, I think, the central fact of my grandmother's life and she bore it like a stone in her shoe, quietly, with a sense of responsibility. She had a quality of innocence, a rarity in adults. When the Ross family came to Winnipeg to re-make themselves, Georgie remained the living emblem of Scotland and their troubles there. So I headed toward the Highland landscape that had formed her and the religion that had briefly sustained her, and returned to Winnipeg, tracing the thin line of blood.

3

LOWLAND

IN GLASGOW the rain was intermittent and the city was a chiaroscuro of greys, the dark grey of the wet buildings set against the lighter grey of the sky. I had been to Glasgow once before, with my family when I was fifteen, a sullen, unlovely age. I remembered the city as besmirched, its buildings black with grime. Now they were clean, sandblasted and scrubbed, the surfaces scoured with swirls that resembled isobars on a weather map. We had landed in Scotland as the starting point for a three-week tour of Europe. Glamorous locales awaited—Paris, Venice—but first we had to find the town that my grandmother had been born in, which was located, inconveniently, on the north coast. The people were so charming; this was the mantra in our cramped rental car. It was repeated after almost every stop, after sparkling sexagenarian waitresses had brought us meat and fish for breakfast, with pale eggs in a shallow pool of water. I had argued against this adventure, chafing to get to Paris. And now I was back, essentially following the same trail. It was early May, though it felt like February.

On occasion, my grandmother had warned me of Lowland Scots, a prejudice that she had received through her Highland roots. Samuel Johnson wrote of the enmity between the two groups: "By their Lowland neighbours they would not willingly be taught; for [the Highlanders] have long considered them as a mean and degenerate race."

I stayed at the Rennie Mackintosh Hotel, named for the city's most famous architect. It wasn't designed by Mackintosh but the building was inspired by him, the woman at the night desk said. "It's what he would have designed had he been alive," she told me. Much is inspired by Mackintosh in the city that spurned him eighty-five years ago. His signature motifs are everywhere, the small aligned squares that mark some of his work are seen at the airport coffee shop, on buildings and posters. Across the street from the hotel was Mackintosh's most famous building, the Glasgow School of Art. The east wing was completed in 1899, the year my grandmother was born. A pamphlet advertising a tour of the school described the building as "the first important architectural monument to the Modern Movement in Europe."

I took the tour of the school, conducted by a woman in her early seventies, perhaps five feet tall, sweet and occasionally confused. She pointed to pieces of Mackintosh-designed furniture that weren't there, beginning her description of them and fluttering to a halt in front of the empty space. "They keep moving them and not telling me," she said. Mackintosh had designed all the furniture and fixtures for the school and the result was a wonderfully integrated, impressively functional whole. Two of the main rooms were temporarily closed, our guide announced, a disappointment. More depressing was the story of Mackintosh's tragic life, which the guide relayed with a genuine sense of melancholy.

After his initial success, Mackintosh and his progressive, functional ideas were largely ignored in Glasgow. The country was too conservative in its tastes and his commissions quickly dried up. In 1927, he was diagnosed with cancer of the tongue and he died horribly a year later, unloved by the architectural world. His estate, including the furniture he had designed, was valued at eighty pounds.

But he had been reclaimed with a vengeance. A couple of years ago a writing desk he had designed was auctioned for $750,000. An extensive exhibition of his work was touring the United States, appearing at the Museum of Modern Art, the Art Institute of Chicago and the L.A. County Museum in Los Angeles. He was being lauded abroad after his rejection almost a century ago. The tour guide pointed to a photograph of him and noted the romantic cast of his features. His story filled me with the kind of sadness that is easily nurtured when travelling alone in a country given to light rain.

I had lunch at Princes Square, a beautifully renovated mall where the tables of the upscale food court looked onto an atrium. On the main floor, Craig McMurdo, billed as Mr. Wonderful, was singing Tony Bennett songs with a sweeping, postwar dance band largesse. A trio of women harmonized behind him. A couple got out on the open floor and jitterbugged with kaleidoscopic precision and dazzling speed. The boy was maybe eighteen, with braces on his teeth and a grim, pugnacious face that communicated the idea that his marvellous dancing ability was a revenge upon those who had scorned him.

In the afternoon, I walked to the St. Mungo Museum of Religious Life & Art. Religion had played such a fundamental role in my grandmother's life. Mungo was the patron saint of the city of Glasgow, the first to bring Christian faith to the area in the sixth century. His mother was a saint as well. She was a Christian who turned down the marriage arranged by her father, the King of the Lothians, and, as a result, was cast out to become a swineherd. She was raped by her spurned suitor and when her pregnancy showed, her father ordered her thrown down from a mountain. She and the unborn child both survived and were set adrift in the Firth of Forth in a boat with no oars. She was saved by fishermen in one account and by fish in another, to become, as the museum's literature states, "St. Thenew, Scotland's first recorded rape victim, battered woman and unmarried mother."

On a wall there was a plaque that stated that the vast majority of Scottish people no longer attended church, although seventy-five per cent still maintained a belief in God. Five reasons for the decline of church-going were listed: the advances of science and technology; increased material wealth; greater freedom; the advent of atheist creeds like communism; and new choices in human relationships, which included contraception, homosexual pairings and common-law marriages. I read this alongside several schoolchildren, who were dragging their way through the exhibits, relieved to be anywhere other than their damp classroom even if it was a religious museum. The other spectators were pious-looking tourists, though the museum seemed to extract that posture from its patrons.

The museum presented the troubled history of the Presbyterian church as a tortured schematic that began in 1690 and went to 1950 by way of a series of parallel and intersecting lines that looked like a map of the London Underground. The first secession in 1733 was over the issue of patronage; there was another split between the Burghers and Anti-Burghers, each of which spawned Auld Lichts, who favoured state connection, and New Lichts, who did not. Reunion in 1839, Disruption in 1843, with the Free Church breaking away, favouring state support. Some of the lines have arrows pointing in opposite directions. Odd geometrical shapes are formed by their intersections. In 1892, the new Free Presbyterian Church broke away when the Free Church became more liberal, allowing the singing of hymns and the notion that Christ died for all men. The lines on the schematic merge and cleave and at the bottom of the chart there are seven versions of Presbyterianism, some with only a few surviving believers. Congregations have been reduced by humanism and television and doubt.

The most recent split was not listed on the diagram. In 1989 Lord MacKay, the Lord High Chancellor of Great Britain and a Free Presbyterian, attended the requiem mass of a Catholic judge who had been a friend of his. This was interpreted as a slouch toward Rome and MacKay was ostracized. A third of the church's ministers and congregants defended MacKay's decision and broke away from the Free Presbyterians to form the Associated Presbyterian Church. Like most of the splits, it was bitter and greeted with mild ridicule in the press. Such believers wouldn't be happy until the church was distilled to a single, grumpy, self-righteous Calvinist, everyone else banished into a sect of his or her own design.

The Free Presbyterians retain the brittle essence of the church, the most conservative of the Presbyterian sects, a wintry, unadorned faith. They are the residual Presbyterians, a small group of a few thousand now scattered across the world, dispersed into small congregations. I had distant relatives who had remained in the Highlands and who were still Free Presbyterians, carrying the torch of the Reformation. I planned to make the pilgrimage north to find them.

———————

The weather was crisp and, when the sun was obscured by cloud, it was suddenly cold and damp. I sat on a bench in George Square, watching the African drummers and a handful of dancers whirling around them. I was killing time, waiting for a 5:30 tour bus that left from George Square and took in the highlights of Mackintosh's work. A man of about seventy came toward me, holding a napkin over his left eye. He took it off and showed me the gash underneath. I said I thought it needed a few stitches and looked around for a policeman. The man sat down beside me and I asked what had happened. His response was unintelligible. He had a thick accent and was still addled from the blow. I assumed that it had been a mugging, or worse, random violence delivered without motive by young thugs. A whole socio-economic model fell immediately into place: disaffected youth out of work, simmering cultural alienation and the kind of nihilism that Anthony Burgess wrote of in *A Clockwork Orange*. There was a look that I had seen, or at least attributed to certain young men. They were around twenty, wearing T-shirts bearing an oblique message and an expression that was equal parts menace and confusion, the look of a captured animal that had been released into an alien environment.

We sat watching the dancers, the man talking in abrupt, co-agulated sentences. At first I thought he was speaking Gaelic, but some words were recognizable. Gradually, his phrases took shape, like ships coming out of a fog, and I could more or less understand him. But I was too late for the explanation of his wound. He was already on his family, a daughter in Stirling and a son in London where the cost of apartments was a horrible thing. I gave him some tissues to replace the bloodied napkin. Two security men with radios walked by and I called them over.

They talked to the man and it came out that he was diabetic and had been weak from low blood sugar and had fallen down onto a sewer grate and cut himself. They gave him some candies and called an ambulance and we waited and compared head-wound stories.

"A cousin, he got hit with a spade, right here," one of the security men said. He indicated his forehead. "Blood. Jesus. A *flood*."

The other security man had sliced his head open on the exhaust pipe of a car, he said without elaboration, as if it were a common injury. The diabetic stared off, sucking on a peppermint, his blood sugar inching upward. The ambulance arrived and took him away. I went to the bus stop and stood for twenty minutes before a friendly bus driver told me that the Mackintosh tour bus didn't start up until June.

———

At 6 p.m. I went into a pool room, ordered a pint of MacEwan ale and played a few listless games of eight ball. A man of maybe twenty-five came over and introduced himself as Alisdair and invited me to join him. Alisdair had black hair and was wiry, slightly bandy-legged. He had a fast, wild game, hammering the cue ball with a flourish and following through so that the cue hung briefly in the air, tip upward. He was fluid, though, and won the first three games handily. Alisdair was drinking two pints to my one. His appetite for both eight ball and beer was raw and impatient, as if the idea was simply to get both of them over with.

At the end of the third game, he sank four balls in dramatic succession. He sighted a fifth along the cue and turned to me and smiled. "It just keeps getting worse, doesn't it?" he said. He held his smile for unpleasant emphasis before rifling the eight ball into the corner. The line was taken from a film about pool, *The Color of Money*, and originally it had been spoken by Tom Cruise. Alisdair had a vague resemblance to Cruise and as the games wore on, he occasionally imitated him and quoted from the film without referring to it.

After the seventh game, Alisdair's encroaching drunkenness and jackhammer game began to work against him. I won three games in a row. Alisdair watched the eight ball go down and approached me, his face about six inches away. "Are ye Rangers or Celtic then?" he asked. It was an accusation rather than a question. The Rangers are a Protestant football team and the Celtic are Catholic. Alisdair wanted to establish fault lines, to gauge the nature of the gulf that separated us. He was a Celtic man, a history of Orangeman wrongs sitting in his head like a pudding. I observed the network of veins already spreading along his cheeks like wisteria and was reminded that my ancestors were a blood-faced tribe of farmers given to outbreaks of hysterical violence. I pleaded ignorance.

"Ye're Rangers then," he said. "Tha's that. I know it for a fact man." Alisdair won the next game and I won the two after that. We were approaching parity. I visited the men's room, which had a machine that dispensed curry-flavoured Lucky Dip condoms.

"Ye're a pommy bastard," Alisdair said thickly when I re-turned. He stared into the green felt. "They're all bastards. I worked there. London. But there's no point ta'it. None a tall. May as well be home, bastards." There was a mood of un-healthy tension, the evening held together by the promise of confrontation. I tried to lose the next game but Alisdair bounced the cue ball off the table twice, scratching.

He rallied to win the last game, lurching around the table, operating on instinct, the dull pulse from his limbic brain. "Ye're a pommy bastard," he repeated.

"I'm not English."

"It's a load of shite, all of it, know what I'm saying." He rammed the black into the side and the cue ball danced into the air but landed safely on the table, spinning crazily. "Fucking pool," Alisdair said. "It's got a mind of its oan." He sat down heavily and finished his pint and stared at the complex swirls of the brown and orange carpet. I thought he might vomit. It occurred to me that the carpet pattern had been selected for that purpose.

"Ye a singer then?" Alisdair asked. His mouth hung open like a landed trout.

"What?"

"Ye sing. Ye a regular Frank Sinatra."

"Sing?"

"Karaoke man. Where ye from. Fucking Neptune?"

"No, I don't sing."

"Ye'll be perfect then. Bastards can't sing, they don't let it stop them." He lit a cigarette and inhaled deeply, his mouth widening with the effort. "A lack of ability is a prerequisite man. It's up ye go and give us 'Stairway to Heaven.' Ten pints and everyone has the gift, know what I'm saying?"

There was a karaoke bar upstairs, he said. He was all in for pool. Game had a mind of its own. I hadn't eaten dinner and the lager felt like bilge water listing in my stomach. It was ten o'clock. I told him I was headed back to my hotel.

"It's your round. I hope that's clear. One drink. It's karaoke, man. You're a bastard."

I went upstairs with him into the dark lounge. We had to go outside first and in the street the threat of violence gained shape. There was something liberating about the space and the air, the relative solitude. Whatever public constraint existed in the bar was gone.

I was relieved when we entered the dark lounge. We sat at a table with four people at it, three women in their sixties and an older man whose thoughts seemed elsewhere. A small smile flickered across his face at random moments. Alisdair seemed to know them and introduced me all around. A couple got up to sing Barry Manilow's "Mandy." They were both blonde and deeply tanned with the kind of waxen beauty that Christian singers often have. When they finished, they kissed each other and held one hand up in salute to the audience. You've been lovely, you really have.

"Daft bastards," Alisdair said. "Malibu Barbie."

"Why don't you sing?" I asked him.

"Can't. It'd be Tom Fucking Jones, man. Women throwing their panties. Close the place down. God's give me a gift. He don't want it chucked away on this group."

Alisdair had emphatically spelled his name three times in the course of the evening, "D not T, got it?" He looked like he was getting ready to go for a fourth try. "Ye know America?" he asked pointedly.

"Everyone knows America."

"Ye been there."

"Yes."

"Ye know what America's about."

"Winners and losers," I ventured.

"Christ." Alisdair's head bobbed. "Yer true nature. Tha's America. Whether you feel like something, it's the green light. Know what ah'm saying?" He finished his pint and looked around for the barmaid. There was a stain on his polo shirt and Alisdair stared down at it as if it were a television show. His head jerked up like a marionette's. "Do you know what a Glasgow kiss is?" he asked rhetorically. It is a head butt, a form of fighting that hurts the perpetrator a lot and his victim even more. It is a particularly Calvinist form of combat, where everyone suffers, as God intended, and a Glaswegian speciality. On the small stage a large bearded man was singing "To Dream the Impossible Dream."

One of the women at the table bought Alisdair a drink, something with Coke, and he entertained her for a few minutes. His eyes were beginning to close. I told him that I was leaving and he lurched to his feet and followed me out. He walked beside me, staggering, his momentum carrying him into the granite wall of a bank. He walked as if this were his natural gait, skittering sideways, bouncing off bus shelters. I thought that for Alisdair, violence might simply be the logical end of any evening, like ordering a coffee and liqueur after dinner.

"I'm gagging for a bite. Man's got to eat. Fuel. That's the thing." He bounced like a pinball through the door frame of an intensely lit Indian fast-food kiosk. Alisdair looked at the options displayed under glass. "What's that one then," he said pointing.

"Onion bhaji," the man said.

"Paki shite." He settled on a vegetable samosa and paid by spilling most of his change on the counter. Some of it rolled onto the linoleum floor and Alisdair leaned down. "Come home ye buggers. Don't leave me." He struggled with a ten pence as if trying to pry a manhole cover. The microwave alarm prompted him to stand uncertainly.

Outside he took a bite and looked into the pie, squinting. "Christ. Shite pie. There's a racket. Paki shite for sale." He threw it against a building. It was raining lightly. "Thing is. I like a pint after my dinner." His speech was clotted into fat syllables. *Ah laikh ah paint afta ma dinnagh.* We were standing on the deserted street. Alisdair was weaving, one foot constantly adjusting for the changes in topography that his brain was registering. "There's a place. After hours." He was looking at me as directly as he could. His vision beamed upward like a searchlight and was jerked back into place. "It's just down this alley." There was a lifeless passageway behind him, a grim narrow space between two buildings.

"I'm beat, Alisdair," I said, backing out of range. "I'm off. Take care." Alisdair looked like he couldn't decide whether to take a swing or not. It would have meant taking at least two steps. So there was risk involved. I walked off, listening for the mad rush of footsteps. He screamed out something, a sentence that sounded like someone gargling kerosene in front of a microphone. Six blocks away I felt safe. A pack of feral dogs suddenly went by at a ferocious clip, turning a corner and disappearing out of sight. They went by so quickly that I thought I might have imagined them.

———————————

In the morning I drove north to Perth, where the grand-daughter of Georgina's biological father, George Ivel, lived. Ivel had settled there and started a new, legitimate family.

Perth was lush and quiet. There was the sound of birds and the rain had stopped. Catherine Bruce was sixty-one, married to John Bruce. They lived in a pleasant bungalow on a quiet winding street. After my parents had learned of Georgie's secret, they had traced Catherine Bruce to Perth and sent her a discreet letter. A correspondence ensued and they knew of our connection. I had phoned from Glasgow and they were expecting me.

Catherine looked a bit like my grandmother, projecting a similar sense of solidity. We sat amid the china and family photographs in her living room and nibbled politely on cheese sandwiches. The room was decorated in waves of brown. Seven volumes of *Times Past* sat on the bookshelf. She showed me a picture of George Ivel, a big man wearing a Highland Railway uniform.

"He was a guard," Catherine said. "Though I think that means something different in America." He wasn't a security guard, but guided the trains onto the right track. He came to Perth in 1903 and married a Gaelic-speaking Highlander, a quiet woman with whom he had a daughter. He died in Perth in 1930 of stomach cancer. Catherine was born in 1936 and had never met him; he existed through anecdote.

"I don't think my mother knew of Georgina," Catherine said. "I don't think she ever knew she had a half-sister."

"*He* may not even have known," John said. "That he had a daughter."

"No, perhaps not."

We ate the cheese sandwiches and biscuits and Dundee cake and drank tea and talked politely. Between us was the odd gulf of distant relatives who have never met and are now meeting under slightly strained circumstances. Perhaps her grandfather was a bastard who abandoned my great-grandmother.

Possibly they were madly in love, or it was just a brief flirtation. These questions lingered between us, unasked. "They may have met in Inverness," John said helpfully. "The railway was the principal means of transportation." Catherine could have been travelling to the south to work. I had heard that she worked as a cook in Edinburgh. The fact that Georgina Ivel Ross had been so emphatically and inelegantly named for her father was a matter of tradition, Catherine told me. I had taken it as an act of defiance, or perhaps love, but it was simply custom.

I was continuing north to Inverness that afternoon and Catherine and John said they would guide me through the city in their car, making sure I got on the right highway. Outside I remarked on the pastoral quality of the neighbourhood.

"Last week someone went up the street and slashed every tire," John said. "Fifty cars." I wondered at the determined nature of the vandal. We exchanged the usual despair about declining values. There was a time we didn't need to lock our doors, John said, the common lament of the urbanite. Though I had always had to lock mine.

"Tell us if you find anything in the Highlands," Catherine said.

4

THE

IMAGINED

HILLS

A BARTENDER with a rabid smile and grey hair the length and consistency of a horse brush told me that the Highlands did not exist. It was a mythic place, he said, like Atlantis only wetter. His arms were stretched out in front of him, hands the size and colour of six-pound boiled lobsters resting on the bar. His eyebrows moved in the contiguous way of an army advancing over rough ground and his voice was low and deliberate, skidding into a higher register as he drove toward a point. It was a hotel bar and there was a banquet in the next room that spilled over as men in kilts left in small groups to have a private drink then return to the speeches. On the bar's television a rugby match was being played and due to the weather and the wet pitch and muddied uniforms, the grey teams played against a grey background and formed a single video organism. The kilted men cheered as the dark mass on the screen moved in one direction, listing like a boat through heavy seas. Technically, we were in the Highlands.

The Highlands aren't easily defined; even their geography is disputed. In some accounts, the islands, at least the outlying islands of Shetland and Orkney, are excluded. The Highland Boundary Fault, which runs from the Firth of Clyde in the west to Stonehaven in the east is the traditional division, though areas well north of the line are not necessarily the Highlands and there are Highland influences in the Central Lowlands. Sometimes the Highlands are defined by their crofting counties, though there are quibbles; the eastern part of Sutherland is sometimes excluded. Linguistically, the Highlands are seen traditionally as Gaelic-speaking, though the language was never spoken in Orkney and Shetland and was spoken in parts of the Lowlands. The Highlands exist most vividly as an idea, a symbol of romantic nationalism.

After the rugby came a televised symposium on Scottish independence. A revolving group of panelists spoke about the need to stay within Great Britain or argued that Scotland would be more successful alone. Pragmatism and emotion twanged inside the bright studio. A sensible-looking man suggested that the spirit of independence was good but the timing was wrong; the North Sea oil, much of which was technically Scotland's, was waning now. They should have leapt when the oil revenues were highest. Instead the money had gone to London. Some of the arguments were familiar from the ongoing

Quebec debate on sovereignty but there seemed to be an energy in the Scottish forum that was irretrievably gone from the Canadian situation. The issue of Quebec's independence had been argued into a grim cul-de-sac. I knew journalists, both French- and English-speaking, who would rather saw off their heads and set fire to them than address the issue of sovereignty again; who were forced to recycle old columns or reinterview politicians who themselves could barely muster enough passion for a twenty-second sound bite. The country's future was at stake, as we were continually reminded, but we were exhausted from two referendums on the question of sovereignty; mentally and spiritually fatigued, browbeaten under harsh lights, threatened with future referendums by politicians who hounded us like evangelists. Collectively, we were at the point where we might be prepared to sign a false confession. Yes, we killed the country. It's true, we did. Just let us sleep.

On the television the issue of inclusiveness was raised. If Scotland was separate from Great Britain, what shape would the new state take? An English woman who had lived in Scotland most of her life wondered what her place would be in the imagined state. It was suggested that the state would need immigrants to bolster the small population: could they be attracted to a country that was celebrating its own identity with such fervour. Scotland would be consumed with nationhood, with being "we." Would "they" feel welcome; would it matter?

The shape of the new state would be modern and industrious. "We" would be a generous group, and would probably take "our" emblems from history. It is Highland imagery that is used to advertise the country to tourists, and clan tartans that cloak the pillars of Glasgow airport. Despite the fact that fewer than 200,000 of Scotland's five million people live in the Highlands, it has come to represent the national imagination.

In 1822, Thomas Carlyle wrote, "With all respect for the generous qualities which the Highland clans have often exhibited, it was difficult to forget that they had always constituted a small, and almost always unimportant part of the Scottish population; and when one reflected how miserably their numbers had of late years been reduced in consequence of the selfish and hard-hearted policy of their landlords, it almost seemed as if there was a cruel mockery in giving so much prominence to their pretensions. But there was no question that they were picturesque."

Picturesque is what a military society becomes once it ceases to have any real power. "The Highlanders," Samuel Johnson wrote, "before they were disarmed, were so addicted to quarrels, that the boys used to follow any public procession or ceremony, however festive, or however solemn, in expectation of the battle, which was sure to happen before the company dispersed." A bloody feud between clans would erupt over poached cattle, which led to a death, then revenge, then a greater revenge, which precipitated a small war and new alliances, which led to innovative betrayals and the destruction of one or both clans. In the earliest recorded feud involving the clan Ross, Finleigh, their leader, was assassinated in 1020 by Maolbride of Moray. Twelve years later, Finleigh's murder was revenged when the Ross men burned Maolbride and fifty of his men alive. A ceasefire flourished until there were enough men to resume fighting or new alliances were forged. Then a grudging peace until a fresh slight occurred. This pattern was kept up for seven hundred years.

"Till the Highlanders lost their ferocity, with their arms," Johnson wrote, "they suffered from each other all that malignity could dictate, or precipitance could act. Every provocation was revenged with blood, and no man that ventured into a numerous company, by whatever occasion brought together, was sure of returning without a wound." By the time Johnson toured the Highlands with James Boswell in 1773, the clan system had devolved. The Scots had lost at the Battle of Culloden in 1746 and the subsequent Disarming Acts had banned weapons, tartans and bagpipes. "The clans retain little now of their original character," he wrote, "their ferocity of temper is softened, their military ardour is extinguished, their dignity of independence is depressed, their contempt of government is subdued, and their reverence for their chiefs abated. Of what they had before the late conquest of their country, there remains only their language and their poverty."

It is the original character of the Highlanders that is being invoked in these days of renewed nationalism. They were given a rich cinematic life in the film *Rob Roy* and in *Braveheart*, which starred Mel Gibson as William Wallace, a key figure in gaining Scottish independence in 1314. Historically, Wallace is slightly obscure, which makes him a perfect candidate for film. But now he is flesh and blood, personified by Mel Gibson's splendid hair and defiant, naked buttocks pointed at the English. Wallace was executed before the Battle of Bannockburn in 1314, the decisive fight that gave Scotland independence for the next four hundred years. The Scottish army was led by Robert the Bruce, who in the film is weak, troubled but finally triumphant.

In August 1996, archaeologists digging in Melrose Abbey found a lead cylinder that was believed to contain Robert the Bruce's heart. He had died of leprosy and was thought to be buried in the abbey of Dunfermline, but a story was told of how his heart had been removed and buried separately in Melrose Abbey. When the cylinder was cut open, a smaller lead casket was found inside with a note dated 1921 that confirmed that the casket held a heart. It had been dug up by His Majesty's Office of Works, which had tucked in the note and then reburied the casket unceremoniously. The archaeologists decided that the casket was too fragile to open, so Robert's heart, if it was his, remained sealed. In these days of renewed nationalism it is a fitting symbol, uplifting but uncertain. Scotland, as several writers have noted, is an imagined country.

It was certainly an imagined country for my grandmother, who had left at such a young age but lived her life within the shadow of its stern religion and romantic mythology. But most countries are imagined. They seize upon the most marketable myths and build a national character out of them, in the way that America, for instance, embraced the gunfighter, a largely manufactured icon who rarely existed in the way of Hollywood westerns (most gunfights took place at a great distance and without warning). The gunfighter came to embody something enviable, something demonstrably American. He defined a New World individualism that had an existential allure. The gunfighters themselves didn't always live up to their reputation. Bat Masterson finished his days as a sportswriter for a New York newspaper and died at his desk of a heart attack. Doc Holliday was a tubercular dentist who was believed to have been from New York. Dodge City wasn't as wild and violent as some other towns, but it had several weekly newspapers that chronicled every skirmish and competed for readers with lurid description. It was a media town.

Driving north, I stopped at the Culloden battlefield, just south of Inverness, where a small museum had been erected, bristling with information. The 1746 battle between the Scots and Royalist forces is one of Scotland's most potent symbols, the historical event used to mark the decline of the Highlands. The Rebel forces were led by Charles Edward Stuart, Bonnie Prince Charlie as he was called. They were pitted against a much larger army made up of Royalist soldiers and some dissenting clans who were led by the Duke of Cumberland. A plaque at the site noted that the Rosses had sided with the Royalists though hadn't fought in the battle. For them, it wasn't a political matter, but a religious one; Charles was a Catholic, born in Rome no less, and the Rosses were Presbyterians.

In the brief preface to his book, *Culloden*, John Prebble wrote, "The book begins with Culloden because then began a sickness from which Scotland, and the Highlands in particular, never recovered. It is a sickness of the emotions and its symptoms can be seen on the labels of whisky bottles. Long ago this sickness, and its economic consequences, emptied the Highlands of people." Eddrachillis, the parish where my grandmother was born, was a fine example. In 1801, it had 1,253 people. A century later it had grown marginally to 1,418 people; in the 1981 census it contained just 645.

It was too early for the tourist crush that would arrive in the summer but a dozen of us milled. It was overcast, with brief showers, not unlike the weather on the day of the battle. There was a viewing platform in front of the battlefield that looked toward the Black Isle and Ben Wyvis. The site was a disadvantage to the Highland army. The ground was marshy and covered with scrub. It was impossible to mount an effective charge, the traditional Highland tactic. Their forces were disorganized and the order for some clans to charge was delayed. Those who did were cut to pieces by cannon fire. The battle lasted less than an hour; by then there were at least 1,200 Rebels dead on the battlefield. More than that were massacred in retreat. The wounded were killed where they lay. Women and children were murdered as the Royalist troops went through the countryside. By contrast, only fifty Royalist soldiers were killed at Culloden.

The fury of the Royalists was partly racial; in the eyes of the English the Highlanders were inhuman savages. And they were making reprisals for the fear felt throughout England when the Jacobite forces had marched to Derby, two or three days from London. A false scouting report given by a Hanoverian spy said a force of nine thousand men was waiting for them at London, so the march was halted. In fact, London was cowering and panicked. The Scots forces retreated, a failure of nerve that has reverberated for two and a half centuries.

There were ten or so people scattered on the battlefield, taking snapshots, shaking their heads. Inside, at the museum, a man stared at the portrait of Bonnie Prince Charlie and said, "We won't see his like again."

He was indeed bonnie. Women swooned and called to him from their windows as he passed. He was also insensitive, ambitious and abusive and had a remarkable capacity for alcohol. Charles was born in Rome, the son of James III of England (who was also James VIII of Scotland) and Clementina Sobieski, the Polish granddaughter of the Victor of Vienna. Before the Battle of Culloden had finished, Charles was led away and hidden in the Highlands, a price of thirty thousand pounds on his head. It was an enormous sum, especially in the context of the local poverty, but no one gave him up. Hiding at Corodale on the island of South Uist, Charles drank with the locals until even MacDonald of Boisdale, one of Scotland's legendary drinkers, was unconscious. According to romantic legend, Charlie covered up the sleeping men with tartan robes and sang *de profundis* over their unconscious forms.

After returning safely to Europe, Charles lived extrava-
gantly and seduced women in the same obsessive and slightly
cold way that he had approached Culloden. Part of his attraction was the air of romantic tragedy that lingered around him
like a perfume. The portraits of him in middle age show a
bloated, thickened, blotchy man, the bonnie prince buried
beneath a dissipated veneer. He converted to Protestantism
in 1750 and had an illegitimate daughter named Charlotte who
loved him when even his mother had tired of him. It was during his decline that Charles finally married, to Louise of Stol-
berg. Their union was a crude sideshow and she eventually ran
off with a poet. Charles died senile, flatulent and stuporous.

Culloden became a symbol of Highland decline but it was
not necessarily its cause; the clan system had already begun
to unravel before 1746, and it continued afterwards. The chiefs
gradually went from being patriarchs and military leaders
to landlords. They married Lowland women, let their Gaelic
lapse and sought entertainment in the parlours of Edinburgh.
They needed money to support their adopted lifestyles and
the military structure of the clans was replaced by a cattle
economy, and later, fatally, by sheep. The chiefs, wrote Thomas
Douglas, the fifth earl of Selkirk, "were reduced to the situation of any other proprietors, but they were not long in discov-
ering that to subsist a numerous train of dependents was not
the only way in which their estates could be rendered of value."

A succession of English monarchs contributed all they
could to the demise of the Highlands. At an uncharitable
glance, the royal line is a list of child monarchs, Germans, alco-
holics, Catholics, malignant dwarfs and pedants, some of the
familiar imagery that Hollywood employs to depict villains.
King James VI was a drooling, alcoholic, gay, unkempt gossip
who assumed the throne at the age of one. Though he was

shrewd and a prolific writer and ushered in the King James version of the Bible slotted in the backs of pews in our church in Winnipeg, Charles II was impotent from venereal disease and died weeping for Nell Gwynne the orange seller. George IV was overweight, tipsy and wore more makeup than Coco Chanel. So the English have been lasting and effective villains, but for the Highlanders, the most potent enemy was themselves.

————————

The Clearances are the other defining symbol of the Highlands, though they are a private wound, nursed among their own. After the Disarming Acts, the chiefs were no longer military leaders and the clan system continued to deteriorate. The older chiefs died and the sons slouched toward the south. Many of them were absentee landlords and they weren't witness to the abrupt decay of their culture.

The land had been grazed with cattle for centuries and dotted with subsistence crofts. But 1792 was *Bliadhna nan Caorach*—the Year of the Sheep. A seer wandered the Highlands with this warning: "Woe to thee, oh land, the Great Sheep is coming!" The Great Sheep was the Cheviot. In the Cheviot Hills that form the gentle border between Scotland and England, a farmer named Robson began to breed his sheep, first with English rams, then Spanish and others, tinkering until he got a breed that was hardy enough to withstand the inclement weather, mountainous geography and sparse vegetation of the Highlands. It was a super-sheep, engineered to specifications. Sheep were more profitable than cattle and required less care. The tenants could be replaced with sheep.

Sheep were first introduced to the County of Ross, the putative home of my grandmother's family. It was warmer even than some of the more southerly counties, due to the lie of its hills, which functioned as solar traps. The sheep thrived there and the Ross men shot the sheep and threatened the Lowland shepherds. The Rosses were still raising cattle and their cattle wandered onto the sheep pastures and were finally impounded by the Cameron clan, who were renting the land from Sir Hector Munro. Led by a local giant named Alisdair Mor Wallace, the Ross men liberated their cattle in a brawl with the Lowlanders.

This small victory was celebrated at a Ross wedding on July 27, 1792, where Rosses had come from every glen. They sang and danced and drank whisky they distilled themselves, which tasted of copper and medicine and earth, and they hatched the idea of driving every sheep in the Highlands back to England. It was a daring plan, a drunken plan. It isn't unusual to come up with grandly ill-conceived ideas when you are staggering and screaming in the wee hours. But four days later, sober now, they executed the plan, which was unusual, especially in the almost fifty years of peace and docility since Culloden.

It was estimated that four hundred men participated in the largest sheep drive in the history of the Highlands. Starting in Lairg, in Sutherland, and moving south they crossed the Kyle of Sutherland, picking up more flocks, an army of Cheviot sheep, six thousand of them mincing dumbly through the heather. When news of this was carried south, it gathered momentum, and the sheep drive grew into an insurrection. Three companies of the Forty-second Regiment were sent out to put down the rebellion. When the regiment caught up to the Rosses at An Corran, it was night. The fires were still burning but the men were gone. Six thousand sheep sat in mute witness in the pale summer night. Some of the Ross men were rounded up. A few were tried. The sheep trickled back north, this time to stay. The Sheep Riots were over.

Getting the tenants off the land presented problems, but in a dismal, extended pogrom, they were burned out, beaten with truncheons and cleared from the land. Over the next century, tens of thousands of Highlanders left for the United States, Canada, New Zealand or Australia. The Highlands emptied out, much of them leased to English aristocrats and Lowlanders for fishing and hunting. The Highlanders had been reduced to peasants, stranded in the wrong century, without even the erratic perks of feudalism to sustain them.

By 1845, there were more sheep than people in the Highlands. The Rosses were being displaced from their ancestral land, first by writs, then by force. In 1845, a group of Ross women who were being evicted were beaten with truncheons by drunken policemen. The incident became known as "The Massacre of the Rosses." Members of the Ross clan drifted north to more marginal land or left for overseas.

A *Times* review of John Prebble's book, *The Highland Clearances*, said, "There is little need to search further to explain so much of the sadness and emptiness of the northern Highlands today." It is a quality that is prized. The Highlands have a historic melancholy, the geographic equivalent of listening to Billie Holiday when your heart is broken. The landscape nurtures a collective grief. Writer Hugh MacLennan wrote, "Above the sixtieth parallel of Canada, you feel that nobody but God has ever been there before you, but in a deserted Highland glen you feel that everyone who ever mattered is dead and gone."

At the same time the Highlands were being dismantled, they were gaining force as a romantic idea. Outlawed tartans became fashionable in the Lowlands and in London. There was an instant nostalgia for a vanished, hostile world that was bound by blood and loyalty. Nostalgia became the Highlands chief export. That and people. In 1777, the Gaelic Society of London was formed and it evolved into the Highland Society, catering to those of Highland descent, many of them the very people who had contributed to its demise. They didn't want to live there, but they polished the idea of the Highlands into a lustrous, heroic, doomed homeland. Other Highland societies formed in Britain and they staged Highland Games and revived stag hunts and Highland feasts.

It was Sir Walter Scott (1771-1832) who gave the movement its most potent voice. Scott was born in Edinburgh but was intrigued by Highland history and several of his novels were set there. His first novel, *Waverly; or, 'tis Sixty Years Since*, was published in 1814 and dealt, in part, with the Jacobite Rebellion. Its central character was an Englishman who essentially has the Highlands explained to him. Scott was the most popular writer of the early nineteenth century, and his books helped cement the idea that Scotland was the Highlands, a tragic, antique land.

Scott's books sold outside Britain and were adapted for the stage and made into operas. Gaetano Donizetti's opera *Lucia di Lammermoor* was based on Scott's novel *The Bride of Lammermoor*. Donizetti's version was the fifth operatic adaptation of the novel. Gioacchini Rossini adapted Scott's *Ivanhoe*. The paperback editions of his books sold like hotcakes and contained advertisements for Frazer's Sulphur Tablets for purifying the blood, artificial arms and legs and Epp's Cocoa. Scott was a relentlessly commercial writer, partly because of the debts he was liable for when his publisher and business partner died, which were estimated to be 120,000 pounds.

Although the Highlands came to be seen in a romantic cast, Scott wasn't a Romantic writer in any real sense; he was pragmatic and opposed to mystery. He was what Scottish writer Tom Nairn described as a "valedictory realist," trying to define a way of life that had recently disappeared, "to illustrate the customs and manners which anciently prevailed," as Scott himself wrote. His prose style was uneventful and his characters were stiff and formal, but his evocations of the Highland geography were poetic and precise. Painters, including J.M.W. Turner, came up to paint the wild vistas he described.

Readers of Scott's books became the Highlands' first tourist boom, drawn to the mythic landscapes and historical sites described in the books. They had been notoriously difficult to reach because of crude roads but between 1803 and 1825 an extensive government road-building program was undertaken; a series of "Parliamentary roads" were built by engineer Thomas Telford. The advent of the steamship, harbour developments and canal construction also made the trip much easier. Railways soon linked the country's major centres. Tourists came north with Scott's revised Highlands sitting in their imaginations and to some degree, the residents responded to expectations.

Scott's house, Abbotsford, became an attraction itself. People flocked there, my family among them. During our European trip in 1969 we wandered through the baronial home in a polite herd. Scott's literary reputation hadn't survived. His books weren't part of university curriculums; they seemed clumsy and quaint. He was famous for having been a famous writer. I was familiar with his novel *Ivanhoe* from the television series of the same name. Etched in stone in Scott's house was the phrase "waste not, want not," my grandmother's signature maxim.

The Highland tourist boom of the nineteenth century was aided by Queen Victoria, a fan of Scott's; *The Bride of Lammermoor* was the first novel she read. She became enchanted with the idea of the Highlands and later with the place itself. She and Albert moved to Balmoral Castle in 1848, and in 1859 the Braemar Royal Highland Gathering—a version of the Highland Games—was held there. It continued to be held there at intervals until the end of the century. The upper class followed the royal example and bought estates in Scotland. The poor fled to America and the rich inched northward to take their place, at least during the summer.

———————

In Inverness I stayed at a bed and breakfast on the banks of the River Ness, the famously shy monster advertised everywhere. At a nearby bar I talked with an Australian who had come to do some genealogical research. He saw the Highlands as a guerrilla theatre version of *Brigadoon*, Lerner and Loewe's Broadway play about a magical Highland village that went to sleep in 1754 and wakes up for a day each century. No matter that there wasn't much magic in the Highlands eight years after Culloden.

"It's dolled up to resemble itself," he said.

In the movie version of *Brigadoon* Gene Kelly falls in love with Cyd Charisse, one of the village girls who's awake for the day. Van Johnson, Kelly's friend, remains cynical about the whole thing. You either buy into it or you don't. The film, due to budget restraints at MGM, was filmed on a Hollywood soundstage rather than on location in Scotland. It was a flop and its ersatz scenery and sentiment didn't make much of an impression, but I could see what the Australian meant.

The next morning, it was breathtakingly clear and the citizens sat on the High Street, staring at the sun the way primitives might view an eclipse. I drove north and stopped in Ullapool on the west coast for fish and chips, taking my lunch down to the sea. A huge black mournful dog arrived and sat beside me and I gave it some fish and watched the ships. It had clouded over. I wandered through the many gift shops on the main street, examining kilts and tweed jackets and sweaters, which were too expensive to really consider. Instead, I bought a box of shortbread. Driving north, the hills became larger and the stone looked like slate, dark with rain. A lamb lay broken in a rocky ditch, a red stain vivid against the white.

5

FALLEN

SCOURIE, like most Highland villages, is built along the road rather than around the bay or a public square. The fishing is famous and in the early evening the parking lot of the Scourie Hotel was filled with expensive cars from the south. A shelf inside the front door was laid with trout, each one named for its owner and offering directions for its use ("Watkins; breakfast"). British sportsmen jostled in the pub and their masculine holiday brio spilled out into the lounge where elderly couples sipped port and read paperbacks.

I had a pint in the lounge and chatted with two middle-aged British fishermen. Tony Blair was poised for victory in the upcoming election. They both felt he was too slick by half.

"If you're going to vote for Tory policies, why not elect an actual Tory," one of them said.

They were grudgingly nostalgic for Thatcher. She looked like one of John Tenniel's illustrations in *Alice in Wonderland*, and she behaved like the Queen of Hearts, but she did the job. They left for dinner and to give instructions to their gillie, the local man who would guide them to where the trout were hungriest. I had an expensive, inoffensive meal in the dining room, delivered by a bustling middle-aged woman. A thin filet of haddock, a mountain of boiled potatoes. Wine was surprisingly cheap, a consolation. After dinner I wandered the walled cemetery by the bay and idly looked for Rosses. There were dozens, and I eliminated most of them as possible relatives before giving up and climbing the hill to Mrs. Macdonald's bed and breakfast. It was ten o'clock and still light.

In the sitting room there were two couples, one Welsh and the other an elderly pair from the south of England who were perfect miniatures, like the bride and groom on the top of a wedding cake. They were travelling in formal dress, without a car, taking buses and riding on mail trucks. The husband was a little over five feet and bizarrely well-preserved. His face was without lines, his lips full and brightly coloured, his eyes un-clouded and his hair cut in the style of a six-year-old boy. He looked like he had somehow avoided life, and the effect was aesthetically offputting, like a hand-tinted photograph. On his way to bed, he stopped and began telling travelling anec-dotes, swaying in front of us in his windowpane wool suit like a schoolboy reciting "Casey at the Bat." His stories were about the weather, the cost of toll roads, shortages of milk, lengthy line-ups. "How old do you think I am?" he finally asked his small audience. This was clearly the finale of his performance, and his strange youthfulness a source of pride. The Welshman answered, "Eighty-four." The little groom looked like he'd been punched. He was seventy-seven, he told us, and then his wife guided him off to bed the way damaged fighters are led from the ring. The next morning at breakfast he whispered to me, "No one has ever guessed eighty-four."

At breakfast, there were three elderly couples at the table, with their steadfast marriages on display. There was the perky wife and sullen husband. The exasperated wife who finished each of her husband's thoughts impatiently and countered his every statement. The bore and the apologist. With their children gone, their jobs behind them, they had become an unhappy unit. A couple named Ferris battled like scorpions in a bottle, betting against one another on the title of a book or the current exchange rate then fetching the proof and waving it in the face of the loser. "*See.* Two point three eight. What did I say? *What did I say?*"

The woman who ran the bed and breakfast took me out to the garden and pointed to the campground below. "If you're looking for relations, you should talk to Mr. Mackenzie. That's him in the green. He knows quite a bit. He's the place to start." He was on a tractor, cutting the lawn. I drove down and introduced myself. He nodded and disappeared into the administration building and brought me out a copy of *Gloomy Memories of Scotland* by Donald Macleod. "Read this," he told me. "The Clearances. It was like Bosnia." He said there were Rosses in Foindle, nine kilometres away. He said the emigrants should all come home: "They've done so well abroad. They are doctors, lawyers, captains of industry. We've given the world so much. We've nothing left to give ourselves. People are afraid to cut ties with England. It's madness." I said that large parts of downtown Montreal had been built by Scots in the nineteenth century. "Exactly," he replied. It began to rain lightly. Mr. Mackenzie thought that the Rosses may have come up from Glencalvie after the Massacre of the Rosses in

1854. But the 1861 census showed that John Ross was born near Scourie in 1813.

I drove to Foindle, twisting along a single lane road for the last three kilometres. Robert Ross lived in the second house in this village that appeared to have three houses, a distant relative, tall and lean with thick eyebrows, an elder in the Free Presbyterian church. We discussed the most recent fissure, in 1989, over Lord MacKay's presence at the Catholic mass for his friend.

"It wasn't just the Lord Chancellor that caused the split," Ross told me. "They wanted liberty of conscience. They wanted the freedom to do things the church didn't approve of. Where's the discipline in that?" I drank tea and ate some biscuits that his wife had wheeled in on a tray. They weren't having any. "Some supported MacKay," he said, "but he doesn't have anything to do with them." The history of the Presbyterian church mirrors the clan tribalism that flourished in the Highlands, a constant winnowing, separating the clean from the unclean, mankind's oldest dance. The local Free Presbyterian congregation was tiny and most of them were related to me.

"We don't have much truck or trade with Rome," Ross said. "The idea of eating the sacrament, the idea that Christ is in this bit of biscuit, that's idolatry to us. It's blasphemy." We were sitting in his pleasant, overstuffed sitting room. Behind the house the loch stretched out among jutting rocks to the North Sea.

After I finished my tea, Ross took me out to show me the ruins of a stone house behind his. It had belonged to the Morrisons, another distant relative. The doors were gone but the thick stone walls were still standing after several centuries. There were two rooms inside. "The family lived in one room and the livestock in the other," Ross said. Lachlan's house had been turned into a school, he told me, and Lachlan had built another up the road. I had passed it on the way in, another solid white house.

I left Robert Ross and drove down the road to the house at Fanagmore. There were tours of Loch Laxford where Lachlan used to fish for salmon. The woman who owned the house was sitting in the glassed-in porch. It was hotter than a sauna in there and she was wearing a thick wool cardigan buttoned up to her throat. Her husband had died, she said. She didn't know much about the house; they had taken it in the forties. She smiled shyly and adjusted her heavy skirt. Behind us the rings of salmon farms floated on the loch.

Lachlan Ross had almost drowned in Loch Laxford as a young salmon fisherman. He was in a small boat that was being towed by a larger one. There were four men in the smaller boat, young fishermen in their thick woollens and heavy boots. When a wave came through and capsized the boat, they were thrown into the icy water, instantly waterlogged. Lachlan saw two of the men go down. He made it to a rock finally and pulled himself up, shivering but grateful. Later in his life, Lachlan told his son-in-law William Matheson this story. Matheson asked him how he was able to get to the rock. "I walked on the water," Lachlan replied. This was the beginning of his spiritual journey. He believed that he had been spared by divine providence. From that point on, he devoted his time to further God's purpose.

I returned to Robert Ross's house and then followed him back to Scourie where he opened the Free Presbyterian church for me and we toured the stern, elegant space, largely unchanged in a hundred years. The corrugated iron exterior had been stuccoed over but not much else had been done. The seats were spare, well-worn hardwood benches. There were four square, unadorned windows and a wooden communion table. Outside we stared down at Scourie Bay and Robert talked of the encroachment of the Catholic church, the result, in part, of the European Union. "The move to Europe, they're all Catholics. France, Italy, Spain. We used to be enemies with Spain . . . the Armada." The relative isolation of Scourie hasn't helped morality, he said. There was satellite television with a multitude of stations, an army of tourists, as well as the Lowlanders and foreigners who now lived in the Highlands, having come for work, an odd though modest reversal of the centuries of emptying out. "The decline in morality," he lamented. "Husbands and wives leaving one another to live with others. The pubs aren't a help. They're everywhere." He gave me a copy of the *History of the Free Presbyterian Church of Scotland 1893-1933*, a gift.

Robert Ross told me that his congregation was now too small to support a minister. Everyone was dead or had drifted. He preached himself, sharing duties with another elder. There weren't any Free Presbyterians left in Scourie. After the split over MacKay, which had led to much local ill will, there was only Robert and his son in Foindle. In Kinlochbervie, four-teen kilometres away, there was Robert's sister and a few more. They had another church there, a larger one. I was welcome to come to Kinlochbervie on Sunday to hear him. "Don't expect much," he said, smiling. "I'm not a preacher."

———

Catherine Ross returned to Fanagmore to have her child in 1899. She was twenty-two, worldly in a village of only two houses. The Ross house held eleven people, a nation protected on one side by the sea and on the other by the hills. It was ac-cessible by a footpath that would be supplemented eventually

by a narrow, twisting road. Georgina was born at home, in a
room facing the sea. Illegitimacy was a mortal sin and her existence was a religious issue. A small bundle, already tainted. On
Sunday, Lachlan Ross, technically her grandfather though act-
ing as her father, would have carried Georgie over the mountain, stepping across the bog and scrambling up the rocks
under the gaping spring sky. It was an arduous two-hour hike
to the Free Presbyterian church. Lachlan would have entered
the church and presented Georgie like an offering. Catherine
was disciplined by the congregation, and had to answer questions put to her by the elders. Did she recognize her sin?
Would she remain on the path of righteousness? The child was
a visual reference for the questions, and drew the gaze of everyone. Lachlan was an elder and held in esteem and this was
taken into consideration. Georgie was baptised in the church
and Catherine left for South Africa soon after.

I asked Mrs. Macdonald about the hike from Scourie to
Fanagmore. She said it was brisk, to give myself enough time.
My grandmother's family sometimes made the hike twice a
day, for morning and evening services. On the map, the walk
looked to be about three miles but it was over a series of hills.
The morning was cloudless, a surprise, and warm enough that
I thought I should get some sunblock. I asked at the Scourie
store and the two women looked at me and laughed. "It's been
a while since anyone needed that," one said. They thought
there might be some in the back from three years ago, when it
was last requested. One of the women rustled around in the
storeroom for five minutes and returned with a small, expensive tube. "It's very dear," she said, "I hope it works."

I drove to Fanagmore and parked my car and started hik-
ing up a small, barely perceptible path. It didn't get much traffic, or perhaps only in summer. In winter the walk must have

been a hardship, stepping through the snow. The ground was still spongy with water now and when the path disappeared, I stepped into brown earth and watched my foot disappear, extracting it with difficulty. I walked to the village of Tarbet, then up through the sheep pasture, over the stone fence. The family would have formed a dark line in their sombre Sunday clothes, following a trail that stayed close to the large rock outcroppings. They would probably have walked in order, with Georgie behind Jean and Jemima, now the oldest with Catherine gone, at the back, shepherding them. The hill opened onto a plateau that had huge boulders that looked like they'd been dropped from the sky. I could see the island of Handa with its bright crescent of beach, like a separate country. The sun came through the holes in the cloud and left circles of light on the sea. There were small lochs up in the hills, dark with peat, that probably stayed cold through summer. The view was spectacular but the footing was so uncertain and the path so narrow that Georgie would have concentrated on following the heels of Jean's shoes, the family moving over the landscape in silence.

The path faded out and I wandered lost for half an hour, not an unpleasant experience when the weather is beautiful. Scourie appeared suddenly, the church glinting dully on the opposite hill. The yellow bloom of gorse covered the south face of the mountains. This bright acreage had a softness to it when seen from a distance but up close the trunks and branches of the gorse were gnarled and twisted and grew at unpredictable angles. Georgie could have looked up now, less fearful of the trail that widened and descended into a pasture. The path ran beside a large white house with a walled garden; exotic plants could be glimpsed through a single opening in the wall, tulips and bright colours. A line of New Zealand palm trees swayed overhead, sustained by the Gulf Stream, an odd tropical note in the primitive landscape.

I walked past the crofts, past the flocks of geese and ducks on the side of the path. Ganders made tentative charges, their glottal aggressiveness trailing off as I passed them. When I climbed the opposite hill and reached the church, I timed the walk at over two hours, though I had been lost for some of that time. To make that walk with nine children during bad weather, to do it twice in a day, would certainly be a gesture of faith.

They would have opened the simple wooden door and filed in, filling two pews with the family. Georgina's earliest memory of the church would have been sitting on the hard wooden bench, her feet not touching the floor, her shoes wet, her feet thawing slowly during the ninety-minute service in the scarcely heated building. Wearing a dark wool sweater that had come through several sisters, her coat mended at the elbows. The interior was pine boards laid the length of the church— floor, walls and ceiling—and varnished to a high shine. As the service stretched into its second hour, she would fidget slightly, though the rigid mood and sombre choreography ensured silence. She rose when her family rose, sat when they sat and listened to their singing of the Psalms. The sermons were dire. Only the elect would enter the Kingdom of God. Georgie's feet dangled in the cold room while she waited for judgement.

I walked back to Fanagmore, getting lost at a different place, the path becoming too subtle to trace. I didn't see a soul up there.

I ate a dinner of apples, cheese and a banana-flavoured granola bar, sitting on a bench looking west over Scourie Bay.

Back in my room I began reading the *History of the Free Presbyterian Church*, which had an element of intrigue. The events that led to the church's formation were described in painstaking detail. Until 1894, it was still a part of the Free Church. William Robertson Smith, disparagingly described as a brilliant scholar, was partly blamed for the split. "He took his theological course at the New College, Edinburgh, and there he got his first taste of the poison that was soon to vitiate the Theological scholarship of Scotland." Robertson Smith also studied in Germany, subscribing to the theory of Higher Criticism, which examined the Bible the way any book would be examined. Science crept into his reading of the scriptures and prophecy was discounted, a disturbing idea to many within the church.

In the book Smith was criticized for his "mental acrobatic gifts" and his "erratic theorizings of the German school." But the church slowly became more liberal. Hymns, accompanied by organ music, began to be heard in some churches, though almost exclusively in Lowland congregations. The Free Church inched away from the unyielding aspects of Calvinism. It became accepted that Christ had died for all men, not simply the elect. Dr Robert Rainy, the Principal of the Free Church, began to lead it toward a union with the United Presbyterian Church, a union that would make the new church the largest in Scotland.

Rainy was opposed in the Highlands, where tradition and simplicity reigned. The two sides mounted campaigns that pitted Highland traditionalists against Lowland revisionists, but the Highlands were in the minority. Rainy was able to get his proposed Free Church Declaratory Act passed in 1892, which moved the church away from pure Calvinism. It gave the General Assembly the power to shape doctrine, where scripture had dictated it before. And it allowed liberty of conscience, which in effect gave ordinands the right to believe what they wished. There was vocal opposition to the Declaratory Act but only two ministers quit the Free Church in protest. Between them, they had 17,000 followers. They had to give up their churches and manses and preach where they could, sometimes outdoors in the snow. This movement was based in the north-west Highlands where my ancestors were and in Skye and Harris. On August 31, 1894, they selected a name for themselves, the Free Presbyterian Church of Scotland.

Six years later, the Free Church merged with the United Presbyterian Church, creating the largest church in Scotland. But twenty-seven Free Church ministers declined to join the United Free Church, as the new body was called and they initiated legal proceedings to retain the name, property and funds. The lawsuit lasted four years, and was bitter. The Free Church congregants were known colloquially as the Wee Frees and were ridiculed in the press. The Wee Frees didn't seek any kind of reunion with the Free Presbyterian Church, despite their commonality; there was too much distrust and bile between them. Both churches became marginalized but waved their independence like a flag.

Sunday was wet with a piercing west wind. In the morning, Mrs. Macdonald gave me blood pudding, a mixture of sheep's blood, suet, oatmeal and onions, and stood over me as I ate it, observing me as if I were an experiment. She smiled proudly as I finished, like a mother with an obedient child. A retired Australian couple at the table vehemently agreed with one another that young people didn't want to work these days.

"If an executive position doesn't just land on their heads . . ."

"Brood like chickens over their hair, but their *future* . . ."

Their conversation was a theatre piece that had been honed in other bed and breakfasts. I left quickly, pleading a religious commitment.

At 9 a.m. I set out for Kinlochbervie where half of the small congregation lived. They alternated between the church there and the one in Scourie. The Kinlochbervie church was one of the "Parliamentary" churches that was erected between 1825 and 1835, financed by the government under the Act for Building Additional Places of Worship in the Highlands and Islands of Scotland. The project was overseen by the engineer Thomas Telford, the famous road builder, though the actual church design was conceived by one of his surveyors, William Thomson. The standard T-plan church sat 312 people, was built of harled rubble, roofed with Ballachulish slate, had grand Tudor windows and a pinnacled birdcage bellcote. The Kinlochbervie church had been stuccoed over and was hemmed in by a fieldstone fence. It overlooked the Kinlochbervie harbour, where boxes of fish were being hauled into a shed on pallets and fishermen mended bright green nets.

I was the second to arrive. Robert's sister was inside, turning on lights and space heaters. A steel pipe ran along the floor in each row, carrying heat to warm the feet. The seats, oddly, were theatre seats, individual, plush corduroy with padded armrests.

"You must be the visitor," she said.

She stood shyly, and backed away when I approached. I introduced myself and chatted a bit and she answered reluctantly. Three others arrived soundlessly and took seats. We were spread throughout the church, no two in the same row, like people at a matinee. Robert Ross came in and took his place below the towering wooden pulpit and began the service without ceremony. The five of us sang Psalm 118, staying in our seats to sing in our separate keys and then standing for a fifteen-minute prayer. Robert read from Revelation and began his one-hour sermon, warning of popery and the modern age, acknowledging the sacrifice of those who had gone before. He talked about how Adam and Eve had enjoyed communion with God before the fall. *I am Alpha and Omega, the first and the last . . . I am he that liveth, and was dead; and, behold, I am alive for evermore, A-men; and have the keys of hell and of death.*

I felt a strange, fleeting envy for their certainty. The United Church had been about doubt and forgiveness and a muted social activism. We had sung Simon and Garfunkel's "I Am a Rock." We contemplated everything and forgave everyone, especially ourselves. The certainty here was from another century. The sparse congregation in this grand church seemed to be hoarding the Truth rather than spreading it. To share it would only dilute it. The church was destined to dwindle down in the coming century to a single, rigid, ancient member who couldn't be swayed from his path. They were already down to five, the congregation largely held together by the will of Robert Ross.

He spoke with an evangelical cadence, the last half of most sentences flattening into an interrogative tone. His voice was strong and he swayed rhythmically from side to side, a subtle version of Ray Charles at the piano, signifying. The light shone off his glasses and it gave the impression that his eyes were closed in some private rapture. After ninety minutes, in the same rhythm as the rest, he said, "There'll be no more just now," and took his Bible and left, followed by the congregation.

Outside, I thanked him for the sermon and he smiled. The others stood at the door. I asked if I could talk to him for a minute. I wondered if he had the session records dating back to 1899, to the year my grandmother was baptised. "We don't discuss secular matters on the Sabbath," he responded. "We don't travel either, except to get to church." The seven of us stared uncomfortably down to the harbour. The wind was strong and blowing the door against the frame. "We're a funny bunch," Ross said. They all got into his Rover without comment and drove home.

———

Two days later I went out on Loch Laxford with Robert's son, John. He was in his thirties, slim with the kind of black hair that seems blue in a certain light. He had a mussel-farming operation. A small motorboat was sitting out in the water and John pulled it in to shore by the rope attached to it. He rolled a cigarette and we rode out onto the loch. It was eight degrees, partly overcast and the breeze off the North Sea felt like a cold razor. I was wearing polar fleece and a windbreaker. John had a thin sweater and jeans, inured to the weather. He motored out to a large flat aluminum boat with a crane on it that was anchored in the loch and we climbed on.

We cruised through the loch, heading toward the sea, while John explained the mussel-farming industry to me. It was expensive to start up; he and his partner had to buy three boats and two hundred miles of rope. They worked every day through the winter, taking the boat out onto heaving, angry water in the bitter cold. It took three years before the first mussels were mature enough to harvest. But the money was good. "I can make more money in a week of mussel farming than I could in a year of crofting," John said.

Ropes were stretched across the bay, anchored at both ends and supported with buoys every six feet. Bright blue ropes were suspended at intervals of ten feet, and millions of mussels attached to them. We stopped and John pulled up a rope thick with clusters of one-year-old mussels to show me.

Closer to the open sea there was a salmon farm, two large floating steel cages containing tens of thousands of fish. A net covered them so they couldn't escape. They were two feet long and from thirty metres away I could see their underbellies flashing in the weak sun and hear the heavy splash of their leaps. There were steel mesh walkways surrounding the tanks and John pulled the boat up and we got out. The tanks were thick with fish, many of them with white deposits on their head.

"It's sea lice," John said. "In the wild, lice are killed by fresh water. When the salmon swim upstream to spawn, the lice die." But with salmon raised in captivity in the salt water at the mouth of the loch, the sea lice have to be killed with a poison that affects other fish. John threw a handful of pellets into the water and the fish churned in pursuit. The pellets contained antibiotics, he told me. A messy business, salmon farming. The mussels were easier. Lachlan Ross had been a salmon fisherman and his boat had tipped not far from the site of the current farm. John pointed out where.

The White House, where Lachlan had once lived, was visible from the salmon farm. The White House had been built for the salmon fishermen but later accommodated the school. Lachlan, my grandmother and the rest of the family lived upstairs and school was held downstairs. Then it was felt that there were too many students for the space and the suggestion was made to the school board to renovate the White House and evict the Ross family. Local records showed that the factor, a Mr. Maclean, wrote to the board, "As due notice has been given to Mr. Lachlan Ross, and that as he could find no other house, the Proprietor would not like to turn him out with his large family unless some other place was procured for him."

He eventually moved up the road, and built a new house. Georgie and her siblings continued to go to the school, barefoot in the summer, wearing boots and avoiding the bogs in the winter. From Orkney, boats came with consumer goods. They were called floating shops and when Georgie and the others sang for the Orkneymen they gave them sweets and clay pipes for their fathers.

The house that Lachlan built was empty now. The former owner had been found face down, dead of drink and hypothermia. His wife was in a nursing home. Above the White House was another house. "Two families lived there," Peter told me. "They had an argument. Didn't speak to one another for thirty years." This was part of the Celtic gift: to live in one of the most isolated parts of the world and to cultivate a war with your only neighbour with the care you'd take to bring a rose garden into bloom. The White House was for sale, John said. He thought it would go for about fifty-five thousand pounds. It shone briefly in the pale sun like a house on a Greek island.

The hills rose up from the bay in picturesque lines. In places the land was flattened into plateaus that had been cultivated and had been part of the crofts operated by the Ross family. John pointed out a large iron ring set in the stone that had been used to anchor ocean going boats. Immigrants left for America from Loch Laxford in the nineteenth century. John pointed to some land along the bay. "That used to belong to Rosses. They were cleared off of it. From Scourie to Foindle. The factor, McIver, he cleared them."

I had read about the man. Evander McIver had arrived in 1845 and acted as factor on behalf of the Duchess of Sutherland, who along with her husband, was the largest landowner in Britain. She wanted to improve on her paltry Highland income and McIver was given the job of doing so. He was essentially his own boss and cleared the tenants off the land in order to make way for sheep and also to expand his own farm. The stone walls behind the Scourie Lodge, an elegant bed and breakfast that was once McIver's home, are reputed to be made from the demolished homes of the evicted families. He was detested then and remains detested more than a century later.

McIver wrote a memoir titled *Reminiscences of a Highland Gentleman*. His version: "The tenants of the crofts wished to go to America, and they marched very awkwardly with my farm, so after the tenants left the land was added to my farm." This is the reverse of what actually happened. McIver wanted to expand his farm, so he evicted the tenants in the name of the Duchess and the families emigrated out of necessity.

Whether the Duchess knew how violent and wrenching the Clearances were is still the subject of debate. She was handsome and plump, a patron of the arts who painted watercolours of the scenery she owned. She had a contempt for the Highlanders, but as their landlord, she had a sentimental attachment too, the kind you have for a lost pet.

In 1883 the Napier Commission was established to investigate the circumstances and abuses of the Clearances and both McIver's name and one of my ancestors, Alexander Ross, were present in its report. The commissioners spent months touring the north, interviewing people as to what had happened and their report was published in April, 1884.

Alexander Ross was Lachlan's uncle. He was seventy-four at the time his evidence was taken at Kinlochbervie and he was McIver's harshest critic. When asked where he lived, he replied, "At Foindale, at Loch Laxford. But I may say I have no residence because I am hated by factors and all in authority."

"What is your occupation?"

"Nothing. I am only a citizen of the world."

Alexander had been chosen as a delegate by the residents of Scourie, Eddrachillis and Badcall to speak on their behalf and he read a prepared statement. His mother, he said, had been turned out of her house at the age of seventy-eight, partly due to McIver's enmity toward Alexander. Four other widows had been evicted so their land could be made into a sheep walk. Others had been removed so that the land could be used by sportsmen from the south. Alexander told stories of corruption and devastation. Fifteen hundred people had been moved to the rocky coastline, replaced by a dozen hunters and several thousand sheep. "It would take a Royal Commission especially for the purpose to unravel the Scourie management," he said.

When asked if he wanted to hear the testimony Alexander Ross had given against his character, McIver replied, "I have not the least desire to hear it."

McIver's one great contribution to Highland culture was the cabbage palm tree in the garden of the Scourie Lodge. He had gotten the seed in a letter from New Zealand, raised it in a conservatory for a year and then planted it outside where it unexpectedly flourished and seeded several young palms.

After our boat tour, I thanked John and drove back into Scourie with the heat on in the car. I stopped again at the graveyard, where McIver's headstone was by far the largest, built on a grand scale, the centrepiece of the site. The stone was eight feet tall with a celtic cross and a mortared wall flanking it that was twenty feet long. He was buried with his wife Mary. The inscription read, "They were lovely and pleasant in their lives and in their death they were not divided." Hugh

Ross, Alexander's father, was buried close to McIver, his grave marked with a dark granite stone laid flat.

My rental car was fluorescent green, a colour that is sometimes used on emergency vehicles, a safety measure by the rental company who had laboured hard to get me to take out extra insurance. The locals had no trouble spotting me. I stopped at the only store in Scourie, which sold groceries, liquor, stationery, newspapers and served as the post office. "Having any luck?" the woman at the counter asked. Everyone now knew that I was searching for dead relatives, a modern epidemic. My absurd car had been spotted as far as thirty kilometres away. I had been seen walking near Kinlochbervie. It was known that I napped at the side of the road at a scenic viewpoint. Everyone knew my business and it was slightly unsettling, like living in a Stephen King novel. I bought a half pint of scotch and wondered how long it would take for this news to get around town.

I stopped for a drink at the Scourie Hotel and talked to a man named Shipley who worked for the government. He had the elongated features of a basset hound and leaned in close to make a point. He was a climber, he said, though not the kind where you needed climbing gear. He took vigorous hikes over well marked trails.

Climbing wasn't his only hobby. Second World War planes was another. And football, though he was quick to point out, as people outside North America generally do, that it wasn't what I knew as football. It wasn't the military drudgery of human draught horses grunting for twenty seconds then taking a two-minute break to discuss their salaries. He asked me if

I had any hobbies and I thought for a moment before saying no. "You're not quite the right age," Shipley said. He might have been five years older than I was. "They'll come," he added, as if in warning. Adolescent boys and men of a certain age had hobbies. Boys had them to take their mind off the gap between sexual desire and the impossibility of relieving it. Men had hobbies to take their minds off the gap between their imagined lives and the one they were actually living. We argued pleasantly for an hour about politics, television and global weather systems. He said it was a shame the way Canadians treated their natives. I pointed out that it was Scots settlers who had first displaced the plains tribes from their land. Ironically, the Assembly of First Nations had recently toured the Highlands, meeting with the Scottish Crofters Union to compare their suffering and their shared cause of self-determination. The crofters apologized on behalf of the Scottish settlers who had left in the nineteenth century and appropriated native land. I left Shipley and walked around the village, looking in the windows of houses from the street.

In the morning Mrs. Macdonald asked me if I wanted porridge for breakfast. I hadn't had porridge in thirty-five years and had hated it as a child. Why not? I tried to swallow a mouthful and a gag reflex quickly followed. The bowl seemed the size of a swimming pool. A skin had formed where the oatmeal touched its concave sides. A modest spoonful seemed to expand in my mouth, exploding into a kilo of mud that filled my skull. I ate all of it, smiling willfully.

Four of Mrs. Macdonald's grandchildren were at the breakfast table. They each looked like a different species of apple, with their round heads and inflamed cheeks. The eldest was about ten and had been to Canada, to Vancouver, Banff, Calgary and Edmonton. He had seen the mountains and the West

Edmonton Mall, the largest in the world. What did he like best? I asked.

"Basements," he said. "They're brilliant."

"Basements."

"Carpets, big screen telly. No parents. Brilliant."

The houses here were built on bedrock and none had basements. So the basement was a place to escape to, a land apart.

———————

What I wanted to do was fish. Except I didn't know how. But Scourie had the same effect weddings have always had on my failed resolution to learn the tango. Fishermen were everywhere. Trout was an industry. Instead I took a tour of Handa Island, one of the largest bird sanctuaries in northern Europe. An ex-navy man from England had an eighteen-foot aluminum motorboat at the dock in Scourie Bay and ran several tours a day. The Welshman from the bed and breakfast and an English couple were waiting at the dock. There were a few clouds and a warm wind.

The boat moved slowly through the choppy water as the tour guide explained the habits of the hundreds of dark birds bobbing in the dark water. The island had beaches on the channel side but facing the sea was a cliff that was several hundred feet high. It was striated and set at a bias and tens of thousands of birds sat on its ledges like the occupants of a condemned apartment. There were holes along the ledges, the result of wind and salt water erosion over the centuries, and they offered shelter. The Gulf Stream flows by and the water was surprisingly warm.

We spotted an arctic skewer, a bird that dives on gulls that are returning with food. They attack the gull or simply scare it until it regurgitates its dinner, and the skewer nabs it before it hits the water. The skewer pays for its thuggish nature with its second-hand diet. The small boat moved slowly along the periphery of the island as we catalogued birds. Everyone seemed to know so much. As we cruised the channel side of the island, the ex-navy man said, "My oldest son was conceived on that beach," delivering the line as if from a play, which, with three tours a day, five months of the year, I suppose it is.

The next day I drove east out of Scourie along the coastal road, which switched from one lane to two and back again at intervals. The scenery altered as dramatically. A long brown valley looked like a glacier had scraped through a few weeks earlier and the land was just beginning its recovery. A moonscape of brown hummocks dotted with lichen surrounded Loch Eriboll. Another valley was almost tropical. A few stands of forest stood isolated. At the head of the loch there was a spectacular beach, contained in a large crescent, walled in on all sides by cliffs of several hundred feet. The sand was pristine and the beach more than a hundred metres deep. The view out to sea showed the mountains receding in separate shades of blue and grey.

I stopped in Tongue, approaching it on a causeway that crossed the Kyle of Tongue. The town was on a hill, a dramatic setting even for this dramatic area. Before dinner I walked up to Varrich Castle, which looked down on the kyle. The castle was on a miniature scale, a single room that must have served as a lookout point. The water was so clear you could see the bottom even from this height.

I stayed at the Ben Loyal Hotel and I told the owner I was going to Bettyhill in the morning, to look for the house of Christina MacKay, another of my great-grandmothers. He told me that Baron MacKay had been staying at the hotel the last few nights. He was a sportsman and a regular visitor. "He's Dutch, you know," he said. The title had been sold, he thought. "The MacKays fought on the side of the English at Culloden. It's not something that's generally advertised. But they were mercenaries, by and large."

I had dinner in the bar, which was filled with tourists, and shared a table with a man from France who was travelling on his own. He looked a bit like Friar Tuck, with sloping, powerful shoulders, a barrel chest and short sturdy legs. His hair was cut straight across his forehead, his eyes were small and he ate with both hands in what seemed like a gesture of defence. I asked him what had brought him to Scotland.

"The isolation, the spaces of nothing," he replied. He worked near Caen, as a mechanic. He was divorced, a confession that was accompanied by a shrug. "You drive, you see some sheeps." He waved his knife in small circles. "You see some mountain. Some people. There is much nature."

He liked driving on the one-lane roads, which he saw as a kind of sport. It was a comfortable country, he said. It wasn't ruled by chain stores and gas bars that sold beer and sports shirts and covered ten acres of roadside.

In the morning I found Christina MacKay's house near Skerray. It was located on the floor of a valley. The sea was less than a kilometre away and the land was defined by rocky outcroppings and gorse, though the valley had the soft green colour of a golf course. Near the turn of the century, Christina's husband, Peter Mainland, had lost the family farm and gone to South America to make a fortune. She and her three young children, including my grandfather Don and his twin brother, were sent here from the Shetland Islands to live with Christina's parents. They must have told her that Peter was no good. The assumption may have been that Peter wasn't coming back.

Christina and the children lived with them for several years as Peter abandoned South America for California and Chicago and, finally, Winnipeg. It was from there that he wrote, asking Christina and the children to join him.

In Bettyhill I visited the Strathnaver Museum, which described the misery of the Highland Clearances. Housed in a church that had been built around 1710, the museum was surrounded by a cemetery, filled mostly with MacKays. On the second floor of the church was the MacKay museum, giving a history of the clan. "Are you a MacKay then?" the curator asked me when I entered. My middle name is MacKay so I had a diluted claim.

I wandered among the artifacts, most of which had been donated by MacKays. There was a couple who looked like they were waiting for visitors. The woman asked me politely, but firmly, how much of a MacKay I was. She was from North Carolina and outlined in painful detail the purity of her own attachment. Her husband occasionally joined in with the relaxed drawl of Huckleberry Hound.

"You kept your maiden name then," I asked, taking the offensive. "You're a MacKay?"

She hadn't kept the name but another lecture followed, and I was caught up in an absurd clannish mudfight.

On one of the downstairs walls there was an excerpt from "The Canadian Boat Song": "From the lone shieling of the misty island mountains divide us and a waste of seas, But still the blood is strong. The heart is Highland and we in dreams behold the Hebrides." It was accompanied by a short history of an uprising in Kildonan in 1813 after a hundred families were removed from their homes. They emigrated to Manitoba's Red River area with Lord Selkirk rather than be relocated to even poorer land in the Highlands.

The villain behind this and other local atrocities was Patrick Sellar, and he looked the part. A photograph showed him in profile, with a sharp, wildly exaggerated nose like a scythe jutting from his thin face. His lips were a hard line drawn on the flesh. Sellar despised the Highlanders, considering them to be ragged aborigines. He had writs from their landlord to evict them from their homes and he enforced the writs with hired thugs and fire. Women were beaten, the elderly abused. Some emigrated, mainly to Canada and New Zealand. Some relocated on the coasts to learn the trade of fishing. Sellar was eventually put on trial for arson and cruelty but he was acquitted by a jury of like-minded peers.

A few kilometres down the road, at Ardlochy, there was the site of a settlement that had been razed during the Clearances. A large map indicated where the buildings had been. From the perspective of the map I looked down onto grass, toward hills—there was no rubble or unrestored remains, none of the usual historical evidence. The site had the framework of a tourist attraction—road signs, listings in books, historical plaques—but there was nothing, in effect, to see, just the negative space of what had vanished. Though it invoked a sombre mood, it had the feel of a clever art installation. I stood at the map, locating the missing points of interest on the lawn below, which were marked with numbered posts. A middle-aged American couple stood beside me, reading and staring in reverent silence. It seemed like the perfect memorial to emigration, the blankness a fitting monument. The once cultivated land, the houses and outbuildings had left no trace on the land.

In his account of a trip he made to the island of Skye with Samuel Johnson in 1773, James Boswell described a dance he took part in. "We performed, with much activity, a dance which, I suppose, the emigration from Skye has occasioned. They call it *America*. Each of the couples, after the common involutions and evolutions, successively whirls round in a circle, till all are in motion; and the dance seems intended to show how emigration catches, till a whole neighbourhood is set afloat."

——— ———

Driving south to Inverness I saw a sign near Rogart that indicated a memorial to John A. Macdonald, Canada's first prime minister, a man of greatness and a significant drinker. South of Rogart was the stone monument, which marked the site of his grandparents' home, the cairn built from the stones of that house and dedicated by John Diefenbaker on July 13, 1968.

I went on to Inverness and had a late dinner in an Italian restaurant. Two American men came in and took the next table. One of them, dressed in a blue blazer, khakis and a striped dress shirt open at the neck, ordered a martini. The waitress blinked quietly at him. "What's in it then," she asked.

"It's gin. And vermouth."

"Vermouth . . ."

"You don't need it," he said, erasing the air in front of him. "Just whisper the word to the gin."

"What."

"I want a double."

"We just have gin in one-ounce glasses."

"Then I want three. And a large glass. And a large glass of ice. And an olive."

"Olive." She wrote it down.

His friend interrupted. "What he's trying to say is, he'd like a large scotch on the rocks."

"I've been driving for three and a half hours on a narrow road and I'm going to have a martini," the first said tersely.

"Ed, we're in *Scotland*."

"Gin. Christ. *Gin.* Is that clear?"

The waitress left. Ed turned to me and said that the Scots could learn a lot about the service industry.

We talked about Scotland for a bit. Along with golf, they were looking up a few relatives. Ed ordered more gin and made everyone ad hoc martinis. As Ed's warm gin warmed us, the Highlands glowed, its rich, plaid history danced and staggered around us. Afterwards, out on High Street, Ed looked in the windows of the tourist shops, examining sporrans and scarves and Black Watch tartan hats. He wanted to buy a kilt, he said, to wear when he washed his car. He wanted to help these people with their insurance needs. It was almost midnight and the dull sky suggested rain.

———

At noon the next day I called Donald Boyd, a minister in the Free Presbyterian Church and asked if there were any central records of kirk sessions. I was looking for a written account of my grandmother's case. The written records only began in 1913, he said, but he invited me to visit and gave me directions to his home, which was nearby. The house was a large, solid manse on a hill. Boyd answered the door, a tall man in his forties with an intensely scrubbed look, as if he had never needed to shave. His hands were pink and soft. The family was just sitting down to lunch and Boyd invited me to join them. "Simple fare," he said.

At the kitchen table was his wife, a pleasant Dutch woman who had the slightly bleak look of some of Van Gogh's subjects.

Their pretty daughter, who was about eight, stared at me as if I were an exhibit. I delicately broached the issue of my grandmother's illegitimacy and how it would have been viewed by the church a century ago. Would she, in effect, have been damned? Boyd laughed at the harsh reputation of the Free Presbyterians: "You might want to brush up on your Calvinism."

The mother would have been disciplined, he said, but she would have remained in the church if she showed the proper remorse. I asked about the current state of the church; were there any congregations in Canada?

The Free Presbyterian church in Winnipeg—housed in a building bought by my great-grandfather Lachlan, he said—had only recently been sold. The congregation dwindled and what assets it had were sent to a mission in Africa. "There was a congregation in Chesley, Ontario," he said. "They broke away from our church though. Over the issue of transportation on Sunday." I knew this story vaguely because it had been a relative of mine, William Matheson, who had been involved in the split. He was the minister of the only Free Presbyterian church in that southern Ontario town. When the Scottish synod decided to allow its members to use streetcars on Sundays, provided it was to go to church, he rebelled, decrying the decision as too liberal. The church threw him out, and he spent the rest of his life trying to persuade people of the church's lack of legal or moral grounds. He preached at his own church, which he called the Presbyterian Reformed Church of Ontario. Yet another split.

"Do you have any ecclesiastical ties whatever?" Boyd asked me pleasantly.

"I grew up in the United Church."

Boyd saw this as the non-answer it was and received it with a thin smile.

"And now?"

I confessed that my interest was largely architectural, which to him may have had some Catholic implications.

After lunch he went upstairs to look for information on Lachlan Ross for me. I waited with his wife in the large dining room. You could have fit the Scourie congregation and all the Canadian Free Presbyterian church members in there without any crowding. We perched on oversized chairs like children under supervision.

"This idea, the Catholic sense that Christ is in a wafer, that's blasphemy for us," she said to me as if it were a standard conversational icebreaker. The room looked like a set from *Citizen Kane*, oversized and unlived-in. Macbeth's castle had been on the site where their house now stood, she said. *Macbeth* is essentially a religious mystery: why do men commit evil? Three innocents were killed in the castle in the service of Macbeth's ambition. We discussed the beauty of her house and how difficult it was to keep clean until Boyd came down with some photocopied documents, Lachlan's obituary among them.

It read, in part, "In common with Adam's family in general, Lachlan Ross showed in his early days that he was born in sin and that he was shapen in iniquity, but when he came of age, he came like Moses to refuse what the world gives for a season . . . He was very free and open in telling about how he was convinced of his sinful and miserable state and how precious Christ came to be to him . . . Mr. Ross was one of the most guileless of men that we ever met. There was nothing of the man of the world about him. He seemed to be without duplicity; simple and single in his desire to serve Christ. We believe he has entered within the veil to behold the Face of Him who drew him with the cords of His love. May the Lord heal the breaches in the walls of Zion and raise up witnesses in connection with his cause in Manitoba."

―――――

In the morning I took a brisk walk along the banks of the Ness, amid the dog-owners and a jogger who looked American. I had a heroic breakfast of bacon, eggs, toast and oatcakes and talked to a woman in thick tweeds who was a travelling saleswoman. "It's the people really," she told me. "That's why I do it. It's like a family." The selling itself was secondary, she said.

I drove south, listening to the BBC on the car radio, the lulling voice of a woman describing the essentials for a successful dinner party. The guests, she said, too many people made the mistake of inviting the wrong ones. The hills softened gradually like a blanket being shaken out and smoothed onto the ground. I drove to Helensburgh, a town to the northwest of Glasgow on the Firth of Clyde. I wanted to see a house there that had been designed by Charles Rennie Mackintosh.

Hill House was an elegant white structure located up the hill from the main street. But it was closed when I got there, due to open at one-thirty. I walked around the town and had lunch at an outdoor café though it was chilly, and read a book about Mackintosh and his tragic life.

He had received the commission for Hill House in 1902. He was thirty-four years old and had designed the first phase of the Glasgow School of Art and he had just married his great love, Margaret Macdonald, whom he had met when they both were art students. He was approaching his professional zenith with Hill House, though he wasn't aware of it.

A few years later, Mackintosh designed the second phase of the Glasgow School of Art. It should have been a triumph, but commissions quickly dwindled. He designed the interior and furniture for a tea house but the large projects went to others. His work was criticized in Scotland as being too modern. It was praised in Europe and in architectural journals but locally rejected. In 1911, he made only seventy pounds from his professional work. Discouraged, he and his wife Margaret left for Walberswick, a village in Suffolk on the English coast, in 1914. But his timing was unfortunate. When war was declared, the Mackintoshes became suspect. Charles had one sleepy eye, which was interpreted by the locals as sinister and he and his wife had accents and they often took long walks along the coast at night, which gave them an opportunity to signal German boats. They were suspected of being spies and summoned before a tribunal where they cleared themselves. But they felt alienated yet again and left the village for London, settling in Chelsea in 1915.

In London Mackintosh worked on textile designs. The couple was permanently broke and Mackintosh sold some of his architectural drawings to a junk shop. But they had a circle of friends in London and one of them, Mary Newbery Sturrock, said when interviewed in the 1980s, "Even in Chelsea I don't think Mackintosh saw himself as a failure. I don't believe he was a disappointed man." Eight years later, he was disappointed. In 1923, he and Margaret left London for France where they lived in the Hotel du Commerce in Port Vendres on the Mediterranean coast near the Spanish border. "When they left London," Sturrock said, "he'd given up hope of being an architect. He was going to be a painter perhaps, certainly he was going to paint watercolours."

France attracted them in part because of the favourable exchange rate, a quality that had drawn Ernest Hemingway and Scott Fitzgerald and hundreds of American expatriates. The

Mackintoshes survived, though barely, on a very small income that Margaret received after her mother died. "As he stayed away in France he became slowly like a lost soul," Sturrock said. "He had nothing else to back him but the love of his wife." When Margaret went to Paris or London, he wrote her long letters, chronicles he called them, describing his painting, his loneliness and depression.

He complained in one letter about how the Americans had ruined French tobacco once they had started manufacturing it themselves. "I think I dislike everything the American touches commercially. His idea is to work for the millions and damn the individual. My ideal is to work for the best type of individual and the crowd will follow. Damn Them . . . Damn Them, Moving pictures—Architecture—Theatres." It wasn't clear what he was damning here: his own stunning lack of commercial success or the profession itself. Mackintosh was stranded between cultures, too much of an aesthete for the modern, industrial world, and yet too modern for his home country. Where once he had been praised in Europe, he had become quaint as the Europeans embraced the modernist ideas of architects like Mies van der Rohe. He was a man who fell completely between the cracks of fashion and geography, another Highland exile.

In 1927, Mackintosh was diagnosed with cancer of the tongue and returned to London for treatment. He wore a radium collar, which was painful. He couldn't speak. A friend led him through exercises in the hope of regaining his speech but he remained mute. He died on December 10, 1928, in a London hospital and was cremated at Golders Green Cemetery.

Looking back on his life, Mary Sturrock said, "I feel terribly, terribly sad at the waste. Here we have this brilliant man whom it would pay you to use. And he wasn't given any real use at all . . . I would have liked to have seen his fiftieth house, with all the edges rubbed off and all his experience and development brought to play. We could have had somebody as good as Corbusier but we weren't able to do it."

In a dispiriting coda to this kind of neglect, I once visited Tom Howarth, a friend of my father's, an architect who had been collecting Mackintosh's distinctive furniture for years. My father and I went to see him in his cramped Toronto apartment, which was filled with the now familiar tall, black, ladderback, not wildly comfortable chairs Mackintosh designed, as well as other Mackintosh pieces. This was well before his recent celebration. I sat in one of the chairs, eating Peek Frean biscuits and drinking tea and thinking the collection carried the air of folly. Ten years later Howarth put it up for auction and profited by several million dollars, the writing desk alone listed in Christie's catalogue for over two hundred thousand pounds sterling.

When I got back to Hill House at one-thirty, there was a lineup, a collection of earnest-looking, middle-aged tourists. We walked through in a line, murmuring approval. It is a stunning house, with all of the furniture, fixtures, colours and interior detail done by the architect before his disappointments, an elegant and functional monument. The living room held a grand piano and the colour scheme was a soft grey and rose with a repeating rose pattern. The bedroom had a domed ceiling above the bed and a steel fireplace. There was stained glass and high ceilings, which lent an ecclesiastical feel, as if we were walking in an abandoned church.

6

ZETLAND

TWO YEARS before Georgina crossed the Atlantic, her future husband left Scotland, also bound for Winnipeg. Donald Mainland was born in Shetland in 1893, near the principal city of Lerwick, and he came to Canada in 1903 at the age of ten after his father, Peter Gavin Mainland, lost the family farm. There are photographs of the Mainland family from that time, formal portraits of men in dark suits staring at the camera as if it were an enemy. The children are in suits as well, solemn and oddly mature-looking. The women loom like icebergs, only their faces showing, the rest hidden below the surface of dresses, bonnets, corsets and boots. But Peter doesn't appear in any of the pictures. I canvassed relatives and didn't turn up a single image. Evidence of his life comes out in wispy anecdotes that trail off. There is a hole in the oral history as well. Peter inhabits the family history like a ghost. There were rumours. He was cross-eyed. He liked to drink. He was a snappy dresser. An aunt thought that he had been albino.

When I wrote to a Shetland genealogist inquiring after Peter Mainland, I received this discreet reply:

"When Thomas Mainland died his son Peter got the farm and what money Thomas had made. About this time the Grand Hotel was built in Lerwick and put in the first billiard table to come to Shetland.

Peter spent his time in the Grand playing billiards and drinking whisky and after a time became bankrupt."

This was the only concrete detail I had of my great-grandfather. He was the antithesis of Lachlan Ross. My grandmother had once described pool as the devil's pastime and perhaps she was right. So I flew to Shetland to see the family billiard table.

———

The flight from Glasgow to Lerwick was in a twin prop Jetstream 31, which taxied drunkenly and then slipped and adjusted in the air, moving like a hummingbird. Each propeller seemed alternately stronger or weaker than the other, and the plane crawled awkwardly through the air. The sky was blue and slightly bleached and whitecaps on the sea were visible from ten thousand feet.

The landscape had a scoured, primitive quality. Shetland sits on a ridge of granite that separates the Atlantic Ocean from

ICU REPORT CARD

Name _____ Room _____

Date _____ Shift _____

CNS:

Cardiovascular:

Respiratory:

GI/GU:

IV Drips:

Other:

the North Sea. It is the northernmost part of Great Britain, almost as close to Norway as it is to Scotland, both geographically and culturally. Shetland is an archipelago of more than one hundred islands, though only fifteen of them are inhabited. Lerwick is at sixty degrees north, the same latitude as Whitehorse in the Yukon, and it is given to the same pale, round-the-clock summers and medieval winters. In Lerwick, I rented a car and drove to Trebister, the farm that Peter had lost with such flair. The wind was gale force eight, strong enough to make walking an act of puppetry, the raised leg shimmying in the wind. The sea crashed along the coast, spray rising in thin, brief suspension. Peat had been gouged out of the hills and the sheep were daubed with bright dye to identify them. A dead hedgehog on the side of the road looked like an inflatable toy. The local radio station was playing country and western music, Garth Brooks mourning a fresh loss. The farm was only a few miles southeast of Lerwick, 430 acres situated on a scenic bay with a small crescent of sand. A chapel stood near the water.

There was a modern house on the site and I knocked on the door and explained to the woman who answered who I was, outlining my convoluted relationship to the farm. She was the owner, Elizabeth Harper, a friendly woman of roughly my age who gave me coffee and spread out the farm's census history on the kitchen table. Oddly, the census records she had gotten from Edinburgh didn't show any evidence of Peter having lived on the land, though I had legal documents that showed he had. She told me that the house Peter had lost in 1894 had been torn down nine years ago and she had built her bungalow on the site. "Come and see the view that your great-grandfather would have seen," she said, leading me into the living room. There was a large picture window that looked over the bay. I stared down to the water, trying to inhabit Peter Mainland's history, without success. The idea of the farm was seductive; this splendid outpost and view. The actual work it took to farm in a land that had few trees, where the wind could ruin a crop, was a much different proposition. Elizabeth phoned a few people on my behalf and wished me luck. Outside it had begun to rain.

I drove back to Lerwick and had a pint of MacEwan ale in a pub that didn't look out to sea. The harbour at Lerwick is picturesque but very few buildings take advantage of the view. The city is huddled against the water rather than built facing it. Lerwick climbs away from the shore, as if escaping to higher ground. The sobriquet, "the Venice of the North"—granted because there are homes built on the water, their doors opening to a dock—is misleading. Historically, the relationship to the sea has been either practical (providing fish, and, more obliquely, oil) or tragic. The sea sustains and punishes but it doesn't represent anything.

The town has just over seven thousand people and looks Scandinavian. Near the harbour, Commercial Street dominates, a narrow stone road that accommodates pedestrians and cars. Stone footpaths run up the hill and the town becomes more orderly as you climb, evolving into a grid of sorts. The people have bright sweaters and faces that are rouged from wind.

In the morning I went to the Family History Society to inquire about the Mainland family. Peter Goudie was the founder of the society, a dapper, white-haired man. "Thomas Mainland stole my grandfather's pig," he said. Thomas was my great-great-grandfather. "He shut it in a shed. Then his son Peter let it out to impress a girl." Another bold act committed in the name of love.

"Did your grandfather get the pig back?"

"I think he went to court."

Peter Goudie offered the names of some Mainlands on the island who might be able to help and steered me to the archives down the street. Peter Mainland came to life in that small room, within the borders of small newspaper entries and in the many legal documents. Amid the favourable notices for The Dandy Darkey Coons Singing Review, articles on the link between tea drinking and insanity, farm tips ("Paying Necessary Attention to the Legs of a Pig"), and ads for passage to Canada or Australia, Peter Mainland's travails were noted in the local paper in unhealthy detail.

I started out with Peter's grandfather. The archivist searched his computer screen. "The late eighteenth century wasn't a good time for the Mainlands," he said. There had been a fist fight over the ownership of a cow, and it had resulted in a lawsuit. Then Thomas and the pig. But it was Peter who really stood out.

When his father died in 1890, Trebister was a large and prosperous farm, free of debt. Thomas was an able crofter and well-respected. Peter inherited the farm and immediately added a second storey to the farmhouse and then planted a flower garden on the roof, which was seen locally as the first sign of folly. He hired two servants as well, which gave him time to set up a business on Commercial Street in Lerwick. Peter saw himself as management, a businessman rather than a crofter. The neighbours accused him of "drooking the miller," which translates as using too much water to make your bread, which in turn is taken to mean something like living off your capital.

At the time he inherited the farm Peter was twenty-one years old and married to Christina MacKay, a Highland girl from Clashleven who had moved to the islands. In 1893, she gave birth to my grandfather Donald and his twin brother Thomas. Peter was already spending some of his time at the Grand Hotel, playing billiards and contemplating larger, bolder schemes. He had one year of living like a gentleman, overseeing both his business and his farm, discussing politics in the bar with an air of wisdom, a father of two sons.

Then, in 1894, Peter's shortcomings as both retailer and farmer were revealed. In June, a case was brought against him by William Adie, who claimed he was owed five pounds sterling for unpaid rent on the shop on Commercial Street. By August, Peter's debts had buried him and he declared bankruptcy. His landlord, Reverend Robert Walker, filed a suit for unpaid rent on the farm. His estate was transferred to a bank agent in Lerwick who acted as trustee for Peter's creditors. His assets were listed as "one black cow with white belly, one grey and white cow, one brown and white cow polled, one red and white cow, one brown and white cow, one calf brown and white, one pony brown and white, one horse dark bay with black points, one old cow brown." He had sold some farm implements to his mother but continued to use them. This appeared to be a legal way to protect some assets. The worth of his coloured cows was estimated at forty pounds. His liabilities were calculated at 1,214 pounds. The long list of creditors included the distiller, draper, miller and shoemaker.

As if this weren't trouble enough, in September, the Inland Revenue authorities brought a case against Peter for keeping an unlicenced carriage. He had been repeatedly warned, the court was informed, but he had ignored these warnings. He was fined, though he was already in the throes of bankruptcy and was unable to pay. At any rate, he no longer owned a carriage.

On the blank cover page of one of Peter's legal documents there is a drawing of a man standing with his empty pockets turned out in a display of penury. He is wearing a suit and his head is bent slightly in supplication. It is the only representation of Peter Mainland that exists. I think that Peter sketched himself, perhaps while the proceedings dragged on, when it became clear that his brief career as a gentleman was over. There is a playful tinge to the drawing, the sense of irony often found in self-portraits.

In his deposition in November 1894, Peter stated that he had started farming in 1890 with between twenty and thirty pounds in working capital. His immediate renovations and expansion resulted in an unreasonable burden of debt. "I cannot say whether I was ever able to pay my debts," Peter told the court. "Perhaps I was in some good seasons, I cannot give a date when I was solvent. I did not keep books from which I could know my position. The trustee asked me for further particulars as to the expenditures and I said I could not give it. I told the trustee that if there had been no expenses other than ordinary expenses of working and reasonable maintenance, there would have been a profit for the past three years of one hundred fifty pounds or so. All of which is truth as I shall answer to God." Though some truths had been omitted. The money he had spent at the Grand Hotel, for one.

The Reverend Robert Walker told the court that Peter didn't in fact have a lease on Trebister. The lease had ended with the death of Peter's father, Thomas. Peter insisted that this wasn't true, though he couldn't produce his father's will. "I promised if there was such a thing, I could produce my father's will," he told the court, "but I found there was none such. I thought it had been in my possession. I told the trustee so but on searching the papers which came over to me with the farm I could not find such a document. I never had my father's will. I only thought I had. My father spoke about making a will, but evidently, he never did."

Except for the receipts he had cleverly made out to his mother for the money she paid for carts, harnesses and carriages, Peter's life was scrupulously undocumented. He didn't live in the cloistered world of marginal numbers the way most crofters had to. He was a big-picture man. The court ruled that the land was rightfully Peter's, or at least, it had been until the bankruptcy. One problem was the inexactness of the lease that Peter's father had had, which specified a period of "between nineteen and fifty-seven years." There was a subjectivity to crofting that deterred most hard-headed businessmen. Not even the size of the farm was exact. In 1877, the Earl of Zetland had sold Reverend Walker six merks of land for two hundred pounds. A merk was the equivalent of 1,600 square fathoms, a fathom being six feet. But the size of a merk was subject to the quality of the land. One merk of poor land was larger than a merk of good land.

Shetland had a disproportionate number of clergymen as lairds, or landowners. "The dovetailing between Church of Scotland ministers and laird was seen more plainly [in Shetland] than I had seen anywhere," wrote David Craig in *On the Crofter's Trail*. "Simply, they belonged to the same class and it is this, rather than any archaic nonsense about driving money lenders out of temples, that typifies these Christian proprietors." Whatever their clerical sympathies regarding the dispossessed, both the church and Reverend Walker were landowners. Peter's antipathy for ministers and religion might have started here.

The *Shetland News* published a running account of Peter's legal woes. The paper catalogued his losses from poor business at the shop (eighty pounds), from death of livestock (one hundred pounds) and from bad crops in two of the three years he had had the farm (eighty pounds). It showed his rapid descent in a way that implied it was not simply business decisions that had been his downfall, so much as his character. Peter made a cursory stand by countersuing Alexander Murray, a drainer who was suing Peter for an unpaid debt of ten pounds. But this dribbled to a close, overwhelmed by larger issues. He had lost everything.

Peter wasn't the only crofter in Shetland who was having trouble. In 1883, before Peter slipped into insolvency, the Napier Commission came to Lerwick, investigating the abuses of the Clearances and the aftermath. What had happened in the Highlands had been echoed in Shetland, where crofters were removed from the land so it could be turned over to sheep farming. The crofters elected local representatives who described the miserable conditions in Shetland to the visiting commissioners. The principal grievances, the commission concluded, were "excessively high rents. The rent charged for land in this locality is much beyond its productive value, land being generally of inferior quality. The crofters have no security of tenure, but are entirely at the mercy of the laird or factor." Most crofters could be evicted on forty days notice, regardless of the improvements they had made to the farm or its buildings.

The memory of the Clearances were still fresh after two generations. Stories were told to the commission of how roofs were burned off homes, doors taken off their hinges. Widows were driven out by force in winter, homes set ablaze, livestock seized. Most galling was that a community as small as Shetland's could find people to carry out this work.

By 1883, the violence was long over, but crofters complained to the commission that they were still trapped in a subsistence life. "Are you continuing to pay the high rent because you cannot better yourself?" one of the commissioners inquired of a crofter.

"To be sure," he replied.

"The croft does not support you?"

"No."

Crofters were barely making a living, and some were supplementing their tiny incomes by fishing. When asked why the poor rate was so high in Shetland, one crofter answered, "The chief cause probably is the number of lunatics; that is the heaviest charge we have, I think."

"Has any reason been assigned why lunacy is so prevalent in Shetland compared with other parts?"

"I have not heard."

The lunacy issue was a nagging one. Perhaps it was simply the consequence of inbreeding, the island's small genetic pool turning on itself. Or the wind, which sometimes sounded like the roar of jet engines just before takeoff and had a persistence that could conceivably induce madness. Or the solitude, or the darkness in winter, or lack of it in summer.

The portrait that emerged from the Napier Commission was of a terminally impoverished crofting class whose lives were defined by hardship and uncertainty. At any point their crofts could be reclaimed by owners and the tenants would have nothing. They were living in houses that hadn't seen any improvements in a century. Many were without leases. The figures that were presented to the commission were paltry; one crofter complained about his annual rent of nine pounds, which he found excessive. It had doubled in ninety years, he said. For improvements that the crofter had made on the property out of his own pocket, the landlord deducted one pound in the annual rent.

By contrast, the figures from Peter's bankruptcy seem from another era: 150 pounds spent on improving the house, one hundred pounds for new roads, fifty pounds for drains, forty for fencing. To lose more than 1,200 pounds in less than three years of operation was a feat. With the farm gone, Peter's options were bleak. To try and start over, renting a smaller croft perhaps, was unthinkable. It would involve actually working the farm, which he had no talent for, and with his well-advertised failure, no landlord would take him on as a tenant. His shop on Commercial Street, which at one point had sold china, had lost money on a smaller scale, but at a regular rate. Peter was without a profession, he was bankrupt and didn't even have a house for his family anymore. At the age of twenty-four, he had effectively exhausted the possibilities on the island. His wife, Christina, took the children back to Clashleven, spending a sick night on the boat on the violent seas and wondering at her decision to go to Shetland in the first place. Peter plotted his escape.

In the small archives building, I leafed through various documents and newspapers, guided by the archivist. In the *Shetland News* I encountered a section titled "Successful Shetlanders." "Well, he won't be in there," the archivist told me. "It's extraordinary that he could have lost the farm so quickly. He must have had a gift."

He did, in a sense. Aside from his documented gift for billiards and whisky, Peter had a gift for possibility. He recognized certainly that there was none for him in Shetland. He felt that the farm and business weren't his failures but the failure of the local imagination. The country was damp and constricting and he needed to get away, to find a place that matched his ambition. According to family lore, he chose South America.

It was a continent that was rich in natural resources. Gold was prevalent, as well as minerals and coffee and rubber. The descriptions that reached Shetland, through hearsay, rumour and the exaggerated claims of commercial travellers, suggested that it was difficult for a man to avoid becoming wealthy in South America. In the Grand Hotel it was agreed over whisky that even a fool, thick as a toad, stunned as a sheep, would get rich. Wealth would land on him, like the weather. And that was another thing. It was warm all year in South America. A bitter wind didn't blow like a curse for eleven months of the year. The soil was fecund, you could grow anything. You could graze cattle. It wasn't a place that was trussed by religious piety; it was wide open and gloriously corrupt.

For Peter, South America was ideal. It was in another hemisphere, thousands of miles from his lamentable reputation. And it was a romantic place, the antithesis of Shetland in almost every way. He would start a company, construction perhaps, or mining. But there were obstacles. Getting there was one. Passage was expensive and Peter was in "embarrassed circumstances," in the polite words of the court. And they didn't speak English in South America. But then neither did he, as people pointed out on occasion. Peter spoke in the local vernacular. The Shetlandic dialect is unique, its twelve vowels rising up unexpectedly and shortened by harsh Germanic consonants. Some of the vowels are palatalized, a Norse characteristic. "*Im tinkin didis waur wadder dan der haen sooth*" translates as "I think this is worse weather than they're having in the south." So language was an issue.

Peter borrowed the money for passage to South America and left his family with Christina's relatives in the Highlands. It would be difficult to get established in South America. The heat was oppressive. But it was the larger world and it confirmed Peter's belief that there was someplace for him other than Shetland.

––––––––

A hundred years ago a Shetland novelist wrote, "We are not Scotch; we have never been Scotch; we will never be Scotch; we repudiate all connection with the Scotch." In 1979, a Scottish referendum on the issue of independence very nearly succeeded, foiled by a last-minute change in the rules. Shetland had its own sovereignty movement, seeking independence from both England and Scotland. The unique character of the island, its determined singularity, stems from its complex history.

The Picts were the first inhabitants. They were in Shetland during the first century AD and left huge standing stones. On nearby Orkney Island the Ring of Brodgar has twenty-seven of the original sixty stones, evoking the same ceremonial mystery as Stonehenge. The Picts also built brochs, circular stone buildings, some of which are still standing. An Orkney historian described the brochs as an "architecture of mortal fear." They didn't scare the Vikings though, who arrived in AD 800 and subsumed the Picts.

The Norse dominated Shetland for six hundred years, and their influence is seen still, in the brightly coloured knitwear, in the place names and language. There were twenty-two thousand on the island in Norse times, only a few thousand less than at present. The Vikings used Shetland as a way station, a place to summer on the way home from a year of plundering. They farmed the land that had been developed by the Picts and built their complex stone buildings over the ruins of the Pict huts. The Vikings believed in equality, free speech and imperialism for its own sake, voyaging as far as Rome to engage a new enemy. The Norse reign in Shetland ended in 1469, when King Christian I of Denmark, Norway and Sweden found himself in the embarrassing position of being eight thousand florins short for the dowry of his daughter Margaret, who was marrying King James III of Scotland, an unpleasant man of ambiguous sexuality, in keeping with the royal trend. James assumed the throne at the age of six and was eventually murdered in 1488 when an assassin disguised as a priest found him cowering in a barn. On his wedding day, Shetland was offered in pledge to James, until Christian could raise the money for the dowry. The Scandinavian king wrote the Shetlanders an open letter, asking them to be dutiful and obedient to their new owner. In effect, the entire island emigrated, moving from Denmark to Scotland, and like most immigrants, retained the language and customs of the old country for several generations. Various Scandinavian leaders tried unsuccessfully to redeem the pledge and reclaim Shetland, but it has remained part of Scotland, though reluctantly at times.

In 1564, Mary, Queen of Scots, granted Shetland to her bastard half-brother Lord Robert Stuart and then to her third husband, the earl of Bothwell. Bothwell was soon hounded out of Scotland by various lords and ended his days in a Danish prison. The property reverted to Lord Robert, who owned the rights to most of the land and could demand revenue from every citizen. He was the chief magistrate as well, making the courts a difficult place to oppose him. In 1571, he gave up the title of chief magistrate and conferred it upon his half-brother, Laurence Bruce of Cultmalindie, who abused the office by ordering guilty verdicts against the innocent then confiscating their land. When a royal commission came to investigate, 760 people came forward to speak against him. Bruce went to jail briefly, but kept much of the land.

Lerwick is the only town in Shetland, a hard-won honour. It was burned in 1614 after Dutch sailors had built a shanty-town of brothels and gin joints on the site. It was ordered torched again in 1625 when sin sprang up like a weed on the same spot. But it developed into a stolid, upright city, with sober brick houses and brown, unadorned churches. There is a historical account in the library of a woman who was caught stealing in 1737. She was stripped to the waist, flogged at three separate sites, then toured around as a cautionary tale. The letter T, for thief, was branded on her cheek. Religion replaced the devil and punishment became the new pornography.

Shetland was once believed to be Thule, the island at the edge of the world that was described by the Greek explorer Pythias in the fourth century BC. There is an end-of-the-world quality to the island, remote and insular. I went into the Thule bar in Lerwick, down by the harbour, and ordered a pint. The wood and tinted glass gave the room the look of a sepia photograph. The air seemed brown. A handful of white-haired men drank quietly and younger men from the North Sea oil industry were discussing how thoroughly, life-threateningly dim their boss was. I talked with a man at the bar about oil. He was in his fifties, barrel-chested, his face the colour and texture of brisket.

"They piss on it," he said of the locals' response to the industry. "Oh Christ, it's killed the islands," he said in a sing-song voice, an octave higher. "Before Sullom Voe [the oil terminal] the only thing here was sheep and wind. Oil created this place."

I suggested that oil was a double-edged sword, that whatever prosperity it brings comes with a price. In 1993, *The Braer*, an oil tanker enroute from Norway to Quebec, spilled 84,413 tonnes of crude oil, 1,700 tonnes of heavy fuel oil and 125 tonnes of diesel fuel into the sea at Garths Ness, at the southern tip of the island. This was roughly twice the official (though unreliable) estimate of what the *Exxon Valdez* had spilled off the coast of Alaska.

"*The Braer.* Fucking *Braer.* There's my point. Everyone crying about the birds, holding them up for the television cameras like they won them at a carnival. A week after she went tits up, not a trace of oil. Gone. Sea swallowed it up. Like spitting in the soup. You don't like it, but if no one tells you, you'll never know. You'd think these half-wits in the Greenpeace boat would have some idea by now how big the ocean is."

"Perhaps the floating garbage five hundred miles from the nearest land makes it seem smaller."

My conversational partner stared stonily at his drink for a moment and I changed the subject to something less contentious. I had worked in the oilfields of Alberta for two years in the seventies, when its boom was at full throttle, and we talked about oil rigs for a while, about apocryphal blow-ins and grisly accidents. Most casual conversation among oil workers has to do with disaster. Derricks toppling into crumpled heaps of scrap iron, drunken motormen falling into the sump tank, prairie fires, fistfights, epic poker games, cruel practical jokes. The criminal stupidity of those in authority is catalogued and the resourcefulness of the worker is celebrated. Oil itself is rarely invoked. It's an abstraction, its discovery incidental to the larger theme of rig life. After several pints I left the bar. Outside, the evening light was fading behind the clouds. I ordered a slice of pizza from a vendor and ate it on the pier, watching the large boats bob silently.

Oil is a colonizing force, one that begins with isolated disruptions of the local geology and moves to the political sphere

before finally inhabiting the social fabric. It arrives with the
rosy tones of a benevolent dictator, explaining that life will be
the same as it was, only everyone will have more money. Then,
the existing infrastructure is overwhelmed by the visiting
army. The pubs are crowded and combustible, the hotels over-
burdened. The roads can't bear the increased traffic and the
airport is inadequate for the crews of rig workers, geologists,
bureaucrats and executives who are flying in and out. Esso and
Shell initially said that only 1,200 men would be needed to
build an oil and gas terminal at Sullom Voe, twenty-five miles
northeast of Lerwick. That figure was revised to three thousand. In the end, seven thousand workers, one thousand of
them local, laboured on the construction. In Shetland, the es-
calating estimates and the fact that the oil companies had
waited a year before announcing that they had discovered oil
were taken as signs of duplicity. The relationship between colo-
nizer and colonized was antagonistic from the onset. Shetland
took on the task of accommodating the new armies. Houses
had to be built for the workers, some of them temporary.
Schools were expanded and new ones raised like barns. Roads
were built and existing ones widened and repaved. Steel crash
guards were added. The airport at Sumburgh on the southern
tip of the island was expanded to handle the increased traffic.
In the end, oil had a greater impact on the island than the Picts
or the Norse or the British Parliament.

Between 1975 and 1985, the Shetland Islands Council received 174.7 million pounds from the North Sea oil find. It was
a considerable part of its budget, though dramatically less
than it had been led to believe it would make. And the expense
of building new infrastructure to deal with the influx kept
rising, though Shetland has done better than some other
hosts. The Shetland Islands Council, through a private bill in

British Parliament, gained substantial powers to deal with the oil companies.

In 1978, the relationship between the people and oil was brought into sharper relief when the oil tanker *Esso Bernica* collided with concrete moorings at Sullom Voe and spilled 1,174 tonnes of marine Bunker C fuel oil into the bay. There are no production standards for fuel oil; it is a heavy substance, more difficult to clean up than crude oil. More than three thousand seabirds died. Other environmental issues loomed. Material for the new roads was quarried from a romantic and visible landmark. Tankers coming in to Sullom Voe were found to be deliberately dumping oil at sea. It saved them time and money and the North Sea was already oily. "The greasiness of the North Sea is next to saltiness its most remarkable quality," the Bishop of Bergen wrote in 1752. If a ship were to catch fire, he said, the North Sea would fuel the flames.

When *The Braer* went aground, the relationship broke into open hostilities. I drove south to Garths Ness to see where the tanker had gone down. It seemed to be an essential part of the island's history now. It was a rare cloudless sky. "Between wadders," I had been warned, between weathers. The hills were worn to gentle mounds and the grass had a tufted quality, as if beaten by the wind of helicopter blades. Stone fences boxed the land.

Near the Bay of Quendale, a tractor blocked the road. I parked my car and got out and stared into the stiff wind. A farmer drove up beside me and unrolled his window, his grey hair angled outward, his head the size of a pumpkin.

"Lost are we," he said flatly.

I said I was looking for where *The Braer* went down. "Was the land here affected by the spill?"

"You'd have to find that out for yourself, wouldn't you." His eyes were bright with resentment. Thousands of journalists had flocked to the disaster when it happened. Environmentalists had come to clean birds and beaches. After a tentative chat with the farmer, he agreed to let me walk across his land.

Along the path that paralleled the shoreline, there was an abandoned eighteenth-century stone building, its roof gone. It was, I had been told, a fish-drying house that had been built by one of my ancestors, who had farmed at Garths Ness when he first arrived in Shetland. The ruins of a croft house were farther up the hill. Three Mainland brothers had come to Shetland in the mid-eighteenth century, possibly fleeing press gangs that forced men to serve in the King's militia. Or casualties of the Clearances. In one version, they were rumoured to be criminals, on the run and changing their name to the generic Mainland.

Half a mile over a rising field, there was the bay where *The Braer* had sunk. The sea around Garths Ness had the deep blue and aquamarine colours of a Club Med ad. The white rocks of the beach shone. *The Braer* was carrying Gulfaks crude, one of the lightest grades of oil, and the violence of the January storm that had beached the tanker also lifted the oil up into the atmosphere and drove it down into the sediment of the seabed. Some of it had been carried southward by the Fair Isle current. Sheep on the opposite side of the island had traces of oil on them. It covered fields and roofs. Prince Charles had flown up to witness the damage first hand and Willie Mainland, a distant relative, had squired him around the land. Charles walked in that deliberate way and listened with practised concern to the local woe. A photograph of them appeared in a magazine and the locals asked Willie who the guy with the big ears was.

Oil spills create their own economies, which, like the tankers themselves, are thoroughly international. *The Braer* was American—managed and owned by Americans in Bermuda, built in Japan, registered in Liberia, carrying Norwegian oil headed for Canada. The technology and expertise to clean up spills comes from a dozen countries. Three separate inquiries tried to divine how the spill happened. Lawsuits ricocheted around the globe. In the wake of each new spill, if it is of sufficient size, new policies and regulations are recommended, and occasionally adopted. You need new spills to make any environmental headway. Without them, the industry would languish. Because of the lightness of the oil spilled by the *Braer*, there wasn't the kind of disaster seen in Alaska when the *Exxon Valdez* went aground. A week after the tanker went down, there wasn't anything to see on the beaches. It was the great, awful, unspoken sentiment that what the environmental movement needed was a dramatic spill in a densely populated, politically empowered place. Shetland, like Alaska, is at a great remove from political power and from the prolonged attention of the media. It was, at some unthinkable level, a waste of a large spill.

On the way back to Lerwick, I drove around Sumburgh, at the southern tip. Seabirds bickered in their thousands on the cliffs. I stopped to view Jarlshof, the remains of a Norse community. It had been mentioned by Sir Walter Scott in his novel *The Pirate*. It was marked by stones, an orderly design. The surrounding grass was as groomed as a golf green, a tropical hue.

In the Sumburgh Hotel bar I talked with a birder. His name was Jenkins, from Sussex, he said, and he came every year. He was tall and hearty, with a dramatic sweep of grey hair. "They're fascinating, really," he said. A local bird, the maalie, had the ability to summon oil from its stomach and spit it at enemies. The oil was corrosive and malodorous and each bird carried almost half a pint.

The Japanese were coming now, he said, drawn by the alarming emptiness of the islands. "You end up watching the watchers, too," Jenkins said. "There are all kinds. It can get quite competitive."

After the *Braer* spill, Shetland had been referred to as "the jewel in Britain's environmental crown." Any further oil spills would seriously compromise that reputation and hurt both trade and tourism. Jenkins agreed. "It didn't look like much," he said of the spill. "But those hydrocarbons have to go somewhere. They don't entirely disappear." Shetland has always existed in the tension between polarities, between Scotland and Scandinavia, between environmental jewel and oil depot.

———

In Lerwick, I stayed at the Grand Hotel, the downfall of my great-grandfather. It was built in 1888 and enlarged in 1908, an imposing, if slightly dour, stone building. The original pub was on the main floor, at street level, but it has been taken over by shops now. My room was expensive and a bit cramped. It was six o'clock and I went downstairs to the pub and ordered a whisky. Yellow and blue lights in the ceiling gave the room an odd glow. The carpet had the familiar brown, orange and yellow swirls I had seen in a dozen places, as if some satanic rug salesman had swept through the Highlands and islands twenty years ago. The barman told me that the billiard table had been gone for years. There was a disco in the basement, he said, by way of compensation. Two oil men were chatting up a table of girls, telling them about their fearless, oil-based lives. The anecdotes came to me in bunched syllables but the inflections were familiar.

The dining room was too expensive; more than $50 for Surf, Turf and Be Fruity, a combination of steak, lobster, banana and pineapple. I went down the street and bought a tattie—a baked potato—from a vendor and ate it outside with a plastic fork as the wind slapped me in gusts. Teenagers hung around Commercial Street, smoking and doing what teenagers do everywhere, talking about going somewhere else.

I walked down a path along the water which led to a cemetery. The stones were thin and faced the sea on a downward slope, like a theatre audience. I looked for Thomas Mainland's headstone in the pale darkness, without luck. Behind me the jumble of stone houses receded in dark shades and the air was filled with the comforting, poisonous smell of burning peat. The sky over Shetland seems remarkably distant. A few people were walking their dogs.

I went back to my room and phoned Toronto, chatting idly, then went to bed early, reading about King Harald of Norway (1015–1066), the last of the dauntless Viking rulers who had harassed England, Rome and Russia for 350 years. When they weren't plundering, Harald's men lived as farmers on Shetland. The extraordinary violence of their travels was mitigated by their utterly peaceful, pastoral lives in the off-season. Harald died valiantly, according to court poets, in a battle for England that took place three weeks before the more famous Battle of Hastings. King Harald's place in history was eclipsed to some degree by this unfortunate timing. Harald's name and that of his half brother, Olaf the Saint, are celebrated in Lerwick as street names.

Sounds from Posers, "the only nightclub in Shetland," filled my room, the blinkered cadence of a bass guitar on a dance track. Unable to sleep, I got dressed and went down to the club and was politely told that it was locals only, a way to keep the peace. I went to The Lounge off Commercial Street, and ordered a whisky. The room was in shades of brown and had a few benches and a large open space. Some men, playing a game that looked like dominoes, yelped in victory. Most people stood and milled. A man of about thirty came in to use the phone. He was wearing a thick tweed Chanel jacket and skirt, the kind of outfit the Queen Mother favours. His bare legs were hairy and he was wearing heels and lipstick.

"Ye're looking lovely Angus," a man at the bar said.

"Do you think so, Jimmy?" he answered.

There was no explanation. Some kind of initiation? The town's only gay bar? Or the odd tolerance of small communities that are largely intolerant. I sat on a bench and talked to a man named Malcolm and his wife. They were in their sixties, out for a quiet drink. The woman said, "There's just a seething mass of young people at Market Cross." These were the teenagers, outside smoking and telling each other lies.

"There every night," Malcolm said.

"That's trouble."

"Large groups like that. Drinking I suppose."

"You wonder where they get the money."

This led to the discussion about drugs and how they have come to the island, oil mostly, you could pretty much count on it. We talked in pleasant generalities for an hour and I left.

It was after midnight and Posers was still working its magic in my room and I slept fitfully and dreamed of Celtic savagery, the heads of enemies paraded on poles, ravens hovering nearby. In the morning I rattled around the small shower stall trying to get wet in the sporadic bursts of cold water. The woman at the desk told me my phone call home cost $144.

Outside, the clouds were a conservative grey and the winds had picked up to gale force nine. When I walked, the wind shoved me around as if it had hold of my lapels. I drove south to Brindister, where the Nicholsons had some information on

Peter Mainland. Their forebears had been neighbours of his. The Nicholsons had more than eight hundred sheep and a four-hundred-acre farm that spanned the island. Mrs. Nicholson had a benign, grandmotherly air and her husband walked with two canes. I asked them about my great-grandfather.

"More of a dreamer than a doer, I think," Mrs. Nicholson said kindly.

We were sitting in the kitchen, drinking tea, eating biscuits. They gave me an assessment of several of the Mainlands on the island. "Oh a terrible drinker," she said of one. "Don't visit him. Though I'd no try and discourage you."

I asked them about crofting and how it had changed.

"In Peter's day a croft might only have one cow," Mr. Nicholson told me. "Sometimes the crofter had so little land he would take his cow and graze him at the roadside."

The crofts look so picturesque, the dry fieldstone fences receding over the hills, the handful of blackface and Cheviot sheep staring out. Some of the fences date from Pictish times, but many of them are from this century. "They were built when labour was cheap," Mr. Nicholson said. "Men would work for sixpence an hour and be glad for it." Once the oil industry arrived, cheap labour was difficult to find.

Most crofters had to do something other than farm to make a living. Fishing was one of the most common ways. But crofting has always been in a state of crisis. The Napier Commission revealed how desperate things were but after the Second World War, another group, the Taylor Commission, was appointed to reassess crofting's chronic troubles. The commission concluded: "We have thought it right . . . to record our unanimous conviction . . . that in the national interest the maintenance of these (crofting) communities is desirable because they embody a free and independent way of life which, in a civilisation predominantly urban and industrial in character, is worth preserving for its own intrinsic value."

The report implied that crofting had little real economic value, that it was a marginal industry, and ironically, given the fact that it was producing food, wasn't producing anything essential. Its value was figurative, emblematic of the island and its history. To allow the crofts to languish would be to lose a critical marker of who the Shetlanders were. The industry has remained in a state of crisis, more or less, during the fifty years since that report. It has had two centuries of crisis. Crofting has retained its convoluted and anachronistic structure. The landowner has no control over how his land is worked and rarely makes much money in rent. The crofter doesn't own the land but he can do what he likes with it and usually makes a little money too. He could buy the land but he would lose some of the grants and subsidies he receives as a tenant. I was reminded of what a Manitoba farmer had once told me, "You don't farm the land, you farm the government."

I criss-crossed the island, seeking out Mainlands and lines that would lead back to Peter. A sea of coffee, a truckload of biscuits. Peter had effectively been excised from the family history. It was too far back for most people anyway. He was limited to anonymous entries in the family tree. Poised above the names of his several children, he couldn't help but look sober and responsible.

The oldest living Mainland on the island was Maggie, who was ninety-nine and lived in Lerwick with her daughter-in-law, Mrs. Tait. I was greeted by Mrs. Tait, a woman of sixty or so. She had been married to Ian Mainland briefly but he had died young. Before he died, Ian asked his wife to promise to look after his mother. So now Mrs. Tait was long since remarried, with a new family, and had her first mother-in-law with her.

Maggie had been married to Andrew Mainland, a relative of Peter. She had wispy white hair and a kind, elongated face. A bit deaf but otherwise bearing up nicely. She smiled, grateful for a visitor.

They had a photograph of four generations of Mainland men sitting in a field. "All the men went to sea," Mrs. Tait told me. "If they weren't crofters or doctors or teachers." She talked a bit about the shipping business and the effect of oil on the island. She had a relative who was an officer on a tanker. "He was the only white man on the ship. It's a scandal. There were eastern Europeans, but they're not really white," she observed without malice. "They don't have the education."

When she and Ian were going to have a son they considered the name Peter, but Ian vetoed it. "There's already a Peter Mainland," he said. "And he's no use."

Maggie showed me pictures of her son, whom she had survived by several decades. "That's my boy," she said, pointing to a picture of him when he was five. Her eyes welled a little. "There he is, growing," she said of a later photograph. "And growing."

When I left I shook her hand and she clasped mine in both of hers and kissed it.

I went to a café, called, eponymously, The Café, which filled suddenly with school children in their teens. They chattered, ate cakes and smoked cigarettes. Two boys with the shadows of a mustache sat at my table. They were pale and thin and the small red wounds of adolescence formed archipelagos on their cheeks.

I asked them if they planned on staying on the island. One was learning the guitar, so he would be leaving, he said. Glasgow maybe. Or London. He had been buying CDs with his money, though he admitted he didn't have a machine to play them on. The other thought he might get married. Then, who knew. "Everyone's *pressuring* me," he said. You shouldn't let them, I offered. "*Now* I'm not supposed to feel pressured. That's *more* pressure." He was smoking a Dunhill and looked like an overworked executive.

"It's okay," the guitarist said of his island. "There's nothing to do. But you do things anyway."

———

After South America, the family story goes, Peter went to California where he dabbled in construction. His family was still in Clashleven with Christina's parents, waiting for good news. It was 1901 and the film industry hadn't transformed the state yet and Peter liked the breezy tropical feel of the coast. It was like stepping into Oz, the colours so vivid and false looking. But there was a torpor, too. He seemed to be afloat in California, hovering in the soft air, not moving. He missed the seasons and went north, first to Denver, then to Chicago.

Chicago was teeming with immigrants: Poles, Italians, Jews. He told people in the bar at the Palmer House that he had an estate in Scotland, in the north, but he was looking for new opportunities. He had disposed of his sturdy tweeds in California and dressed like a sportsman who had done well at the track. He possessed an American jauntiness. But he still sounded like he was gargling stones when he talked. And he still had a restlessness. He wondered if there was somewhere better for him.

Canada was a possibility. As a member of the Commonwealth, he would be less of an immigrant there. The West was opening up. Land was cheap, free even, though he'd had enough of land. He liked the urban life.

An article appeared in the *Chicago Record Herald.* It read: "All roads lead to Winnipeg. It is the focal point of the three transcontinental lines of Canada, and nobody, neither manufacturer, capitalist, farmer, mechanic, lawyer, doctor, merchant, priest, nor labourer, can pass from one part of Canada to another without going through Winnipeg. It is a gateway through which all the commerce of the east and west, and the north and south must flow. No city, in America, at least, has such absolute and complete command over the wholesale trade of so vast an area. It is destined to become one of the greatest distributing commercial centres of the continent as well as a manufacturing community of great importance."

In 1902, Peter went north to Winnipeg. Christina came over with her sons, Don, his twin brother Thomas, and the youngest, James. They took a boat to Glasgow where they boarded the *Sarmatian* in September. Christina had brought her jewellery box with Celtic brooches and a dozen rings. On the boat, the twins took the rings up onto the deck and threw them, one by one, into the sea. The family landed in Quebec City and took the train to Winnipeg, which Peter had said was the centre of the world. There was money and opportunity and Scotsmen there, but he would overcome this last hurdle. The prairie was like a huge unpainted canvas, and in his heart, Peter felt that he was an artist.

I flew back to Glasgow where I was seized by an inconsolable loneliness. My daughter was eighteen months old, a caricature of a Highland child—curly hair and naturally rosy cheeks the size of softballs—and I was reminded of her continually. I pined for that hand on the back of my neck as we read about all the Whos in Whoville. I had a bronchial cough and a stubborn cold and my head felt like it weighed twelve stone though I didn't know what a stone was.

There was still a week left on my plane ticket, which had been bought at a discount and was non-refundable, non-transferrable and unchangeable. I drove to the airport with the intention of trying all of those things. A uniformed woman told me there might be an Air Canada flight with an empty seat but it vanished inexplicably from the computer while we were talking. Heathrow was in flames, she said, a fire that had started at a Burger King, which scuttled any plans to route through London. I tried other airlines, other uniformed, helpful women who tilted their heads slightly and gave them a subtle shake as they stared pessimistically at their computer terminals. After each failure, my despair grew and the need to leave became more pressing. Maybe there would be something tomorrow, one of the women said sympathetically.

The next day a seat emerged on the computer, tentative and shimmering, conditional and primed for heartbreak; I could be bumped, the woman warned. But I checked my luggage and held my breath and with a prolonged rush into the air I was free.

7

THE

FORTY YEARS

AGITATION

VIEWED FROM THE AIR, Winnipeg has been described as a bullet hole in a windshield, the small central wound giving out to roads and rail lines that appear as cracks in the landscape. It's an improbable city, especially in winter when the prairies are a vast, sterile desert. There wasn't a good reason to settle at the junction of the Red and Assiniboine rivers and the settlement that was founded there in 1812 represented the triumph of ambition over geography. The city was a bad idea. It was the bad idea of a Scotsman, Thomas Douglas, the fifth earl of Selkirk, and was settled initially by Scottish Presbyterians from the Highlands who starved and endured.

But, within a century, Winnipeg went from improbability to inevitability. It was the hub of a new empire, a brilliant idea. It was a city thrilled with itself. Both my maternal great-grandfathers arrived in Winnipeg shortly after the turn of the century, stepping into the happy maw of its booster spirit. Peter Mainland arrived in 1902, invigorated by its growth and excitement. Lachlan Ross arrived three years later, dismayed at the unprincipled expansion and shameless materialism. They each came to inhabit a different Winnipeg, though both versions were contained within the earl of Selkirk's original vision for the settlement, and contained within Selkirk's own nature, which balanced philanthropy with personal ambition. It was Selkirk who had wished the city into existence. For years the idea of Winnipeg had sat in his head like a curse.

———————

It was a child's nightmare; pirates had come looking for his father. They were standing in the large parlour, their swords drawn, muskets at the ready. Their clothes were unkempt and they were bearded, brown-toothed and bright-eyed from rum. Their hair was knotted and fell like damp cloth to their shoulders. Only it wasn't a dream. The seven-year-old Thomas Douglas was standing in his nightshirt in the large parlour of his family's ancestral home on St. Mary's Isle, on the southwestern coast of Scotland. It was 1778, two years after the United States declared its independence. The American privateer John Paul Jones was standing in this Scottish home with his scrofulous mob, demanding blood. Jones had been born on the Selkirk estate, the son of the head gardener. He followed his father into that trade but was fired and took to the sea. He eventually hooked up with the American cause, raiding the

British coast. The pirates looked around the Selkirk manse with contempt and envy. Jones intended to kidnap Thomas's father, the fourth earl of Selkirk, and use him to engineer a prisoner exchange between England and America, but the earl was away on business. Jones wasn't prepared for this anticlimax. Take the children? It would seem cowardly. The earl's wife perhaps. But how would she fare with his crew? He finally took the family silver and left. The young Thomas watched the pirates disappear down toward the shore. Outside, Jones stared at his men carting the Selkirk silver down the hill and was struck by despair. It was a mockery, a student prank rather than a political act. He asked his men for the silver but they refused to give it up. He later bought it back from them, a vaguely noble gesture, and returned it to the earl. Although he wouldn't have fared much better had he gotten what he had come for. The fourth earl of Selkirk was a free-thinking, minor nobleman and the government wouldn't have traded much for him. Thomas always remembered the crude, ghostly pirates. Later he would write, "This was a momentous event in my life. I was terribly frightened . . . I developed an antipathy for the United States due almost solely to the buccaneering of John Paul."

Thomas Douglas was a timid boy, red-haired and slim and thought to be too delicate for the military rigour of the Edinburgh High School. He was educated at Palgrave, a short-lived (1774–1785) school that would be described today as "progressive." It was concerned, its prospectus said, with the present. He went on to the University of Edinburgh where he associated with Walter Scott, who would become Scotland's most popular novelist. David Hume, the philosopher, was in Edinburgh and Adam Smith, the great political economist, had retired there. It was a centre of learning, the "Athens of the

North." Douglas was the seventh child of the earl of Selkirk, separated from the family estate by four brothers. But his brothers died in rapid succession and at the age of twenty-eight, Douglas became the fifth earl. He was a member of a privileged class and was able to associate with intellectual celebrities, dining with Thomas Paine and going to Paris to hear Robespierre debate in the National Assembly. Selkirk himself debated William Wilberforce on the best methods for the improvement and civilizing of the Indians of North America. One of Selkirk's ideas was to create reservations for them.

In 1792 he toured the Highlands, and the area became a passion of sorts for him. He learned Gaelic and wrote extensively about the region. His first book, *Observations on the Present State of the Highlands of Scotland, with a View of the Causes and Probable Causes of Emigration* was published in 1805. Selkirk was criticized for romanticizing the Highlanders, who were viewed as lazy, and for endorsing emigration, seen as feeding the crisis. He felt that "emigration was an unavoidable result of the general state of the country . . . the only solution to a bad situation." Selkirk put forth an early proposal to relocate Irish Catholics, arguing that it would suit their "Religious and National prejudices" and it would rid Ireland of "the most dangerous subjects." But he was persuaded by Lord Hobart of the Colonial Office that the government of Canada would likely object to an influx of Irish immigrants. Hobart advised him to seek settlers that were "more tractable than the Irish" and suggested that "Scotch & German families" be used for his plan. Selkirk settled finally, on the Highlands. He witnessed the deterioration of their culture in Scotland and thought that it might be preserved in North America. "Admiring many generous and manly features in their character, I could not observe without regret the rapid decline of their genuine manners, to which the circumstances of the country seemed inevitably to lead. I thought, however, that a portion of the ancient spirit might be preserved among the Highlanders of the New World."

After the Clearances, those Highlanders who remained in the hills were largely destitute and those who had come to Glasgow were defeated. Selkirk's dream, the one that consumed him, was to ship these men to the New World where they would be free to remake themselves. If emigration was inevitable, then organize and harness it. Rather than have the emigrants assimilated into other cultures, give them the means to establish themselves as a British settlement. In the Canadas they could reconstitute their proud spirit. They could work hard, build a community and bring their families over. They would be free, landowning citizens. The benefits were political and humanitarian, Selkirk argued, and the presence of British settlers would be a deterrence to the Americans' imperialistic whims. His critics responded that his goals had more to do with personal profit and that he shouldn't meddle in national policy. Selkirk had tried unsuccessfully to gain a foothold in British politics and, as one observer noted, "in many ways pursued the same dreams as the settlers he hoped to recruit: a chance to start afresh."

Selkirk's first attempt at colonizing in the Canadas was in Prince Edward Island. It was a difficult but modestly successful project and the early hardships were quickly romanticized. A settler wrote back that the climate was much like Italy's. But a second settlement, in Upper Canada, was a disaster. The land was boggy and disease broke out. The settlers felt abandoned by their benefactor and they became "discontented, violent and rapacious."

But Selkirk still wanted to pursue a settlement on a larger scale. He toured the United States and Canada, making notes. In Montreal, he dined at the Beaver Club, whose members were with the fur trade. He ate bear and buffalo tongue and toasted the industrious beaver and shyly joined these men in their vulgar songs. It has been reported that Selkirk kept his nails extraordinarily long and had the odd habit of making notes on them in shorthand, though this eccentricity seems far-fetched. The men of the Beaver Club reminded him of the pirates who had crowded the family parlour twenty-five years earlier. At times he still felt like a boy in a nightshirt, helpless, insulated by money and title and a shrewd wife. But he had some of the pragmatism of his ancestors. He knew that the Hudson's Bay Company legally held the charter to the land he wanted as the site for his settlement, an area where the Red and Assiniboine rivers met. He had given a copy of the charter to several different lawyers in London and was assured that it was valid and binding.

In Montreal, Selkirk showed a good grasp of the local cultural frictions. "The English in Quebec cry out in the true John Bull style against [the French settlers'] obstinate aversion to institutions which they have never taken any pains to make them understand—& are surprised at the naturally and universally experienced dislike of a conquered people to their conquerors & to every thing which puts them in mind of their subjection . . . the only chance of reconciling the people would have been either to use every effort to change them entirely in language and Institutions & make them forget that they were not English—or keeping them as French to give a Government adapted to them as such, & keep every thing English out of sight—neither of these plans has been followed & the policy of Govt. has been a kind of vibration between them."

Napoleon had been wreaking havoc with continental trade and as a result British goods had suffered. The market for beaver pelts was stagnant and Hudson's Bay stock dropped from 250 pounds a share to sixty pounds. Back in Scotland, Selkirk began to buy up stock in the summer of 1808 and beseeched family and friends to do the same. They came to own almost one-third of the shares. Using his influence, Selkirk then persuaded the Hudson's Bay Company to sell him 116,000 square miles, an area almost four-fifths the size of Scotland, for ten shillings, another of the august land deals that heralded civilization. He placated the Indians who lived there by promising them one hundred pounds of tobacco annually.

He had the site for a colony. Now all he needed was colonists. In his "Advertisement and Prospectus" he outlined the area's reported advantages. "A tract of land, consisting of some millions of acres, and in point of soil and climate, inferior to none of equal extent in British North America." He had not actually visited the Red River Colony, but had read Alexander Mackenzie's *Voyages*, which had warned against trying to settle in the area. Selkirk said the area had some of the qualities of the Russian provinces. It had, in fact, most of the qualities of the Russian provinces, including the brutish winter. Selkirk suggested the settlers grow hemp. Bishop Strachan, rector of York in Upper Canada, described Selkirk's advertisement as "one of the most gross impositions that ever was attempted on the British public, and must be attended with the most baneful consequences to all those unfortunate men, who, deluded by the false promises held out to them, shall leave their homes for such a dreary wilderness." Strachan hadn't been there either, nor had most of those who joined the debate. The Red River area was so distant as to be an abstraction, it was like debating the existence of God.

Despite the abject conditions in the Highlands, it was difficult to recruit settlers for the Red River settlement and Selkirk hired agents to scour the country. There were articles in Scottish papers warning against emigration agents and countering their sunny reports. Selkirk's agents were able to find only 105 people who would go to the Red River. Thirty-five of these were indentured servants who would help prepare the colony, the rest were settlers. They left from Stornoway on July 26, 1811, on a mouldy hulk named the *Edward and Ann*. The group quickly formed cliques and fought. Miles McConnell, who Selkirk had hired to deliver the settlers, and who eventually would become governor of the new colony, described the national traits of his passengers. "The Orkneymen were naturally slow and clumsy; the Glasgow recruits were lazy and faultfinding; the Irish were addicted to quarrelling and fighting." There was only one cleric on board, Reverend Charles Bourke, a witty, dissipated Irish priest who had abandoned his bishop. The few Catholics felt he was too dissolute to be of any use except as entertainment.

The weather was terrible and the crossing took sixty-one days, the longest of any Hudson's Bay vessel, and it was almost October when they landed at Hudson Bay, the latest in the season a boat had landed. It was too late to make the trek to the Red River so they wintered there. Scurvy was a problem and the cold was frightening. Where winters had been miserable and damp at home, here they were life-threatening, with a coldness that was not of the earth. The settlers became exhausted past description. This kind of hardship sometimes binds a group but within this impossibly small society the competing nationalisms resulted in violence. On occasion, they tried to beat one another to death and a temporary jail had to be constructed. In the spring, the trip to Winnipeg was a hellish seven-hundred-mile trek in which they had to portage the ungainly boats around the many rapids, dragging them through unbroken brush. The mosquitoes feasted on the men and the noise of these insects at night was a mechanical drone. It took the settlers fifty-five days to reach the fork of the Red and Assiniboine rivers. Only nineteen survived the journey, the rest were dead, or discouraged and on their way back to Scotland. But in June 1812, eighty Highland Presbyterians arrived, and then a third wave, ninety more Highlanders from Kildonan. They were a colony.

The New World was as unyielding and vindictive as the Old Testament. In winter, the land was a great blank desert that stretched for a thousand miles. The cold froze the breath in your lungs. Animals and men died in the bleak calm of January when the air itself was filled with ice. The snow came in violent bursts and reordered the landscape in extravagant drifts. In the spring, crops were planted but migrating blackbirds ate the seed out of the fields. Women and children chased them, scattering them into the air where they reconvened like a storm cloud and then descended two hundred yards away. The children rushed to scatter them again but they grew too weary to run and then even to walk, and in this way the fields were stripped. The Red River flooded, the muddy water engulfing the land. Later, locusts came like a plague, a great grey mass that could be seen twenty miles away. For several months, the settlers lived on wild parsnips and boiled nettles. "The emigrants suffered greatly," wrote Alexander Ross (not a relative) one of the original settlers, "especially from cold, wet and walking in English shoes." The Red River Valley presented "a picture to the imagination of civilized men as gloomy as Ultima Thule."

They had other problems, too. The North West Company was in a bitter struggle with the Hudson's Bay Company, and the settlers were harassed by the Nor'Westers, who felt that this new settlement infringed on the fur trade. Dealings with the Nor'Westers, which initially involved as many as six languages—English, Gaelic, French and various native tongues—led to "Anarchy and confusion . . . Retaliation and mutual recrimination followed, till the whole body of settlers were driven from the colony, and their houses burned to ashes."

On June 19, 1816, a party of sixty-five Nor'Westers arrived at the settlement, plumed and painted like demons according to one account. A party of twenty-eight settlers, including Governor Semple, the governor-in-chief of the Hudson's Bay territory, went out to meet them. Faced with the colourful and oblique enemy, the settlers stopped and discussed their strategy. While they were huddled, a shot was fired and a settler by the name of Holt fell from his saddle. Another shot was fired and Semple was dead. Fire was returned by the settlers but only one of the raiding party was killed. Twenty-one of the settlers were massacred and some of them scalped and mutilated. The whole colony was driven into exile, moving to Norway House, on the northern tip of Lake Winnipeg.

The raiding party had been made up of Nor'Westers, natives and Metis and of the sixty-five involved, twenty-six met with violent deaths within a few years. This fact was noted among the settlers, interpreted as a sign. Ka-tee-tea-goose, the native who was believed to have fired the first shot, ran into the Gros Ventre tribe and was shot and scalped. His body was cut into pieces and his fingers and toes were kept as souvenirs, the rest scattered on the plains. Ne-de-goose-ojeb was gored by a buffalo. Pe-me-can-toss was shot by his own people. Thomas McKay died of intemperance, Lavigne drowned in the Red River, Coutonahais dropped dead while dancing, Duplicis was impaled by a wooden pitchfork when he jumped onto a haystack, Dechamp dropped dead while crossing the frozen Red River. His dog mysteriously died at the same moment. Most telling was the death of Wa-ge-tan-ne, who was hit by lightning. The biblical nature of the deaths and the sheer numbers had a resonance that buoyed the settlers. God had not forgotten them.

One of the conditions of immigration for Selkirk's settlers was that a Presbyterian minister would be sent out to their community, to bring the relief of the gospel to this hostile moonscape. Ministers arrived, but no Presbyterian. John West was the first Protestant minister. "Oh! for wisdom, truly Christian faith, integrity and zeal on my labours as a minister, in this heathen and *moral desert*," he wrote. "Thousands are involved in worse than Egyptian darkness around me, wandering in ignorance and perishing through lack of knowledge. When will this wide waste howling wilderness blossom as the rose, and the desert become as a fruitful field."

The Scots reluctantly attended the Church of England services conducted by a Reverend Jones, who replaced West. In 1827, Jones wrote, "I lament to say that there is an unChristian-like selfishness and narrowness of mind in our Scottish population; while they are the most comfortable in their circumstances of any class in our little community." By contrast, those natives who had converted showed an unsettling generosity of spirit. "The half-breeds in particular," Jones noted, "walk in simplicity and godly sincerity." They were happy to give up any possession that was coveted by a friend. They abandoned prizes with cheer and grace. *Thou shalt love thy neighbour as thyself.* This was one area of the Bible the local Christians didn't interpret literally.

After twenty years of settlement, there were two Protestant churches and a grand Roman Catholic church built of stone but no Presbyterian church. The Scots quickly became a minority in the colony they had founded. "It is as if [the Scots] had come to Red River merely to endure its hardships," Alexander Ross wrote. To make matters worse, the Church of England was developing Popish tendencies. By 1850, there was still no Presbyterian minister despite a letter-writing campaign that was in its fourth decade. Their collective grief now had a name, "The Forty Years Agitation." *But the more they were oppressed, the more they multiplied and the more they spread abroad. And the Egyptians were in dread of the people of Israel. So they made the people of Israel serve with rigour, and made their lives bitter with hard service, in mortar and brick, and in all kinds of work in the field; in all their work they made them serve with rigour.*

In one of his many missives to the governor and the committee of the Hudson's Bay Company, Alexander Ross wrote, "Your petitioners are mortified to see year after year Roman Catholic priests brought into the settlement—at present no less than six over a population of some 3,000—and Church of England missionaries, no fewer than four over a few; while your petitioners are left to grope in the dark, without even one. And yet our petitioners were the first, the only regular emigrants in the colony; and on the faith of having a clergyman of their own Church they left their native country." The animosity between the Presbyterians, who reluctantly and skeptically sat in the Church of England congregation, and their fellow parishioners reached a head when the reverend announced, "No Presbyterian will ever enter the Kingdom of Heaven!"

On September 19, 1851, after forty years in the desert, the Reverend Mr. John Black arrived and three hundred Presbyterians left the English church with bitter relief. In 1853, they erected a stone church on Frog Plain that seated 510 people and cost 1,050 pounds sterling. It was filled every Sunday and carried no mortgage. Their farms were prospering. A second generation was on the land. "No farmers in the world," Ross now reported, "no settlement or colony of agriculturalists, can be pronounced so happy, independent, and comfortable as those in Red River."

Selkirk himself didn't live to see how his unlikely settlement had prospered. A series of lawsuits had pitted him against his detractors in the NorthWest Company. The cases were argued in Quebec and Montreal before moving to Upper Canada, a travelling sideshow that was marked by "connivance, laxity, ignorance and prejudice," according to historian E.E. Rich. Selkirk's health was beginning to fail and he was disheartened by the lingering, destructive lawsuits and felt his name was being maligned. Among other things, his motives for starting the Red River Colony were impugned. He returned to England and in 1818 went to Pau, near the Pyrenees in the south of France, as a curative measure, hoping to restore his fragile health. He died there in April 1820 at the age of forty-eight, and was buried in the nearby village of Orthez because Pau had no Protestant cemetery. His grave was unmarked for 156 years until a University of Winnipeg professor rediscovered it. It was restored by Aquitaine, the French oil company, and bears the inscription: "*Mais le sentier des justes et comme la lumiere resplendissante qui augmente son eclat jusqu'a ce que le jour soit en sa perfection.*"

Despite the singularity of Selkirk's vision and the extraordinary obstacles that were overcome in the Red River settlement, he wasn't really mythologized. Part of this is because the town in Manitoba that is named for him lost the bid for the rail line to Winnipeg. Northeast of Winnipeg, Selkirk is home to several thousand people and a mental hospital. The hospital was built at a time when pastoral care was felt to be a necessary part of rehabilitation, though most of the patients spent their time in the locked building. The pastoral location also kept them out of sight. When I was in school in Winnipeg, the town of Selkirk was a euphemism for the mental hospital and, finally, for mental illness. It was years before I found out that it was a town. I had no idea that it had been named for anyone. To be in Selkirk was to be insane.

Selkirk's motives for spending so much of his time and money trying to establish a colony at Red River were various. He genuinely wanted to better the lot of the Highlanders. He had expansionist dreams and he wanted to keep the Americans at bay and he saw Manitoba as a wilderness where agricultural experimentation could proceed unfettered. He had hoped for fame. He was young, rich, intelligent, filled with ideas. His maiden speech in the House of Lords was one of the dullest on record. His thoughts were sound, the peers noted, but he was a spectacularly untalented public speaker. His voice was low and small and he was stiff and humourless. Selkirk wanted to have some political impact and a successful colony would help. But he wasn't widely recognized at home for his feat. Red River simply became part of a larger settlement effort, people wandering the few acres of snow, as Voltaire had called Canada. There remained a hint of folly to his project. In the New World, Selkirk wasn't canonized by the settlers. Red River had been his vision, but he hadn't been out there eating nettles, breathing locusts, freezing in his London waistcoat. He was appreciated as a rich man's son.

By 1903, the extraordinary difficulties of the Red River settlement had been efficiently romanticized. *The Romantic Settle-*

ment of Lord Selkirk's Colonists, by "Dr. George Bryce Of Winnipeg, President of the Royal Society of Canada, etc., etc." as he was billed in the book, described the pioneering struggles in a way that Hollywood would applaud. Even Bryce, a Presbyterian minister, was seduced by the romance.

Much of the romance was state sponsored. When Clifford Sifton became the minister of the interior in 1896 under the Liberal government of Wilfrid Laurier, he made it his mission to populate the West. A western businessman himself, Sifton succeeded beyond expectation. Between 1896 and 1914, the population of the Prairies climbed from 300,000 to 1.5 million. Sifton used a variety of schemes to attract settlers. He gave American reporters tours of the West and offered American farmers free land and sent agents throughout Europe to recruit farmers and give speeches. He surreptitiously gave money to steamship agents who brought immigrants from western Europe, setting up a clandestine government shell, the North Atlantic Trading Company, to pay them. Sifton offered the Doukhobors, religious dissenters and able farmers, forty thousand acres in Saskatchewan and persuaded Leo Tolstoy to donate the royalties from his novel *Resurrection* to help finance their resettlement.

But Sifton's most effective means was a propaganda campaign using pamphlets and posters. He put advertisements in foreign papers, announcing free land (160 acres), fertile soil and unfettered freedom. The West was first described in poetic, Utopian terms, then placed within a realistic context. "It is no Utopian dream to look forward and see these endless plains thickly populated with millions to whom Western Canada has given a happy home, larger opportunities in life, and the assurance of a prosperous future."

The weather was described as being perfect for wheat and

healthful for people. The winters were "bracing" and "invigo-rating." The climate was "the healthiest in the world." Thomas Spence, an early pamphleteer, incorporated some of the racial theories that were extant; northern peoples were superior and one of the reasons was the cold, which invited virility in men and fertility in women and promoted clear-thinking and in-dustry. "Climate gives quality to the blood," Spence wrote, "strength to the muscles, power to the brain. Indolence is characteristic of people living in the tropics, and energy of those in temperate zones." There was a subtle implication that one could become more Nordic by moving to the Canadian West. You could not only alter your economic circumstances, but within reason, you could refine your racial characteristics as well. "The future citizen of the North-West of Canada will have Norse, Celtic and Saxon blood in his veins. His counte-nance, in the *pure, dry* electric air, will be as fresh as the morn-ing. His muscles will be iron, his nerves steel. Vigor will characterise his every action." Photographs of homesteads were shown in development, observing the metamorphosis from rough hut to home with barn and fences and trees. A poster showed an endless blue sky, a woman of Nordic beauty holding a perfect baby amid stacks of cut wheat with the caption, "Canada—The New Homestead." The soil was ex-cessively rich, the pamphlets warned, the climate "a veritable Eden for four months of the year." There wasn't any mention of the remaining eight months. "The frontier of Manitoba," one pamphlet said, "is about the same latitude as Paris."

Thomas Spence was quick to grasp a fundamental tech-nique of modern advertising; it was not enough to celebrate your own product, you had to denigrate the competition. He wrote of Manitoba's "unparalleled Salubrity, Growth and Pro-ductiveness in comparison with the Older Provinces." He hinted at tropical wasting in the more southerly United States. "Thousands have left comparatively healthy Canadian and European homes to find untimely graves in the prairie soil of Indiana, Illinois, Iowa and Missouri." Testimonials were used; an Englishman arriving with $1.75 and seven children becoming a land baron in a few years, or sickly urbanites from the United States who were transformed into robust, landowning men.

A pamphlet entitled "Manitoba, True Stories of Success in Farming" contained stirring testimonials. One of them was from a man named James E. Maynard, who had worked in England as a ropemaker, then a shoemaker, and finally a tailor before coming to Manitoba. He overcame hardship to eventually own 640 acres of land and in 1911 he went to the New York Land Show and returned with first prize in the Red Fife wheat category and third prize for the best wheat grown in the world.

The science of wheat was trumpeted. Red Fife had been developed to ripen quickly, to avoid the killing frosts that could arrive in September. Then Marquis wheat came along, an improvement on Red Fife. In 1885, a wheat farmer named Angus Mackay developed the concept of summer fallow. In 1918, two farmers, Leonard and Arie Koole, refined the idea by planting crops at right angles to the prevailing winds to protect fallow fields from wind erosion. There was a spirit of innovation that was lacking in Europe.

But the reality of farming in Manitoba wasn't nearly as sanguine as the pamphlets suggested. Near Moosehorn, a small community 120 miles north of Winnipeg, the free quarter sections offered by the Department of the Interior went mostly to Russian and Scottish immigrants, the only two groups with enough inherent fatalism to embrace the stony, unproductive ground and eclipsing winters. Some of the Russians' experience of farming was recorded in an anecdotal history. "When I think of all the hardships we went through," wrote Julius Weigelt, who was born in Russia and came to Moosehorn in 1917, "I sometimes wonder why we stayed. The younger people today will never understand what problems we had, so I think it is best to forget those early years." The nearest doctor was in Winnipeg, a two-hour ox-cart ride and seven-hour train ride away. Typhoid and influenza winnowed the large families. Babies died in infancy, men were trampled by oxen, horses died of swamp fever. One journal had only daily entries of "Went for wood," for several months, punctuated finally by, "Baby died."

Sifton's campaign was a tremendous success. In 1901, the number of homestead applications was 8,167. A year later it had gone up to 14,633, many of them from Americans who sold their farms in the United States and applied for free land in nearby Canada, the border an arbitrary line to them. Some of them were less than a generation removed from Scandinavia or Germany or Scotland. In 1905, the year Lachlan Ross arrived in Winnipeg, the number of homestead applications had ballooned to more than forty thousand.

It was an exclusively rural campaign; Sifton wanted only farmers. But the farm was pitched differently to different audiences. Independence and space were the notions presented to clerks in London who laboured at desks in windowless rooms. A kind of heroism was implied. The oppressed became free. The scale of the farms was emphasized to those farmers working on twenty-acre plots in eastern Europe. He went after most Europeans though he tried to avoid Jews.

Some pamphlets exploited a theme of religious freedom. The Canadian West was described as Edenic, unsullied by civilization. Man could exist here in an idealized state, as Adam had before the Fall. Instead of hardship and isolation, the

Prairies offered spiritual purity. Various groups came west and flourished; Doukhobors, Mennonites, Hutterites and Mormons. Utopian communities with a religious nucleus sprang up. At Beulah, Manitoba, a community named Harmona was established by radical socialist Protestant farmers. Theirs was a collective inspired by British Utopian writers like John Ruskin. They failed to attract many followers in that time of foaming capitalism and they lacked a railway link to Winnipeg, so Harmona withered. But it was, as people still claimed ninety years later, God's country.

One of Sifton's pamphlets came to Lachlan Ross in Fanagmore and he read of the life of a Manitoba farmer. "With a farm free from debt," it said, "his fields of ripening grain ready for harvest; with herds of cattle on his pasture lands, and flocks of sheep feeding on the hillside; dairy and poultry providing the household with groceries and many other comforts; schools for his children in the immediate neighbourhood; churches close at hand, and such other social advantage as he desires within easy reach—what more is required for a happy existence? And that is the condition of the Manitoba farmer." If he agreed to emigrate, Lachlan would receive a plot of 160 acres of prime land. His croft at Fanagmore was less than an acre of thin soil surrounded by rock. He had a cow, a few sheep. The image that was presented in the pamphlet was of an unbounded sky and limitless land. Manitoba offered both economic freedom and a respite from the secret that the family harboured. In a poster that arrived in Scourie there was a man in the position of a carnival barker, one hand pointing to the mark and the other indicating a tree that spelled out the words CANADA WEST. Beside each capital letter was a quality to be found there: Contentment, Abundance, Nationalism, Affluence, Democracy, Ambition, Welcome, Encouragement,

Sociability, Thrift. It would never have occurred to Lachlan that this was advertising.

———————

In 1905, when the ship carrying the Ross family landed in Montreal, Lachlan Ross was burdened with secrets and fifty years old, though he looked older. He was of modest stature, slope shouldered and bald. His full grey beard drew his face into a naturally lugubrious expression, as if he had just witnessed something heartbreaking. No one would have been surprised that he was a grandfather. His wife, Bessie, was short and stern and her face was cast in an expression of disapproval. They had seven of their children with them, eight if you counted Georgina. They had been two weeks at sea, a heaving, unpleasant crossing. Montreal was filled with grand stone mansions, many of them built and owned by Scots. There was a common grave that held hundreds of victims of typhoid, mostly Irish, though some Scots. The train from Montreal to Winnipeg took almost three days, a cramped, hopeful journey. Their room had detachable tables that hooked to the wall, a small kitchenette and a compact furnace, which they didn't need in June. A sea of spruce and poplar went by in a blur. Georgina sat with Jean, staring out the window. When Georgie looked back, following the motion of the train, the trees stood still briefly then returned to a blur. Occasionally the view opened up to large fields planted with flax and barley and corn.

The train stopped at Ottawa and White River and Rosport and Port Arthur. There seemed to be no end to the wilderness. The train went along the north shore of Lake Superior, through rock that had been blasted to expose a jagged face. The air was cool in the evenings but in the day the family members perspired in their thick woollens. An hour east of Winnipeg the train left the trees suddenly and arrived on the endless prairie. When you came out of the woods it was as if days of unbroken noise were suddenly relieved by a magnificent silence. After seventy hours in the train they had reached only the midway point of this vast, uninhabited, lush, stubborn country, to Winnipeg, one of the few cities with a climate harsher than the one they had left.

Lachlan had been told that there were Scots in Winnipeg, most of them Highlanders. The climate was favourable and a hard-working man could do well. He had fished for salmon in Loch Laxford but there would be no fishing here. He could see that the minute he set eyes on the Red River. Each morning he looked into that water, which was the colour of coffee. He had seen men take crayfish out of it and cook them in pots over open fires. There was carp, maybe. But this wasn't the river for trout or any cleanly fish.

For a time the Ross family lived in a tent, camped on the riverbank near where Osborne Street and Corydon Avenue met. There were other families, a city of tents, and each day ended in a wreath of foreign smells. They were surrounded by rank mud and underwear drying on poles. Men sat defeated in their undershirts and women boiled dinner. The children ran in herds, excited by this raw society. Lachlan read his Bible while there was light and took grim comfort in its words.

They had to boil their drinking water. It was ironic that here in the unspoiled and indefatigable prairie there was no fresh water. The Red River was thick with silt and in 1904 there had been a deadly epidemic of Red River fever. The Assiniboine was no better. The water was hard, like "taking a gulp of shingle nails," according to one resident, and it was polluted by cattle and sewers. The water was worse than in the crowded cities of Europe. In the North End of the city, where the immigrants lived in their multitudes—Jews, Galicians, Hungarians, Slavs, Scandinavians—a typhoid epidemic struck and the casualty rate was among the highest in the world. Fewer than half of the homes in the North End were connected to the city's water system. Winnipeg wavered between the optimism of the new millennium and a plague that invoked the Middle Ages.

After rising before 6 a.m., Lachlan walked north to Main Street. It was a city consumed by growth, he thought. An editorialist in the paper agreed. "The fact is that Winnipeg in her feverish desire to grow, only to grow, was not in the least concerned to grow properly and healthfully, to develop sanely. Her insistent demand for figures to prove growth, and only growth, be it by building permits, or by bank clearances, or by customer receipts, or by pavement mileage, or peradventure by the price of vacant land, any process of growth demonstration, has blinded her to the fact that cities cannot live by growth alone."

Main Street was filled with men applying at Mike's Standard Employment for work. They looked like bees clustered around the employment offices, waiting to sign onto bush clearing or railway crews. But Lachlan couldn't leave his family to go and work in the bush, without even a roof over their heads. And he didn't like the thought of living with these dark, unhappy men for weeks on end.

The adjustment from the Highlands to Winnipeg was difficult for Lachlan. The city was elusive; he couldn't seem to grasp its energy. He was a spectator. In summer, the family lived on the riverbank, in a tent. In the winter, in boarding houses. Lachlan worked as a labourer, digging, hammering, lifting the city toward its prideful destiny. In the winter, there wasn't always work. Sometimes it was too cold, a still dry cold that froze your breath while it was still in your lungs. Usually no one worked in construction in the winter, but the demand for housing was so great that men braved the weather. It wasn't until 1911 that Lachlan had a permanent address, on Corydon Avenue. By then he had become a carpenter and the eldest girls had found work as domestics. Jean and Georgie were at the Gladstone School, a grand stone building not far from where they had camped. His wife, Bessie, had a job at the T. Eaton Company, the huge department store that Scots immigrants favoured.

In 1913, Lachlan resolved to do two things: one was to leave the city and become a farmer; the other was to establish a Free Presbyterian Church. God made the country and man made the town, William Cowper had said. There was a belief that spirituality was equated with rural life while the city promoted materialism. It was hard not to believe this, living in a boom town, watching the city's behaviour the way a teetotaler watches a drunkard's progress. On June 9, Lachlan applied for a homestead under the provisions of the Dominion Lands Act. On July 2, using funds he had raised among the city's Free Presbyterians, he purchased a building on McGee Street, north of Portage Avenue. It was a small bungalow, suitably unimpressed with itself, and was held in trust by Lachlan, William Sinclair, who was Lachlan's cousin, and a Mr. D. Kennedy.

With the church established, Lachlan left for his farm. Under the Homestead Act, he paid ten dollars and received 160 acres of land. In return, he had to cultivate at least thirty acres, build a house worth a minimum of three hundred dollars and reside on the land for three years. His land was near Moosehorn, a village that was almost 120 miles north of Winnipeg, located between Lake Winnipeg and Lake Manitoba.

He took the train to Camper, sitting stiffly for seven hours observing the thousands of orange lilies that grew along the railway line. From Camper, he took a team of oxen to his land, a quarter section of scrub and swamp with a ridge of stone where the Canadian Shield jutted through. First he had to dig a well using a crowbar and a spade. On the prairies, settlers looked for buffalo-willow, waterweed, badger holes or anthills as signs of water. Lachlan's land was too swampy for any of these indicators. The hole had to be six feet in diameter in order to be wide enough to throw the dirt out. Each foot he dug down meant almost thirty cubic feet of dirt to throw out. It was back-breaking, suffocating work and the flies and mosquitoes filled the damp hole. He dug twelve feet before abandoning the first hole as dry, an accomplishment, given that the land was essentially a swamp located between two of the largest inland lakes on the continent. He found water on his second attempt and shored up the walls and built a wellhead.

He built a two-room log house and chinked the cracks with clay. He rose early and worked to clear the land, hacking with an axe and grub-hoe and picking the hundreds of stones from the soil. The mosquitoes and horseflies never gave him any peace. The oxen were dumb brutes that laid down when they were tired, and he couldn't get them to do his bidding and he didn't have the heart to beat them. At night, moths circled the coal-oil lamp by the hundreds and the light was a flickering mosaic. The land was wet enough that horses died of swamp fever. He drove the oxen into Moosehorn to buy supplies, a trip that took the full day. He bought sugar and flour from Sam Zechoval, who ran the store. Other immigrants were there, most of them Russians. Few of them spoke English. The women bought flour bags at ten cents each to make clothes for the children. Zechoval used to put a gum-drop in the coal-oil cans to seal the spout, and Lachlan saw a Russian child take the oily candy and put it in his mouth, chewing solemnly.

He worked through to November, alone in the prohibitive cold, reading his Bible for sustenance and practical advice. *The earth bringeth forth fruit of herself, first the blade, then the ear, after that the full corn in the ear.* In the morning, the sky was depthless and night arrived in the afternoon. The snow was driven into drifts outside and Lachlan bought moose and elk and rabbit meat from Russian hunters and roasted it in the fireplace. The wind from Lake Manitoba came through fissures in the clay and as it diminished and changed direction, it suggested the cadences of speech, a keening cry that rose and fell. Whispered hisses leaked in. He imagined that it was God's voice, speaking to him. Why was he here, Lachlan asked, alone in this wilderness? The touted spiritualism of rural life was contingent on living in harmony with nature and Lachlan hadn't found anything resembling harmony. He was a discordant shriek on the landscape.

Songs of the day celebrated the farm as a symbol of both progress and Christianity. A song called "Harvest" described the nobility of the calling.

Manitoba, from thy prairie,
Won by God's especial grace,
To a nobler, fuller mission
Than the battle or the chase,
Rises up the song of harvest
As the thankful people raise
From the oat fields and the wheat fields
Fervent notes of thankful praise.

Lachlan couldn't call his meagre output a harvest. There were probably gardens in Winnipeg that yielded more. Was his a higher purpose or exile? he wondered.

He returned to Winnipeg for two months in the winter and preached at the Free Presbyterian Church. In the spring he went back to Moosehorn with Bessie and their son William, while the rest of the family stayed in Winnipeg. There was a small society forming among the settlers. The Sabbath was observed among the small community of Scots in the area, which came to be known as New Scotland. They worshipped in both English and Gaelic in the small log church and the children memorized five hundred Bible verses to be eligible for a summer camp at Gimli. Lachlan was an earnest presence leading them through the psalms.

Lachlan and his son optimistically built a granary though they were only able to break half an acre of soil after a summer of brutal work, fighting the entrenched scrub and the predatory clouds of blackflies and mosquitoes. The grain could have been held in a basket. They bought two cows. The next year they planted barley and oats and some vegetables in the half acre but there was frost in July and it killed the barley and some of the vegetables. That summer they were able to clear another half acre of land and add two more cows. William played the bagpipes in the early morning and the horses came to him, curious at that inhuman noise.

The soil on Lachlan's farm was stingy and mean. He kept a handful of dirt in his pocket and when he was too exhausted to work, he would take it out and examine it the way gypsies looked at tea leaves. That something so elemental as dirt could hold so many secrets. One handful could raise carrots but reject wheat. His soil grew potatoes to the size of marbles and corn that was stunted and sandy. Wild sunflowers stood like a crowd watching a tennis match, their animate heads following the sun and observing his defeat.

The advances in agriculture weren't any help. After Red Fife and Marquis, two new strains of wheat followed, Garnet and Reward, both developed for the northern prairie. But science wasn't going to save him. His farmland wasn't the land that had been advertised in the pamphlets. The dangerously rich soil had gone to someone else. The Doukhobors had gotten a huge tract not that far away. They had once tried to walk to Winnipeg in a mood of religious fervour, looking for the Promised Land, but had run into the prairie winter and returned to their farms. Lachlan had heard that they ran naked and burned their own homes in purification rituals and he thought them extreme, but he admired their talent for renunciation.

The Dominion Lands Act allowed for each qualified settler to claim 160 acres of free land, though it didn't automatically grant them ownership. They had to meet the requirements and then apply for patent before they assumed title. One of the requirements was to clear thirty acres but after seven years on the farm, Lachlan had only cleared three and a half. He had expanded his cattle herd to twelve and had fenced the land, but this wasn't enough. The assistant secretary to the minister of the interior, a Mr. Nelson, wrote to Lachlan in 1919 informing him that they had initiated cancellation proceedings on his patent. The government was reclaiming the land. Lachlan appealed, citing ill health; he had been plagued with kidney problems for five years and he was still recovering from a bad fall. He also pleaded financial hardship. They had made little money from their picayune crops. The assistant secretary continued his stream of letters, signing them, ironically, "Your obedient servant" and demanding proof that Lachlan was unlucky and ailing rather than shiftless. Mr. Nelson knew from correspondence with others in the area that it was farmland in name only. Few were prospering. Still he wanted full value for the money it had taken to advertise and subsidize their journey to Canada to clear the brush. He finally took into account the fact that Lachlan had one son in France during the war and the cancellation proceedings were abandoned.

Lachlan was granted the deed but he didn't stay long at Moosehorn. After more than a decade of farming he had less than five of his 160 acres under cultivation. The area flooded during his last year on the farm and men dipped fish out of the ditches. He wasn't the only one to leave. Many of the original settlers abandoned their farms after more than a decade of making a marginal living. The land "should have been left to the Indians," one of them said. The Ross farm never came to resemble the posters that Lachlan had seen in Scotland. At no point was there any threat of youth and Aryan vigour and golden possibility. It was unproductive and debilitating; it was an anti-farm. When he left it, Lachlan was seventy, ailing and defeated. He had a luxurious beard, the only thing that grew. When he had been a young fisherman in Scotland and watched his friends drown in Loch Laxford, Lachlan had become uncomfortable with the sea and its unpredictable vengeance. Now he was lost on the soil, growing as awkward and unyielding as his crops. His wife was worn and shrunken and the children didn't want anything to do with farming. He had flayed himself in the wilderness for fifteen years and had made little mark. The house, buildings, fences and cleared land were valued at only $1,410. Within two years of leaving the land, it had reverted to scrub and dogwood and vines, eclipsing any sign of Lachlan's toil.

He returned to Winnipeg in 1929, to Ashburn Street, north of Portage. It was a relief not to face that stubborn, silent land in the spring. The Free Presbyterian Church couldn't afford a minister and Lachlan sometimes preached there. He stood at the front of the church, staring at his family sitting stiffly on the hard pew. Those in the church knew Georgina's secret. She was thirty now and married, a large, moon-faced woman, ungainly. He watched her sing the psalms, her voice robust but undistinguished, an honest voice. Not one for entertainments. Though she had a quiet dignity, he thought, her mother in South Africa, her father under God's eye.

8

GATEWAY
TO THE WEST

LEWIS FOOTE came to Winnipeg in 1902, the same year my great-grandfather Peter Mainland arrived. Foote had been born on an island off the coast of Newfoundland. He had a lopsided, unhandsome face and a goofy charm and he became the city's pre-eminent commercial photographer, handing out business cards that read "The Man Who Foote-e graphs the people with a smile." Much of the photographic record of Winnipeg in the early part of the century is composed of his images. The most notable thing about Foote's photographs is their remarkable symmetry. A fox farm shot in winter shows rows of uniform, miniature houses and identical cleared pathways that resemble roads. Foote's photographs, like the settlers themselves, brought order to the wilderness. The flat waste was marked off in grids for farms and the city superimposed its own grid, first on the land and then on the people. Foote's record is one of almost unblemished optimism, reflecting the city as its civic leaders wanted it represented: ordered, ascendant, a square-jawed place with a good Christian raising.

One photograph has the nurses of Grace Hospital standing in line, all of them dressed in identical whites, each holding a baby wrapped in white. Workers installing the copper roof on the Hotel Fort Garry stand and face the camera. The multitude on the floor of the Grain Exchange stare upward at him as one. A photograph of the Eley Brothers plant shows lines of perfect machinery, bathed in a white light. The factory is unsullied by workers and looks as if it could function without them, a prevailing wish of the owners and a view that Foote's work supports. One photograph shows the clean, erect line of the Knox Presbyterian Church. In another there are uniform rows of Fuller Brush Men behind a banner ("We're Fuller Pep!"), graduates of the Fuller Field Manager School. Foote was a commercial photographer in every sense and celebrated the commercial class on film.

To look at his photographs as a record of the times would be like taking Frank Capra's films as a defining document of America of the 1930s. But Foote captures some of the city's insistent enthusiasm. In 1911, only 1.5 per cent of Winnipeg's population was over the age of sixty-five. It was the youngest city in the country, its awkward energy celebrated in the cheer of the Young Men's Section of the Winnipeg Board of Trade:

Winnipeg, Winnipeg, Gateway of the West
Always growing greater, never growing less
Winnipeg, Winnipeg, we are not so slow
We are always boosting, everywhere we go!

———————

Boosterism has many of the qualities of a religion and its central theology is growth. Winnipeg's boosters used the mad arc of statistics to convey the city's prosperity. They thrived on numbers: seventeen and a half miles of asphalt pavement, thirty-three miles of macadam, twenty-three miles of stone roads, 190 miles of plank sidewalks, eighty-four miles of sewers, thirty miles of streetcar tracks. Boosterism was self-idolatry; the city worshipped itself, it was the alpha and the omega. To be a knocker was to be a heathen.

The city's business leaders were largely transplanted Ontarians and predominantly Presbyterian or Methodist. This elite group also dominated politics, controlling the provincial legislature, city hall and the Board of Trade. It was an oligarchy that spent more money on promoting the city than on sanitation, health and welfare. You needed to own property to vote, a criteria that kept the voting register small. In 1906, there were 7,784 registered voters in a population of 100,000. As the boosters prospered and Winnipeg grew, the North End became a kind of parallel city that was regressing. The infant mortality rate there was twenty-five per cent. There was little sanitation, inadequate education, no social services. Winnipeg was like one of those western film towns; a series of authentic facades.

The downtown plan was on a grand scale. "It is as if some mighty force were astir beneath the ground," one pamphlet read, "pushing up buildings—warehouses, business blocks, office buildings, hotels, residences." Both Main Street and Portage Avenue were impressively wide, though the width was initially to accommodate the awkward Red River carts. The buildings were solid and occasionally elegant. The business leaders were aware that they were building a monument to themselves. The result was often photographed by Foote and others with a Kodak Circuit camera, which produced panoramic views and further exaggerated the scale.

The photographs and testimonials were used to advertise the city, to attract citizens and investment. A pamphlet titled "Canada as Seen Through Scottish Eyes" was distributed abroad. It read, "Winnipeg, where we spent our first Sunday on the plains, is the gateway of the west, and destined to become one of the very greatest of Canadian towns. It came into being as if by the touch of a wizard's hand." The promotion of the city was like a telethon that went on for a decade.

The West was its own religion, a sunny, bountiful paradise. But within it the various cities sparred and competed like sects of the Presbyterian church. Saskatoon declared itself respectively, "the fastest growing city in world," "the Largest City in the World for its Age," as well as "the greatest example of town and city building in the world's history." It wasn't enough to trumpet your own strengths; you had to denigrate the competition. The Regina *Leader Post* ran this headline in January 1913, "Girls Cannot Live Morally in Calgary." None of the cities could afford self-criticism or introspection, which could have a negative effect on investment, commerce and growth. Edmonton would become "the largest city in Canada" according to its newspaper, the *Journal*. The *Calgary Albertan* declared Calgary, "Queen of the Plains and Mistress of the Gateway to the Great Canadian Rockies."

It wasn't just the larger centres that had this outsized vision of themselves. Towns that never attracted more than a few hundred people drew parallels to Rome. Villages that quietly disappeared did so announcing that they were the Empire's Jewel. Medicine Hat was the "Minneapolis of Canada." Selkirk, Strathcona and Lethbridge all saw themselves as vital hubs, their charms defined by businessmen and politicians and repeated by editorialists.

But Winnipeg was the most established city on the prairie. Despite the fact that it only had 1,600 people in 1873 when it officially came into being, Winnipeg was incorporated as a city, rather than a town or village. It had an early confidence. Within twenty-five years it had become the central handling point for the nation's wheat. By 1902, it was the largest grain handler in North America, 51.8 million bushels to Chicago's 37.9 million. The 1905 wheat crop had increased by five hundred per cent from ten years earlier as Sifton's settlers began to produce. "Winnipeg is founded on the prairie," one of the city's immigration pamphlets read, "and the vitality, the immense potentiality and ever advancing prosperity, of which the prairie soil of Western Canada is the greatest reservoir in the world, is in Winnipeg's blood. The city is only on the threshold of its greatness. The transformation that is being wrought now is for all time, and is only beginning."

Not everyone agreed with the boosters, of course. The British poet Rupert Brooke visited Winnipeg in 1913, before he found his subject in the First World War, and had a mixed, decidedly English view. He saw the city as less offensive than America. "The people have something of the free swing of Americans," he wrote, "without the bumptiousness; a tempered democracy, a mitigated independence of bearing. The manners of Winnipeg, of the West, impress the stranger as better than those of the East, more friendly, more hearty, more certain to achieve graciousness, if not grace. There is, even, in the architecture of Winnipeg, a sort of gauche pride visible. It is hideous, of course, even more hideous than Toronto or Montreal; but cheerily and windily so."

Journalist George Bain, who visited Winnipeg in 1906, found it alarmingly cosmopolitan. "The Red Indian, the dusky Kaffir, the yellow Chinaman and the bronzed Mexican, the heavy Scandinavian or Russian Pole, the perky Italian, and the melancholy Greek are all to be met with in the surging crowd of an evening, but the Anglo-Saxon race happily predominates." In fact it occupied virtually all positions of power, setting the tone for language and custom. And this would eventually become the city's downfall.

An unsubtle racism permeated government, business and religion. The Methodist publication *Missionary Outlook* candidly outlined the dominant position: "If from this North American continent is to come a superior race, a race to be specially used of God in carrying on His work, what is our duty towards those who are now our fellow citizens? Many of them come to us as nominal Christians, that is, they owe allegiance to the Greek or Roman Catholic churches, but their moral standards and ideals are far below those of the Christian citizens of the Dominion. These people have come to this young, free country to make homes for themselves and their children. It is our duty to meet them with the open Bible, and to instill into their minds the principles and ideals of Anglo-Saxon civilization."

And who wouldn't want to embrace those ideals? they wondered. Who wouldn't want starched collars and cricket? The immigrants would be relieved to give up garlic and an uncertain god, anxious to embrace devilled eggs and boiled meat and a pipeline to salvation. The women would wear white and volunteer. Their voices would join the chorus that celebrated Winnipeg to the world.

"How the sun shines here in Winnipeg!" wrote Emily Murphy in *Janey Canuck in the West*. "One drinks it in like wine. And how the bells ring! It is a town of bells and light set in a blaze of gold. Surely the West *is* golden—the sky, flowers, wheat, hearts . . . Winnipeg has something western, something southern, something quite her own. She is an up-and-doing place. She has swagger, compelling arrogance, enterprise, and an abiding spirit of usefulness. 'What I like,' says an American to me, 'is the eternal spunk of the place.'"

———

Peter Gavin Mainland wasn't a booster in any real sense. He didn't believe in the innate superiority of the citizens and he understood their Christian cheers to be the exclusionary cry of a private club. The boosters celebrated the city's growth but lamented its actual people: the Jews, the Galicians, the Ukes, Douks, Polacks and Hunkys. He was a knocker by temperament, rejecting any religion, even one as secular as boosterism, but he recognized its advantages. When Peter arrived alone from Chicago in 1902, the city had a sprawling fervour that he enjoyed. The train station itself signalled excitement, designed by the same architects who designed Grand Central Station in New York, a fact that was often mentioned. Crowds were everywhere and speculation was rampant. Along the bars on Main Street, Peter heard stories of people hitting it big. Elaborate theories of history unfolded over Three Swallows whisky.

Location, he was told. Power was an act of geography. Winnipeg was the centre and nothing, no gimcrack Ottawa

politician, no suffragist steamroller, no Bible-dragging crea-
tionist orator could stop the trade of North America from
going straight through the city. It was an unalterable fact.
Peter sipped at his whisky and felt that he had come home.

There were dozens of bars on Main Street alone, among
them the Nugget, Alberta and Iroquois on the east side. On
the west, the Maple Leaf, Club, Bell and the Exchange. Just
off Main there was Jimmy's, Queen's, Reno, Bank, Grange,
George, Seymour, Leland and Roblin. Most had pool rooms.
Some had nickelodeons. Several had prostitutes.

In 1904, more building permits were issued in Winnipeg
than any other city in the Dominion, an amount equal to
Montreal and Toronto combined. The next year, thirty apartment blocks were constructed and three million dollars spent
on commercial buildings and hotels. Peter heard these statistics, often inflated, repeated like a litany. The city was alive as
if it were an independent organism. The West was still empty
enough that there was talk of empire.

At the Dominion Theatre, he went to see the comedy gym-
nastics of Frank and Little Bob and then Harney and Haynes
doing their Octamaroon impersonations. Peter found himself
laughing, though he couldn't have explained why.

On Labour Day, he went to watch the car race sponsored
by the Winnipeg Automobile Club. Oldsmobiles, Packards,
McLaughlins, Mitchells, the Royal Tourist and the Canadian-
made Russell all competed over forty-nine and a half miles of
uneven land and dirt roads. They hit the mud and sank like
ships. He noticed the way the people sat in their motorcars, elevated and swaddled against the chill, looking down as if in-
specting the peasantry. After the exciting start, Peter retreated
to the hotel bar to discuss whether this was a sport in any real
sense. Russell Macleod came in first in the cross-country race,

posting a time of two hours, nine and a half minutes. Peter preferred the baseball games at Wesley Park and the occasional boxing matches. He sometimes went to the International Club in St. Boniface to watch the visiting fighters train. They drank olive oil and had it rubbed into their skin, burnishing those hard bodies like they were furniture, bringing them to a shine. He evaluated them for wagering, judging the speed and force of their hands, observing the dull violence of their fists against the heavy bag.

The advertisements in the *Manitoba Free Press* indicated a society obsessed with itself. The Blatz Wiener beer ads were followed closely by "The Keeley Cure for Drink and Drug Habits." Women bought Dr. Charles Flesh Food for removing wrinkles and developing the bust. Men spent their money on Dr. McLaughlin's Electric Belt, to eliminate puniness, rheumatism, nervous debility and liver trouble. They used Newbro's Herpicide for Beautiful Hair and brushed their teeth with Sozodent tooth powder. Moving pictures were playing at the Kinodrome, frantic comedies where everyone moved as if they had been prodded with a hot poker.

Prostitution was flourishing. The city had an official policy of segregated vice. There was an understanding between the prostitutes and the civic leaders that the brothels would operate only at the edge of the city. For one thing, it made them easier to visit discreetly. But as the city grew, the relationship deteriorated and market forces took over. By 1909, there were more than one hundred brothels within the city limits.

Winnipeg became a moral battleground. Presbyterian minister J. G. Shearer told the Toronto *Globe* that "Winnipeg has the rottenest condition of social vices to be found in Canada." He was denounced in the media and the Presbyterian church then denounced the media. A judge was appointed to investigate the state of the city's vices and found that prostitution flourished and was condoned by the police.

Peter established himself as a stone contractor, and sent for his family in 1903. He built a home for them on Mulvey Avenue that had touches of grandeur: small pillars on the front porch, a second-floor balcony. It was a large home, graceful in its proportions, comfortable for what became a family of nine. There was another son and three daughters. Peter wore a suit to supervise the men he hired. Occasionally, if it was late in the day, he wore a dinner jacket with tails. Against great odds, he had retained a shining sense of his own aristocracy.

Peter prospered as a contractor. Houses couldn't be built fast enough to accommodate the new immigrants. He rode the boom though he retained some of the business practices that he had learned in Shetland, sometimes paying the men with worthless cheques. Most of them simply moved on, vowing never to work for him again. But labourers and carpenters were easy to find. He was lax in his payments to suppliers and his cheques occasionally bounced there, too. On November 30, 1907, two policemen came to the door on Mulvey Avenue. They were nice enough, beefy and broad-faced and without malice. They asked Peter about certain cheques and told him that hē was being charged with obtaining money and goods under false pretenses, reading the information from a small pad. Charges had been laid by a Mr. Max Warshaft. Other charges were laid by Percy Brawed and a third complaint made by Elias Tapper. There had to be a mistake, Peter said amiably. Certainly there was, the men said and took him to the York Street jail and asked him to empty his pockets. Peter gave them his rule book, which contained scribbled reminders and tips on horses. He gave them his knife, his pencil, his keys and his mittens and sat in the cell with two Irish drunks named Gilboy and Donnally. Gilboy was a singing drunk and Peter thought that this punishment might be taken into account by the courts.

His nationality was listed as Scottish and when he appeared before the judge, Peter acted as his own counsel, describing his role in the city's expansion. His concern was that people needed to be housed. He had seen the great tent cities and the men wandering the North End. There were homes by the railway yards made of earth. Winter was here already and bitter as the devil. His crime was in trying to provide solid homes for employed Christians. Houses were the cornerstone of civilization; homes created neighbourhoods and led to paved roads and sidewalks and churches and order. As God was his judge, he had been caught up in the effort of providing relief. He tried to employ those who needed work but they weren't always grateful for the opportunity. They gave you half a day's work and moved on. In his haste, his accounting had suffered, but something had to give. The judge sentenced him to three months in the hoosegow. Donnally and Gilboy were gone the next morning, which was something.

When this anecdote was related within the family, Peter had always managed to get himself off with a combination of guile and oratory. His successful defences became part of the necessary, unverifiable myth that make up the family.

December, January and February, the three worst months of the year. The construction business had slowed anyway and Peter was content to wait out the winter in jail. Christina had enough money to keep things together though it was now a large family. In addition to the three boys born in Shetland, there were two girls, Jessie and Mary, and two more boys, William and Gilbert. When she came to view him through the bars, like a gibbon sitting at the back of his cage, she cried.

She had a witchy Highland vision that this was her place; to live with grief, to wait for another knock at the door. She told the children that Father was away on important business. She didn't tell the neighbours anything. She took care of the children and read from *The Poetical Works of Robert Burns*.

> The wintry west extends his blast,
> And hail and rain does blaw;
> Or, the stormy north sends driving forth
> The blinding sleet and snaw:
> While, tumbling brown, the burn comes down,
> And roars frae bank to brae;
> And bird and beast in covert rest,
> And pass the heartless day.

She had "the Highland disease," as it was called, a slur that implied laziness. She languished, suffering from real and imagined ills that were treated with Lydia E. Pinkham's Vegetable Compound. In middle age, she believed she was dying and held to that belief until her death at ninety-two. In 1913, when she learned that a Free Presbyterian church had been established on McGee Street, she joined the small congregation. She had found herself longing for the Highland community of her youth and here, certainly, was a Highland religion. In Shetland, she had been an outsider and in Winnipeg she was stuck between the teeming immigrants dressed as though for a costume party and the ruling class and their vanity. She found the two-hour services lulling and she loved the preacher's voice, revelling in his accent as much as his message. His voice had a musical quality. She was accompanied by the family, everyone except Peter, who had crucial business each Sunday morning, he said. The supply minister from Scotland told

Christina not to read her beloved Robbie Burns, that he was a wicked man. But she forgave the minister.

On Windermere Avenue, Peter built himself an elegant house, the finest for a mile. They had the first gramophone on the fledgling street and each night Christina listened to "His Master's Voice," the scratchy hymns coming out in rhythmic waves. At night, Peter would return from the bar and his Three Swallows whisky and the conversations about the size and shape of the future and climb heavily up the stairs. He lay on his bed, the dark swirling around him, the whisky no longer his ally, and took stock of his life. He had a fine home and a lovely family, as he was regularly reminded. The boys were athletic and industrious and the girls were slender and graceful. His business, despite ongoing irregularities with numbers, was sailing. He was forty-three years old and in good health, all things considered. He should walk more and drink less, perhaps. He took a spoonful of Perfect Headache Powder and then a shot of Dr. Shoop's Sarsaparilla With Iron Sure Cure. A tornado had hit Regina and plucked buildings from the ground like a farmer picking weeds and Peter had bet a man at the Hotel Fort Garry bar that Winnipeg would be hit with one as well. He didn't believe in God but he didn't want to bet against Him.

Peter Mainland had a pattern to his contracting business. He built the family a modest home then took out a mortgage on it, sometimes several mortgages, and built a much grander house next door. The first home was sold or abandoned for unpaid taxes. He understood the city's momentum and could see that it was lurching, unchecked toward the future. Bad debts, a criminal record, unpaid taxes were all part of the past, something that was of no interest and little consequence in Winnipeg. What mattered was the future, the homes that

Peter would build, the land he was buying, the money he was borrowing. He knew that boom towns are conscienceless, neither cruel nor compassionate, but like nature, simply indifferent. Peter was able to thrive, leaving his mark on the city. The houses he built are still standing with a sense of muted grandeur. While Lachlan Ross was struggling in the wilderness, Peter Mainland was embraced by the amoral city, which recognized him as kin.

9

DETROIT

ALL THE MAINLAND BOYS were welterweights like their father, five foot seven, just under 150 pounds, compact. They had sandy hair, grey eyes and lean faces. Tommy, my grandfather's twin brother, was the athlete. He pitched in the Winnipeg baseball league and played soccer and hockey for Fort Rouge. He was quick and wiry, with an athlete's anticipation of disaster, and at twenty, he was young enough to believe that these qualities would help him in the war. He was the first of the brothers to enlist, joining in December 1915. The next summer Jim joined on, and in May 1917, my grandfather, Don, enlisted. All of them were fit. They all answered no when asked if there had ever been any trouble with their Nervous Systems, Integumentary Systems, Osseous and Joint Systems, their Special Senses. There had been no Disturbances of Mentality. Their teeth were good.

For a lot of Winnipeggers, the war was a rite of citizenship. Germans and Ukrainians were further reviled and bullied, their loyalties challenged. But Scots were embraced. For my grandfather and his brothers, the war defined them as Canadians.

Jim was shipped to Liverpool and spent the war as a mechanic. Don joined the Thirty-fourth Fort Garry Horse and trained in Winnipeg, digging trenches in sharp geometric lines near Main Street. Barbed wire was strung along stakes cut from poplar trees. The men laboured beneath a billboard advertising Maltum, "The New Malt Beverage." Boys lingered enviously, women waved. This would turn out to be the best part of the war. In February 1918, the Fort Garry Horse sailed to England on the SS *Grampian*. Don had a brief layover in London and went to Valentine's Photography Studio and had a picture taken of himself in uniform. The photo is sepia-toned and in it he is standing with his legs apart, his hands clasped behind his back, probably a standard, authoritative pose directed by the photographer. Behind him is a painted mural, an impressionistic sweep of foliage. The upper-left-hand corner is a square of grey light, a glimpse of sky. Beside Don, in front of the mural, is a small stone ruin, two pillars perched on a foundation that have been torn from some grand structure. It is a romantic evocation of a battlefield, a commercial artist's rendering of war, slightly gloomy, but ennobling and ancient. The desired illusion is the dawn-after-battle with Don looking weary and grimly victorious. The photograph was laminated onto a postcard, which could be sent home, a marketable image of the war. It was a backdrop that was designed for those on their way to the front, not for the ones who were returning from the surprising slaughter.

There was more training in England. They dug neat, dry trenches and sat in them smoking, staring up at the uneventful sky. After two months, the Thirty-fourth Fort Garry Horse went to France. The Germans had begun a large-scale offensive on March 21, 1918, hoping to capture Amiens. On March 23, Don's outfit took up a position between Le Four Croix and the Faillouel-Villequier-Aumont Road. Two battalions of enemy guns pounded their position. It was my grandfather's first taste of war, a confusing, uncoordinated experience, scrambling in a pack, everyone moving at the garbled bark of the officer. The trenches were overrun by rats and filled with stagnant water. The men burned lice off their shirts and rubbed their feet with whale oil to staunch the swelling of trench foot.

Within two weeks, the German general, Ludendorff, abandoned the attack on Amiens. For three weeks the Fort Garry Horse rested west of the city. They were blooded now, relaxing in the aftermath of battle, able to make grim jokes. In early May they went to Hallencourt to dig trenches and, on August 8, the Allied offensive began. They were buoyed by rumours that the war would end soon.

On August 10, the Fort Garry Horse tried to encircle the town of Roye. C squadron was ordered to ride straight down Roye Road, heading for Hill 100, one of the numbered sites that had seen so much blood. They had to stick to the road because the trenches and barbed wire made riding through cover impossible. Their charge was down the road, in full view of the enemy. The horses thundered past the trenches and Don watched the dust rise above them and settle like snow on their uniforms. The entire cavalry was cut down by machine-gun fire, the horses and men splaying into awkward heaps in the desert between the two armies. This happened two hundred yards away from the trenches but even this news arrived mostly third hand. Few had raised their head above the lips to watch.

By October, the Allied advance was rousting the Germans. The Fort Garry Horse was seven miles north of St. Quentin. They drove the enemy out of the Bois de Gattigny, rushing the woods on horseback and killing with their swords. Though casualties were high a general described it as the best cavalry action of the war, his perspective somewhat tempered by four years of fighting. They advanced to the Bois du Mont-aux-Villes and cleared the town of Bertry.

The Garrys led the advance along the Roman Road and captured Maurois. In their final manoeuver of the war they continued to Inchy. German resistance was sporadic but occasionally fierce. Don had survived the worst campaigns and the sense of impending victory buoyed them. On October 15, he was moving over undulating ground in a scrambling run when he was hit by two bullets, one in his right thigh, the other on the left side of his chest. He laid on the field, immobile, bleeding.

He was taken to a stationary hospital in Rouen, then transferred to Birmingham. He was discharged in January 1919, his wounds healed, most of the world at peace. Jim was already home. But not Tommy.

———————

Tommy had the recklessness and lack of discipline of the natural athlete. In his first month in the military, he forfeited seven days pay for being absent without leave. Two months later, he forfeited another two days pay for the same offence. Tommy went to France on September 11, 1916, with the 101st

Battalion and later transferred to the Twenty-fourth, the Victoria Rifles.

In the summer of 1917, Tommy was in the trench listening to the symphony of guns, a dozen different calibres, each with a distinctive sound. When the Strombos horns sounded, warning of a gas attack, there were only a few minutes to react. The Germans had waited for the ideal wind conditions then lobbed gas canisters into neutral territory and the chlorine gas formed a thick white cloud that rose from a greenish-yellow base. It moved with the wind, hugging the ground, the heavy gas pouring into the trenches, invading the lungs of the unprepared. Tommy covered his face with a dirty cloth and coughed convulsively. Around him men hacked and vomited. He was taken to a nearby hospital, his symptoms comparatively mild. Others had died horribly, their faces blue then black, their lungs in spasm. The gas burned and left blisters which filled with blood and clung to the men's faces like bloated insects. In the hospital he noticed that the brass buttons of his uniform had turned green. He spent three weeks recovering.

Tommy was gassed again the following year and again recovered. In early November 1918, the Twenty-fourth was in Aniche. Rumours that the war would soon end had reached a critical mass. There had always been rumours and then disappointments and he had learned not to invest too much in their veracity. But the men made jokes about French girls and wine and going home. On November 5, the sun was out and there was the snap of a fall day. The Twenty-fourth organized a soccer game between themselves and the Twenty-fifth battalion. Tommy, who had been a stalwart for the Fort Rouge team, played for the Twenty-fourth. He loved the feeling of release, sprinting in the crisp air, finding that flow, the familiar movements. For a few hours, France was what he had expected and not a sea of mud contaminated by chlorine and mustard gas, a country of ruined villages with people huddled in cellars with their wine.

On the sixth, they marched east pursuing the enemy, the road blown by mines. The Germans shelled them intermittently. On the tenth, Tommy attended a church parade at Petit Wasmes, a Protestant church. It was the first time that Sunday service for the Twenty-fourth had been held in a church since they left Canada. The church was on a grander scale than his modest bungalow in Winnipeg and Tommy sat amid the cold stone and chanted with the men, victory at hand.

The Armistice was being engineered in a railway car near Rethondes in the Forest of Compiègne. At 5:10 a.m. on November 11, the Germans finally signed the Armistice agreement, ending the war. The ceasefire would officially begin in six hours, at 11:00 a.m. but the war was technically over, a victor declared, terms dictated and accepted. Ten million were dead, six million of them civilians. Germany's weapons had been seized in principle: 5,000 tanks, 5,000 train engines, 150,000 railway cars, 25,000 machine guns, assorted warships and submarines. The geography had been claimed. The six-hour interval between the Armistice and the communication of it to the troops on both sides afforded a symmetry—the eleventh hour of the eleventh day of the eleventh month. It was a bloody limbo where those who were still fighting were literally fighting for nothing, a time outside of history, war distilled to its essence, beyond politics and geography, reduced to death and habit and survival.

In those hours, Tommy was in his trench. It was a muddy dawn that broke the same colour as the field, removing perspective, rendering the battlefield a brownish-grey borderless sphere. Tommy moved to the top of his foxhole, scanning the puddled waste. A sniper's bullet hit him in the chest, a fatal surprise that sent him backward, clutching the air briefly and landing on the wet mud of the trench, staring upward. Someone had gotten up before the light, staring at the pocked brown landscape through the sights of his rifle, patiently waiting for the first inquisitive target.

Tommy was taken to a field hospital and listed as "dangerously ill." By the time he got there, the news that the war was over had reached the lines. He had four days to ponder this attendant irony, while around him celebrations began cautiously then grew delirious. Soldiers, doctors and nurses reeled with joy then slumped with relief as if they had been holding their breath for four years. Tommy died on November 15, while the nation still danced drunkenly and embraced strangers. He was one of the last casualties of the war, buried in a veteran's cemetery in France. My grandfather had lost his twin brother, the closest one to himself, the most wrenching loss.

Instead of bringing the city together in unified victory, the war etched Winnipeg's divisions even deeper. It was, in effect, a partitioned city. The North End was called New Jerusalem, a pejorative term. Eighty-seven per cent of the city's Jews lived there, as well as eighty-three per cent of the Slavs, two groups who were openly reviled, referred to in an editorial as "the scum of Europe." Until an underpass was built, the North End was sometimes literally cut off by freight trains sitting on the track, preventing traffic from entering or leaving. The mortality rate in the North End was more than twice that of the south, a gap that was ascribed to the immigrants' ignorance and immorality, though it was due to the lack of an effective water system there. They were economically and politically disenfranchised and as the cost of living went up and their wages didn't, they became increasingly militant and restive.

In January 1919, a group of veterans went on a spree in the North End, smashing windows and breaking into homes and demanding that suspect foreigners kiss the Union Jack. They were unhappy that there were few jobs for returning soldiers, while the "alien enemy," which included Germans and Ukrainians, were working. With a sense of drunken righteousness, the veterans destroyed the Edelweiss Brewery and the Austro-Hungarian Society's building. No charges were laid.

———

After recuperating in a Birmingham hospital, my grandfather left Liverpool on the SS *Belgic* and landed in Halifax on April 23, 1919. Three days later he was in Winnipeg, carrying two wounds, basking in the concern of family. He was quiet about the horror, glad to be away from it. Tommy was a fresh ghost in the family parlour.

The talk was not of death but of work. In March, representatives for western labour unions had met in Calgary where they endorsed the One Big Union. The OBU was an alliance of both skilled and unskilled workers. This megalith would be able to engage management on a level field. At the meeting delegates sent warm regards to the new Soviet government in Russia, prompting fears of Bolshevism in the powers that be.

On May 1, a metal shop went on strike over the issue of collective bargaining. Five days later the Winnipeg Trades and Labour Council called a strike vote that carried easily. On May 15, a general strike commenced. Twelve thousand union members and more than twenty thousand non-union workers walked off their jobs. Printers, teamsters, postal workers and railway workers all stopped work. There were no newspapers. Milk went undelivered. Police joined the strike but stayed on the job. Garbage piled up as all the collectors walked off the job, with the exception of eighty-six-year-old Ginger Snook, who defiantly picked up the trash, carrying a club for protection. On his military papers, Don had listed his profession as teamster and he returned to find that he was part of the bitter strike. His father, Peter, wasn't so sure which side he was on. He dressed and acted like he was on his way to have tea with the queen but his sympathies were with the aggrieved, unless they were aggrieved with him, an ever-expanding group. So he hedged his position; he was for the strikers as long as nothing actually changed.

The city came to a halt in the surprising heat of mid-May. Business leaders allied into the Citizen's Committee of One Thousand, pitted against the Strike Committee of Three Hundred. The Citizen's Committee warned of Bolshevism and denounced the strikers as alien and seditious and asked for the deportation of agitators. The entire Winnipeg police force was fired when they refused to sign a statement saying they wouldn't strike. They were replaced by two thousand newly appointed police, "Specials," as they were called. For six weeks, the city was suspended, the two sides hardening their positions, drawing the enemy in bolder, cruder lines, refining their hatred.

On June 13, Richard Ernest Bray, a war veteran sympathetic to the strikers, spoke at Victoria Park. A North West Mounted Police report called Bray "the most dangerous man in the City, in view of the fact that he is a Returned Soldier and is using this to influence other Returned men." Bray was wearing an undershirt and suspenders and leaned forward on the plank stage, rallying his crowd around support for labour and denouncing the Citizen's Committee. He gesticulated like an angry preacher and his words came out like an assault.

In the early hours of June 17, eight of the ten strike leaders, including Richard Bray, were arrested in their homes at gunpoint, charged with seditious conspiracy and taken to the Stony Mountain federal penitentiary. In protest, returned veterans organized a silent parade for June 21 in front of city hall. They were now on the side of the workers, the divisions redrawn along class rather than ethnic lines. Mayor Charles Gray had issued a proclamation that there would be no parades until the strike had been settled and the date was anticipated like a heavyweight prize fight.

On the morning of Bloody Saturday, Don and Jim left their home on Fleet Avenue and walked north up Osborne to Portage and east to Main Street. Other veterans moved north singly or in small groups, none in uniform. Don recognized one or two of them, he thought. Though it could have been simply that look from the war, subdued rather than euphoric, the twenty-three-year-old faces unnaturally lined. In front of city hall there were already a few thousand men milling, their straw boaters shining in the sun. They were in dark suits and ties and the heat crept through the wool as they spoke of the war in the technical terms of generals, sharing battalion allegiances and troop movements and avoiding the grotesque imagery of death. Teenaged boys loitered among the heroes. They were giddy with the defiance and the mood of expectation.

Mayor Gray observed the gathering crowd and went to the Osborne Barracks and commandeered fifty-four North West Mounted Police to keep the crowd in order. They came on horseback, riding three abreast up the empty street and made a dignified pass on Main to disperse the crowd. A few of the Mounties were in their army uniforms. The veterans moved to the sidewalks and let the procession pass and closed around the vacant space after it passed. Mayor Gray read the Riot Act, his voice stiff with historical certitude. His unamplified voice died quickly on the wide street; he was a small muffled figure waving one arm stiffly.

Don and Jim milled among the veterans. It was like the war; the chain of command was distant and abstract and, on occasion, absurd. Whatever the precise plotting of those in charge, you were faced, finally, with chaos and smoke and screaming. You were in a group that swelled in one direction, then another, moving on instinct, on whispered intelligence and rumour. On Main Street, the men formed loose cliques and discussed the situation. They had no plan, other than to demonstrate support by their sombre, blood-invested presence. The precise nature of their support wasn't entirely clear. They weren't Bolsheviks certainly. They didn't have much use for foreign labourers either. Four years in France hadn't done much for their respect for authority. They were against a number of things; they weren't sure what they were for.

The Mounties turned around and came back down Main, at a trot this time. Don felt the mood of randomness that he had hated in the war, dressed for church this time instead of battle, standing amid the comforting architecture of home. The crowd moved out of the way of the advancing horses and swelled back once more, like the breathing of a large organism.

A streetcar passed in front of city hall, run by the Citizen's Committee in defiance of the striking operators. A group of teenagers approached it, fed by the sense of affront in the crowd, by hormones and stabbing regret at not having fought in the war, seizing this chance to do something. They lifted the streetcar off the rail and it moved up slowly then fell on its side like something fatally wounded.

The Mounties passed again and were met this time with stones and bricks taken from an idle construction site. Two fell from their horses. The Mounties regrouped and charged toward the men on William Street, .45-calibre revolvers in their right hands, firing as they rode. An old man standing by the Union Bank slumped onto the pavement. Don moved with the crowd, dispersing and regrouping in rhythmic, purposeless waves. Stones and bricks flew. Bullets went through the crowd and worked the arbitrary magic they had in France. He understood the nature of bullets, the way they simply arrived with their stunning velocity, burrowing through flesh, deflecting off bone, pushing through soft tissue until they were exhausted. In front of the Manitoba Hotel, a man reached for a brick lying on the street and was shot through the heart. He collapsed on the street, dead.

All of this was captured on film by Lewis Foote, who was on the third floor of a building near the corner of Portage and Main, leaning out the window with his camera. Below him the mob spilled into irregular shapes. He watched the rigid, orderly lines of the Mounties and the army approach. The mob dispersed and reformed in kaleidoscopic patterns. Foote was probably cheering for the forces of order, if for no other reason than his appreciation of the crisp aesthetics of authority. Three shots were fired at him as he leaned over the street. One bullet went through the window above him and two others hit the building. He thought it must have been one of the strikers but it was probably the other side; they were the ones who had the guns.

Reinforcements from Minto Armouries arrived to assist the mounted police and my grandfather was surprised to see that it was his outfit, the Fort Garry Horse, riding up Main Street armed with baseball bats. This completed the circle of confusion. Now he was opposing his own outfit, men he had stood beside at Amiens. He didn't have time to ponder this irony.

The Specials arrived in their suits with white armbands and clubs. A streetcar was set on fire. Don and Jim were separated in the confusion and Don went down Banatyne, west a few blocks and down to McDermot, south on Spence, over the river. The veterans retreated along Maryland, through alleys, down the empty streets. They went north and west and south. Two strikers were dead, hundreds injured. The Mounties had a few injured as well. Blood streaked the road and straw hats were discarded and crushed.

The Specials formed a line near city hall. In the afternoon, trucks mounted with machine guns patrolled the downtown streets in quiet menace, waiting for a counterattack from the veterans or the strikers. But it never arrived. The veterans had had enough blood. Don was at home on Fleet Avenue, wondering at this new war, which held some of the baffling elements of the last one. The enemy was unclear; was it the city's leaders? the immigrants? the federal government? (This would prove a lasting target.) In the end, like most battles, it was soldiers fighting soldiers; they were at war with themselves. As it had been in France, it was difficult to gauge the importance of the ground gained or lost.

The General Strike haunted the city for thirty years. It was a pyrrhic victory that signalled Winnipeg's decline, though the strike wasn't the only reason for the decline. The Panama Canal had opened in 1914 and it became cheaper to ship by boat to Vancouver than ship by rail across the prairies. The wheat economy was stagnant. Winnipeg was the youngest city in the country and had suffered commensurately from the war. But the strike had taken away the booster spirit. The ditties were joyless, the claims unfounded. The campaign was still marked by exclamation marks and vigorous boasting but it was hollow. The city was no longer the Gateway to the West, though it held on to that sobriquet for decades. Vancouver was the new Gateway, and in the 1920s it surpassed Winnipeg as the country's third-largest city. Winnipeg's industrialists started to resemble the entrenched elite they had come west to avoid. The city stagnated under their leadership as other prairie centres gained ground. Calgary and Edmonton began to draw energy and resources away from Winnipeg. But the General Strike became the symbol of all this, a few bloody and dramatic hours that broke the city's spine.

What had happened and what was won or lost was debated for years. The city leaders felt the strike was a victory over the forces of communism and chaos. In his summary of the riot, Lieutenant Colonel J.S. McMahon described it as a heroic moment that prevented the strikers from overthrowing the capitalist system of government. He praised the Fort Garry Horse for their loyalty and bravery. But the citizens elected eight of the ten strike leaders to office over the next few years, a vindication. A school was named after one of them, R.B. Russell. For my grandfather, the strike was a victory by his army unit over his colleagues.

Jim Mainland surveyed the local landscape in the wake of the strike. He was a mechanic and Detroit was where the cars were. It was where the future was. He left for Michigan, telling his brother that he was a fool for staying in this damned town.

My grandparents met in the relative gloom of the Free Presbyterian Church on Magee Street in the North End. Lachlan Ross was an elder there who preached on occasion and his family sat dutifully in the back row. Christina Mainland had been drawn to the church by its Highland roots, finding in the church some of the sorrowful qualities of home. She took her children along and Georgie and Don saw each other mutely each Sunday, forbidden to speak on matters not related to the church.

They were married on June 30, 1921, at a friend's house on Home Street. My grandmother wore a navy-blue tricotine suit and a blouse of shell-pink georgette crepe and a large mohair hat trimmed with French blue flowers. She wore a corsage of bridal roses and lilies of the valley. Jean was the maid of honour, wearing a blue suit and maise organdy hat, surprised that her twin was first to the altar. There was no dancing or singing or outward sign of celebration. They were joined by the Reverend Malcolm Gillis in the eyes of an unforgiving God amid the best wishes and mutual suspicion of their families. Peter Mainland regarded his pious, lugubrious in-laws with the natural animus he felt for the clergy, who had snapped up much of Shetland in the wake of the Clearances. Lachlan wasn't too sure about Peter, who carried with him the scent of the racetrack and the tavern, but his wife was a regular churchgoer and the sons were industrious. And Georgie was happy, breaking into an awkward smile outside the church, as if something was escaping from her. She and her husband had a curious symmetry: Don had lost a twin to the war and Georgie had gained one through sin.

They moved into the Kitchener Court apartments, a handsome building trimmed in oak with a courtyard. Georgie worked at Eaton's mail order and Don worked in the building trade. Jim wrote regularly from Detroit, telling them that the place was on fire, construction was booming and Don should come down and get on the bandwagon.

Winnipeg seemed lustreless after the strike, though Don may have felt it was a failure of his imagination as much as the city's failure. Like his father in Shetland, he could no longer imagine a place for himself here. Winnipeg had been populated by the Great Lie: it was the civic equivalent of a blind date who is advertised as having a great personality, neat handwriting and all her own teeth. Not a great beauty, but not homely either. She was empty and flat and you could project what you wanted upon her. In 1923, he went to Detroit, leaving Georgie at the Kitchener Court. He said he'd send for her when he got set up. He took a train to Port Arthur and then the boat to Detroit to join his brother.

Jim was working for Packard Motors. He was familiar with the Packard engines because he had worked on them during the war, manufacturing the Liberty motor, an aviation engine that was based on the twin six automobile engine. Jim liked the luxury of the Packard car. It was a grande-touring automobile, sleek and powerful next to the upright rectitude of Ford's Model T. Jim had come through the war unscathed; the only one of his brothers to do so. But he lost three fingers in the Packard plant, watching in silent horror as they were ripped away, caught in the unrelenting ironworks, pulled from him without effort. Now all the Mainland boys carried a wound.

On the train to Port Arthur, Don alternated between watching the scenery and talking to other men in the club car. Canadians were going down to Detroit by the thousands. They talked of opportunity and recast what they had heard in even more favourable lights. A sober, hard-working man could make himself a tidy sum. Add a little imagination and you had yourself a millionaire. Sales was one route. Personality equalled Pulling Power and that spelled Profit. If you had pep, if you had drive. If you were a booster and not a knocker. The automobile was the future, they agreed. Detroit needed men like them. Don had a newly ironed shirt and an ice-cream linen suit that was starting to wrinkle. His sandy hair was flat beneath his straw boater and he contemplated its thinning.

On the boat from Port Arthur to Michigan, the water was wide and grey and the boat rolled slightly in the waves and the brisk wind. Lake Huron had the scale of the sea but was a bit lifeless. Detroit looked like Zenith, the mythic city in Sinclair Lewis's novel *Babbitt*, which had been published the previous year. "The towers of Zenith aspired above the morning mist; austere towers of steel and cement and limestone, sturdy as cliffs and delicate as silver rods. They were neither citadels nor churches, but frankly and beautifully office-buildings . . . a city built—it seemed—for giants." Jim was waiting for Don at the docks, waving his damaged hand as if he were ordering a round of drinks.

Detroit was a wicked town; even Henry Ford said it was the devil's playground. Ford embodied the city to many, though his plant was in Highland Park to avoid city taxes. Michigan had gone dry in 1918, a year before the passage of the Volsted Act and Prohibition and this enabled Detroit to get a jump on the rest of the country as the main distribution point for bootleg liquor. Boats came across the Detroit River carrying whiskey and gin, crossing just east of Windsor where the river was narrowest and good cover was provided on both sides. It was the same spot that escaped slaves had used to cross in the previous century, coming from the United States to the Promised Land. Enforcement of the Volsted Act in Detroit was negligible.

Speakeasies were easy to find; you could drink a few ounces of rye from teacups in the back of restaurants. Drugstores sold both the ingredients and the recipe for bathtub gin. Because Detroit was the automobile capital, there was a well-developed series of highways leading out of town. Outside the city it was impossible to police all the roadways and the trucks went east to Cleveland and west to Chicago and south to Cincinnati, the bottles rattling in the back of the Ford one-tons.

Detroit was dominated by the automobile, by its existence and possibilities. The future here had a more tangible and specific focus than in Manitoba. You could see it every day, as shiny as sin. There were 113 exhibitors at an automobile show in 1923, among them Packard, Hupp, Hudson, Maxwell, Dayton, Brush Runabout, Paige-Detroit, Saxon, King, Liberty, Lincoln, Stutz, Studebaker, Columbia, Gray, Commerce, Willys, Denby, Dodge, Peerless, Pierce-Arrow and Chevrolet. Legendary flying ace Captain Eddie V. Rickenbacker was promoting a car named for him. But Henry Ford was king. His Model T dominated the industry.

It wasn't just Canadians who were coming to Detroit, but rural boys from farms in Iowa and Ohio, unemployed men from burned-out timber towns in Michigan's Upper Peninsula, blacks from the south. Irish, Germans, Swedes, Poles, Greeks and Italians all came looking for work, leaving the ruins of Europe. America was producing forty per cent of the world's manufactured goods and provided its own mass market. So men flocked to America and Congress appointed a nine-member commission to look at the impending moral collapse due to the foreign influx. Like Winnipeg, they needed the men to fuel the overheated economy, but the commission reported the immigrants "were poisoning the pure air of our otherwise well-regulated cities; and if it were not for them there would be no congestion, no filth and no poverty in the great industrial and commercial centres of America." The Irish, the commission discovered, were the most susceptible to insanity, caused mostly by alcohol and venereal disease. The stolid Germans weren't far behind. This was a surprise to the commissioners, who had previously viewed both groups as among the most reliable and established immigrants to the United States. Canadians accounted for 6.9 per cent of the juvenile delinquents, somewhere between the law-abiding English (5.7 per cent) and the insanity-prone Irish (20.5 per cent). Virtually all of the country's ills were attributed to immigrants. It had been an Eden until the foreigners arrived. The report concluded, with some prescience, that the "conditions of American life are conducive to an increase in insanity."

Based on the commission's report, the Immigration Act was revised in 1924 and quotas were reduced. But Don had already arrived. At any rate, he was only nominally an immigrant, being a Canadian of Scots descent. He was sober and industrious, he spoke English and ate meatloaf and was Protestant. No one could accuse him of being an "International Jew," one of the categories the revised Immigration Act had been designed to keep out. Henry Ford's views had appeared in a pamphlet titled *The International Jew*, which accused the Jews of fomenting labour unrest in Europe and of being Bolsheviks. They would cause problems in the United States if given half a chance, he thought. Ford also feared Catholics, particularly Pierre Du Pont, who controlled General Motors, his chief rival. The twin evils of Judaism and Catholicism, coincidentally, represented Ford's two chief concerns, labour and competition.

Despite the congressional view that American life made one insane, there was no shortage of immigrants wanting to be Americans. When my grandfather arrived in Detroit, there were twenty-seven thousand people enrolled in Americanization classes, learning to use a handkerchief instead of their sleeve, to brush their teeth once a day and to greet one another with a wide smile and firm handshake. These were the kind of people who could take advantage of Henry Ford's profit-sharing plan, which extended, not to every employee but to the sober and decent, to he who led "a clean and constructive life, and is of proved thrifty habits."

The Mainland boys liked the singular focus of Detroit, its tangible progress, but neither of them went to work for Ford. Don took advantage of the boom in the construction trade; Detroit was behind only New York and Chicago in the building of skyscrapers. Housing had to be built for all the workers arriving in waves and factories had to be built for all the car companies who felt they had claim to the future. Don bought one of Henry's cars though, the homely, affordable coal-black Model T, a car that was thought of as old-fashioned even while it was in production. At the annual automobile shows there were bright colours and modern gadgets, rounded lines and cars that sold get-up-and-go. The Ste. Claire car company had built a car that was so mechanically advanced that mechanics couldn't understand it and Ste. Claire went bankrupt within two years. Ford stuck to the basics. He had created the People's Car, as it was called, and he was trying, as best he could, to create the people.

——— ———

Don had a flat in a house in a respectable neighbourhood and he had a Model T and some money. He sent for his new wife. Georgie wore her good dress and a hat from Eaton's for the trip. On the train she watched the northern forest go by in a blur for the second time, retracing that first journey when the Ross family had come from Scotland. She had picked up tips on marriage from the *Winnipeg Tribune*, in the "Of Interest to Eve" column, tips on cooking and how to kiss without making too much noise. She had her Bible and a Scottish recipe book with her. The way to a man's heart was through his stomach, the *Tribune* had warned. The book had recipes for Black Pudding ("Clean and wash one sheep's stomach inside and out. Mix in 8 oz. of suet, 8 oz. of oatmeal, one pint sheep or pig's blood . . .") and Crowdie ("Let a gallon of milk from the cow stand until thick and sour. Place in a pan and heat slowly until a curd is formed . . .") and Cormorant, eventually to become a protected species ("Pluck the bird and singe with a hot iron. Boil for 1–2 hours . . ."). And there was Sheep's Head Broth ("Using a red hot poker, rub over the sheep's head until a nice brown colour, remove ears, horns and burn off any remaining wool. Split head with an axe or saw. Remove brains and rub them well into the skin of the head. Put the head into a bowl of cold water with a handful of washing soda and soak overnight. Place in pan of boiling water. Add barley.") But Don had a Canadian palate now; meat, potatoes and gravy. Pumpkin pie and pork chops and applesauce. He would be eating fried liver and onions and mashing his potatoes with butter. Still, there would be brose, there would be porridge. Robbie Burns had written a poem about it, "O gie my luv Brose, Brose, O gie my luv Brose and butter." Two handfuls of oatmeal in boiling water, add salt and butter. Eat with a spoon.

Georgie slept on the train and chatted politely and daintily adjusted her thick dress, a married woman. She read her Bible: *But the Egyptians pursued after them, all the horses and chariots*

*of Pharaoh, and his horsemen, and his army, and overtook them
camping by the sea, beside Pi-hahiroth, before Baal-zephon. And
when Pharaoh drew nigh, the children of Israel lifted up their
eyes, and behold, the Egyptians marched after them; and they
were sore afraid: and the children of Israel cried out unto the
LORD. And they said unto Moses, Because there were no graves in
Egypt, hast thou taken us away to die in the wilderness?*

Lake Superior was endless. Before she got off the boat, she
sprayed herself with *eau de toilette* and felt a tremor of risk.
She was coming to a country that her parents had avoided
because of its constitutional commitment to the pursuit of
happiness. Don was waiting for her, waving his hat, the Yankee sun shining off his brilliantined head.

In the mornings, Don ate cornflakes and drank his coffee
and went off to work in the building trade. He had a small
crew of men to supervise. Georgie decided that she would
look for a job. She didn't have any formal training; she wasn't a
secretary or a nurse or a teacher. But she had zeal for hard
work, she was clean-living and had a pleasant personality. The
downtown sidewalks were filled with smart grey people, moving toward offices. The traffic was a scandal, the cars like a
black sea. Don had tried to teach her how to drive but it had
been a disaster. She couldn't see the patterns in the traffic,
couldn't imagine a place for herself and the Model T among
that chaos. She felt that if she entered the dark stream of lurching cars, she would never get out. So each morning she took
the streetcar downtown and looked in the windows of a few
stores and imagined herself working there. At Hudson's department store, she left an application at the personnel department. The buyer in the children's department was a Canadian
and she hired Georgie as a clerk. Now, in the mornings, she
joined the grey bustle with purpose.

They saved their money. On weekends, Don and Georgie and Jim would drive to Dearborn in Don's Model T to see the mansions of the new aristocracy and speculate on their unhappiness. Georgie made a lunch; cold chicken, potato salad, cucumber sandwiches and cherry pie, and they stopped in the countryside for a picnic, sitting in their dress clothes like a Monet painting. Driving was their pleasure. The sheer joy of being self-ambulatory was its own reward. They would get out of Detroit, which was filled with a thick black smoke when the wind conditions were wrong and didn't carry it away. Every Saturday night, Georgie and Don bought a chocolate cake and a box of chocolates and this was their extravagance.

Georgie was promoted from clerk at Hudson's to assistant buyer of children's wear. She earned a good salary and she had a modest discount, which she used to buy children's clothes. She wanted a child and she would be ready in the event they had one. In 1925, she accompanied the buyer to New York on a buying trip. They took the train and stayed at an affordable midtown hotel. Al Jolson had returned to the stage in the musical *Big Boy*. The Charleston was all the rage and Charlie Chaplin's *Gold Rush* had just opened. Georgie was impressed by the New York cabbies; they had just started to wear white collars as part of a city ordinance after complaints by citizens who said they were rude and ill-kempt.

In Detroit the Purple Gang was bringing in bonded whiskey from Windsor by the truckload. There were underworld battles over the liquor trade. Some of the Mainland sisters came down to visit and Don and Jim told them stories of the Purple Gang and the wicked character of the city. But they kept a distance themselves. They weren't here to enjoy themselves, they were here to save.

On May 25, 1927, Henry Ford shut down the assembly line

of the Model T, a car that had become a rolling anachronism. He had produced more than fifteen million of them. Automobile production in 1927 dropped twenty-five per cent from the previous year and since seventy-five per cent of Detroit's economy was tied in some way to the automobile industry, unemployment rose. Two years later, the stock market crashed on Wall Street and the reverberations were keenly felt in Michigan. By November, the state had 212,500 unemployed. The construction trade, which had been booming, stalled. The credit economy, designed to allow the middle class to afford an automobile, faltered. Some of the workers who had come from farms and small towns returned home. But the immigrants stayed and a sullen xenophobia set in. Hudson's department store was hit hard as the discretionary income of the middle class disappeared. Don thought that the few remaining construction jobs would go to native-born Americans. As money got tighter, the definition of immigrant would become more refined; he and Georgie would become progressively more alien. My grandparents drove back to Winnipeg in their Model T filled with children's clothes to weather the Depression in the comfort of the northern prairie.

10

DEPRESSION

MY GRANDMOTHER described
the Depression as if it were her oldest friend. A bit tough to
live with, but still, they had gone through so much together.
The 1930s formed her world view. She distrusted debt, for one
thing, something my generation embraced like a lover. There
was never a mortgage on their home. She was wary of credit
cards and owned the opposite, the long-defunct debit card,
which Eaton's offered. She deposited money with the department store and each purchase was deducted from her balance,
a system that played to the insecurities of her generation. Her
sense of thrift, of money as something to be stretched and
massaged, was pervasive. She followed me around the house,

turning off lights. When we talked, she often started sentences with the phrase, "During the Depression . . ." The rest would be about how they had made do, or how far a dollar went. Sitting by the warm hearth of the middle class in the 1960s, these stories seemed like fables.

She told me about men who rode the rails. During the Great Depression, at the time when the Prairies were blown out and men were moving across the country in desperate un-employed armies, Winnipeg was a way station. Whether you were heading to British Columbia in the hope of work or going back east to relatives, you came through town. Men rode in on the trains, black from the dust and smoke, white-eyed, scorched or frozen, stiff from the ride.

My grandmother's house was a quarter mile from the tracks and in the 1930s a neighbourhood hadn't yet formed around it—it was isolated. Occasionally, and then almost daily as the Depression ground on, she would hear a knock at the door and there would be a man with skin like a coal miner wearing dirty clothes, asking politely after yard work. There wasn't anything to do around the house but she usually made them a sandwich while they stood outside, silhouetted by the screen door. She gave them the sandwich and a glass of lemon-ade and they stood there eating and drinking as politely as they could manage. Georgie watched awkwardly and waited for the glass and plate to be returned, thinking of how she would scrub them clean.

They usually came in summer and there was no shade as the trees had just been planted. Flies moved in the still heat and Georgie had a brief flutter when she opened the door to these rough men. Some of them seemed poised between na-ture and civilization. Their eyes were predatory and looked past her into the house, searching for something valuable maybe, or the sign of a man, or a glimpse of what they had had themselves a few years earlier. Others were apologetic. They wanted to tell their story, but it was always the same story. Once they had had a life, not an easy one maybe, but they'd never complain again if they ever got it back. But it didn't seem possible. Even if the Depression ended in the next five minutes, something had been taken from them. They would carry the betrayal and doubt for the rest of their lives.

Winnipeg itself had been based on the idea that the future held deliverance. It was more than economics, it was closer to physics, a fundamental principle that was suddenly gone, as if gravity had been replaced with something new. The Depression altered their concept of time, which had once moved in lockstep with progress and was now at a standstill, something to be endured. The men usually thanked Georgie, though some didn't, and then they left, heading back to the tracks or north toward downtown where they exchanged their stories with one another.

One day a man asked her if she got a lot of drifters coming by looking for handouts. She did, she said. She didn't mind so much but she and Don weren't rich and sometimes there were two a day. The man said a sign had been left, a chalk mark on one of the small brick pillars that flanked their sidewalk, which meant that her house was an easy touch. She had been singled out. The man erased it and moved on and Georgie had mixed feelings about being rid of it.

My grandmother often invoked the Depression as a cautionary tale. It had been God's judgment, punishment perhaps for a nation's hubris, a country that celebrated itself too loudly. There had been seven years of plenty as Pharaoh had seen in his dream of the gaunt cows devouring the seven fatted ones, and they would be followed by seven years of lean. *The famine will consume the land, and the plenty will be unknown in the land by reason of that famine which will follow, for it will be very grievous.*

———————

Lachlan Ross lost a son, Johnny, who died at the age of seven in Scotland. His daughter Robina died in the flu pandemic of 1918. He lost his oldest daughter, Catherine, in a different way, gone to South Africa; he never saw her again. He lost his friends in the boating accident in Scotland, he lost the house at Fanagmore and the farm at Moosehorn. When his wife died in 1929, he moved back to Winnipeg, in time to experience the full weight of the stock market collapse.

From his house on Ashburn Street he heard how other farmers, those with good land, were failing. There was a grim parity at hand. All of the Prairies now looked like "the land that God gave Cain," as Jacques Cartier had described Canada. Occasionally, Lachlan could actually see the farmers' plight, the topsoil from a hundred farms lifted into the air, forming a dark cloud that looked like a prairie thunderstorm until the first stinging grains of dirt hit the expectant faces staring westward.

On May 12, 1934, the Associated Press reported that clouds made of topsoil from the American midwest had been sighted at an altitude of ten thousand feet over the Atlantic Ocean. Three hundred million tons of topsoil had been blown eastward, leaving a residue on the ledges of New York skyscrapers. The dust continued east, caught in updrafts and delivered to the troposphere and falling finally into the ocean without effect. The Canadian prairies were turning to dust as well. Almost fourteen thousand farms had been abandoned, three million acres of land left untended, turning to desert. John

Palliser, an Irishman commissioned by the British government in 1857 to do an inventory of the Canadian West, had described the plains as arid, not suitable for European settlement, though they eventually came to be the most productive wheat-producing area in the world. The Palliser Triangle, as it was called, stretched along the American border, beginning near Cartwright, Manitoba and extending almost to the Rocky Mountains. It went north past Calgary and arced through Saskatchewan and down through southern Manitoba. It wasn't shaped like a triangle; when drawn on a map it looked like a snowdrift blown by eastern winds, piling up at its western terminus. And now it was returning to the desert that Palliser had described. There were photographs of farmhouses with sandy soil blown up past the windows, drifted like a January snow. The prairies were being reclaimed as wilderness and the immigrants who had tried to make it a paradise were leaving the land, many of them going to the cities. Five thousand single men, most of them from farms, came to Winnipeg, looking for work or to go on relief. The drought spread upward from the United States like a stain. The groundwater dried up and the soil blew. In 1933, the grasshoppers came in their millions and ate the grain in the fields. They chewed clothing and sheets that hung on lines and ate the residue of human sweat on axe handles and shovels, leaving them pockmarked, as if they were mocking the labour that had built these farms. They ate gardens in a matter of minutes. You could hear them, a sound like swishing silk, the devil's masterpiece; an animate cloud moving east, aided by a tailwind. The Red River became a brown trickle and the clay on its banks hardened and cracked. On those few days when it rained, the first drops bounced off the riverbed as if it were asphalt. When it softened slightly there was a renewed smell of decay.

On Christmas Day, 1935, Lachlan was at his home on Ashburn Street staring at the holiday as if it was a stranger. He had a cold and his breath was short. His cousin, William Sinclair, co-founder of the local Free Presbyterian Church, came by to visit and retrieve a book, *Simply Trusting*, that he had lent him. They chatted amiably about God and their conversation had the usual hint of competition; who could sing His glories highest? It was a competition that Lachlan usually conceded. Two days later he took a turn for the worse. He was eighty-one and his various ailments—kidney problems, aches, poorly mended bones—and his quiet defeats had piled up within him. He was spent. Sinclair came to visit him again, this time to say goodbye.

"Are you going to leave us?" Sinclair asked him.

"Not today," Lachlan said. He was wizened and small, his face heavy.

"Is there not something you are to say to me before you leave. Surely you're not going to leave with all those secrets stored away in your heart."

Lachlan said he had something to tell him but he couldn't remember what it was.

"Well, if it comes to you," Sinclair said, "tell Georgie." He knew Georgie's secret though he and Lachlan had never spoken of it. It was an official lie that everyone knew but no one spoke of. He pressed Lachlan to reveal it but Lachlan wouldn't.

Sinclair stared at him. "What is the Lord saying to you at this time to comfort you. Surely you can tell me that much."

"It's a secret," Lachlan said.

Sinclair kept on about what the Lord was saying and it was hard to tell if he was there to comfort Lachlan or torment him. "What you could tell me at this time might encourage me on my own wilderness journey," Sinclair persisted. "Will you not say a word?"

Lachlan considered this. "The Lord is saying to me, 'I will never leave thee nor forsake thee.'"

Sinclair was looking for more detail but it was clear that Lachlan wasn't going to budge. His Book of Psalms was on the dresser and Sinclair picked it up and turned to Psalm 121 and read aloud. *Yes I to the hills will lift mine eyes from whence doth come mine aid, my safety cometh from the Lord Who heaven and earth hath made . . . The Lord will keep your going out and your coming in from this time forth and for evermore.*

Sinclair stayed until 11 p.m. then went home unsatisfied. Lachlan died four hours later, at three in the morning, January 3, taking his secret with him, though he knew it was a secret he kept only from himself. Sinclair wrote a cousin, describing Lachlan's passing. "He had no pain or no struggle and his appearance was that sweet calm which was his portion in all his storms of life and the Lord who cared for him in life took him gently through the Valley of Death and he was no trouble to anyone and only one week in his bed and now it is all over and it is for us to follow in Faith and Patience the path he followed and our end will be Peace as well."

My grandmother had been with him that day and had held his hand while he slept. They kept their secret silently in those last hours. Her real father, George Ivel, had been dead for five years, dying painfully of stomach cancer in Perth, Scotland, surrounded by his own family, though Georgie didn't know this. Perhaps she had ceased to wonder after him. The child's sense of romance, if she had been able to cultivate it against long odds, had withered; her real father wasn't a prince or a millionaire but a distant fable. Lachlan was her father and she prayed and wept at his grave.

Catherine was in South Africa with a new family and a new name, Catherine Scott. She and Georgie corresponded over the years, but always as sisters. They maintained this fiction even between themselves, even in the cold remove of print. They never saw one another again after that first parting in Scotland. Catherine died in Johannesburg in 1951, and on her deathbed she told her children her story: *Promise me you'll always stay in touch with Georgie. She isn't your aunt, she's your half-sister. Family is important. There was a man in Edinburgh, it was years and years ago, a lifetime. I had a past.*

———————

When my grandparents came back from Detroit they paid cash for a piece of land in Fort Garry. Don built their brick house himself, paying for the material and labour as he went. There wasn't much other work around. Occasionally he worked with his father but the construction industry was shuddering to a halt. In 1929, $11.1 million of building permits had been issued in Winnipeg. By 1934, the figure was down to $700,000. During the Depression the tax base shrank, unemployment soared and manufacturing declined. Being the largest grain handling centre was like being the best dance band on the *Titanic*. The whole point of Winnipeg was being challenged. It was still the hub, but now it was at the centre of a vacuum. The Age of Boosterism came to an abrupt official halt in 1930 when a federal Order-in-Council banned all immigrants to the country, with the exception of self-financed farmers.

My mother was born in 1931 and there are pictures of my grandmother sitting in the open field in front of the house in a wicker chair, holding her baby with unfettered pride. Don's work was seasonal; they didn't lay bricks in the winter because the mortar wouldn't set. But even in the summer, there wasn't much to do. Don started going farther afield, travelling to Regina with his father for a project, going to Medicine Hat and northern Ontario. His disability pension was small and they took in Jean as a boarder in 1933 to help make ends meet.

Jean had a job with Winnipeg Hydro, a working girl who smoked Black Cat cigarettes and acted the way women did in movies. The tension between her and Georgie grew in that dark house. But they were one another's best friend, linked by history, a secret and attrition. Jean was looking for someone to change her life, someone who cherished her sharp tongue. Money was tight and they played cards and drank tea and sometimes went to the grounds near the zoo to watch cricket. They were left to their own devices.

My grandmother still attended the Free Presbyterian Church and sometimes took my mother, who sat and played with her gloves and ate peppermints and waited for the wave of relief that came at the end of the ninety-minute service. Don didn't go to church. When Georgie told him to take my mother to an evening service, he took her to Dell's for ice cream instead and then to a parade on Portage Avenue. She looked like Shirley Temple, red-haired and freckled with perfect features. She placed second in a Shirley Temple look-a-like contest sponsored by the *Winnipeg Free Press* and got her picture in the paper. She pulled out of a freckle competition, despite being the clear front-runner, able to walk away from celebrity. Such were the amusements of the Depression.

Jim Mainland returned from Detroit and worked as a mechanic at Pellessier Motors on Jubilee Avenue. His father and mother and brother Gilbert all lived nearby in a small bungalow on Somerville Avenue, the elegant house on Windermere lost to unpaid taxes. The family huddled together during the Depression like cattle in a storm.

The whole city huddled together. At one point in the thirties, half of the families in Winnipeg were on some sort of relief. As the farms failed, the city's relief roll grew. Some rural communities paid families' train fare to Winnipeg and paid their expenses until they qualified for public assistance. The relationship between town and hinterland, never great, deteriorated further. Ethnic tensions remained high. The Scots remained mostly in Fort Garry, Fort Rouge and St. James. For the purposes of demographic surveys, they were grouped under "of British origin" though their resentment of the English was deeper than anyone's. Still, they weren't in a rush to embrace the Galicians. They were, as reputed, clannish.

In 1939, with a fresh war to boost the economy, men and women went back to work. But by this time my grandfather was unable to do much. He had complained of severe abdominal pains in 1919, after he was home from the war. In 1928, it was finally diagnosed as renal colic. By the start of the next war he was at home much of the time. He was diagnosed with angina soon after, while he was still in his forties. He and my grandmother were housebound and turned to each other for amusement and torment. There are staged photographs of their marriage—Don holding a rolling pin like a club with an exaggerated look of reprimand, like a character from the Maggie and Jiggs comic strip. In another photograph, he has a saw, about to cut one of my grandmother's stolid pies. They presented their marriage as a cross between light opera and war, Ricky Ricardo staring bug-eyed and innocent as Lucy lowers the boom. When my grandmother voted for the Conservative Party once, impressed with the local candidate, Don didn't speak to her for two weeks. They argued for days on a single issue. Was a kettle boiling when the whistle sounded or was it *beginning* to boil? A series of non-scientific experiments failed to dissuade either of them from their views. For a month they argued over who the dog liked better. The issue was decided in a *High Noon*-style showdown where they both went out to the yard and paced off ten steps in opposite directions from the dog. They called him at the same time and he went to my grandmother, who fed him.

The neighbourhood filled in around them. In 1944, Jean married Leslie Barratt, an Englishman she met at City Hydro and they eventually moved to a bungalow on Windermere Avenue, the next street over. Les was tall and alarmingly thin. Jean was 45 and had played the field, flirting through a series of beaux. Their wedding photo looks like Grant Wood's "American Gothic."

After the war, Winnipeg was like Don, ready to work, but not entirely able. The prosperity from the early part of the century never returned and the city had lost its confidence. The first war, the 1919 strike and the Depression had all taken a specific toll. The next war didn't help. Winnipeg continued to grow, but at roughly half the rate it had between 1921 and 1946 and less than a quarter of the rate during the boom years. But it settled in and, to some degree, made peace with itself.

———————

I was born in 1954, the year the Edmonton Eskimos were playing the Montreal Alouettes in the Grey Cup. The West had won only four of the thirty-three championships since 1921, a constant source of frustration. My grandfather was at home listening to the game on the radio, lying on the couch, pulling for Edmonton, a five-to-one underdog. With three minutes to play, the score was Montreal 25, Edmonton 20. The Alouettes had driven to the Edmonton fourteen-yard line. It looked like a done deal, another notch for the East. On the next play, Montreal quarterback Sam "the Rifle" Etcheverry pitched out to Big Chuck Hunsinger who came around from his halfback spot and tried to find blocking behind pulling guard Ray Cicia. But Ted Tully knifed in from the linebacker position and hammered Hunsinger, followed by Rollin Prather who pancaked him, and the ball came out like a lemon seed and bounced on the cold field. Edmonton's Jackie "Spaghetti Legs" Parker picked it up and sprinted toward the end zone, eighty-five yards away. Etcheverry limped after him but Parker crossed the line untouched, bringing victory to the West. The Eskimo fans screamed until their lungs gave out. Montreal coach Peahead Walker slumped as if he had been shot. My grandfather sat up and had an angina attack and fell back onto the couch, his heart tightened suddenly into a knot that took his breath away. He recovered, but five months later he was again lying on the couch in the evening, listening to the radio when he abruptly sat up and suffered a fatal heart attack.

His father, Peter, was still alive, retired, living in the bungalow on Somerville, a few blocks away. He had outlived two of his sons. Gilbert still lived with them but didn't work, and the three of them became an odd society of Scottish hillbillies. The house was the smallest of all Peter had built, a miniature house. His daughters were all married and living in Winnipeg but he rarely saw them. He drank, as they said in that unsubtle euphemism. He had become a pariah, as he had been in Shetland. Peter's life mirrored the city's dramatic arc. He had been corrupt and successful at the turn of the century, had revelled in the city's growth and entertainments. He had lost a son to the war and been humbled by the Depression. For the rest, he endured and dwindled, his house, his family, his business and himself all getting smaller. Christina was thin and delicate. For forty years she had held to the idea that God might claim her at any moment. Weather permitting, she sat on their small porch, staring at the tall hedge that eclipsed them, and recited Robbie Burns.

> Farewell to the Highlands, farewell to the north,
> The birthplace of Valour, the country of Worth;
> Wherever I wander, wherever I rove,
> The hills of the Highlands for ever I love.
>
> My heart's in the Highlands, my heart is no here;
> My heart's in the Highlands a-chasing the deer;
> A-chasing the wild deer, and following the roe,
> My heart's in the Highlands, wherever I go.
>
> Farewell to the mountains, high-cover'd with snow,
> Farewell to the straths and green valleys below;
> Farewell to the forests and wild-hanging woods,
> Farewell to the torrents and loud-pouring floods.
>
> My heart's in the Highlands, my heart is no here,
> My heart's in the Highlands, a-chasing the deer;
> A-chasing the wild deer, and following the roe,
> My heart's in the Highlands wherever I go.

Peter died in 1957, at the age of eighty-six, three years after I was born. I wasn't conceived in drought or war or hardship, and arrived at the still point when history had come to an end.

11

FLOOD

THE ONLY THREATS my family faced in Wildwood Park were floods and nuclear war. In 1963, the featureless hostility of the Cold War was marked with rumour and expectation. At any moment, Khrushchev could fly into a peasant rage. At Oakenwald Elementary School there were regular drills to protect us from atom bombs. A shrill siren, more fearsome than the fire alarm, sounded and I filed into the hallway and sat against the wall cross-legged, my hands pressing my head into my lap. The hall lights were turned off and the mood was oddly intimate. I remained immobile, waiting for the explosion until the lights came on and I filed back into class, relieved and disappointed.

Winnipeg was particularly vulnerable to nuclear attack because of its location. An over-the-pole attack from Russia

would put us right in the path of the bombs. I had seen dia-
grams of these deadly parabolas, drawn in bold red strokes
with oversized arrows, heading south. What if the bombs ran
out of steam before they got to Washington and landed on us
instead? When I saw the purposeful, disintegrating contrail of
a jet in the blue sky, I was sure it was a fighter sent up to deal
with a Communist plane carrying an atom bomb. If you held
your breath for the first ninety seconds after impact, the
schoolyard physics expert told us, you escaped the worst of it.

Our teacher, Miss Morden, tried to allay our fears with a
slide show, demonstrating the benefits of the Distant Early
Warning system—the DEW Line—that protected us. It was a
series of more than sixty radar stations along the seventieth
parallel—the bleakest, wildest territory on earth—where they
maintained constant vigilance. Completed in 1957, and manned
not just by Canadians but freedom-loving people everywhere,
the DEW Line radar was sensitive enough to detect a seagull
flying in its territory. We saw slides of brush-cut men in horn-
rims and plaid shirts, staring unhappily at electronic equipment. The temperature outside could be minus 50° F we were
told, the winds up to 90 mph. We sent the men a letter, composed by the class. ("Thank-you for being awake so that we can
sleep.") We sent them a gift, too, wool socks, or a fruitcake.

I was in the bluebird row, intellectually circling above the
earnest robins, barely a speck to the idiot sparrows. Miss Morden would drape herself around me to help with my erratic
writing, her hand guiding mine, both of us gripping the
messy fountain pen. In memory, her breasts were pressed
softly to my head, though this can't be true. Her lips almost
touched my ear and her hand moved in concert with mine,
creating a line of elegant script. She was slightly zaftig and her
hair was cut in a Doris Day bob. She wore angora sweaters in

the winter and the overheated classroom ripened her perfume (was it only soap?) to a disturbing bouquet. Caught in her soft grasp, the torpor of the alphabet and stuffy air invited a dopey intimacy.

Partway through the school year, Miss Morden announced that she was getting married and invited the class to her wedding. She gave us a talk about finding that other acorn in the forest to grow with. I drew circles on my construction paper, stung.

On Saturday, my mother and I went to the wedding, in a Catholic church in another part of town. The interior was vast and gloomy and serious, the opposite of our United Church, a sunny bungalow on Point Road. There was a sense of religious heft. Miss Morden walked down the aisle in her white dress, radiant. How could she leave me for another? I wondered, how could love die? I prayed for the comforting white blast of the atom bomb, our men on the DEW Line asleep in their new wool socks, the world destroyed to avoid this pain.

––––––––––

Nuclear winter was the backdrop for our quotidian sins, but the atom bomb was an irregular menace, as fleeting as Halloween. Our neighbourhood was defined by the Red River and its implicit threat of flooding. Wildwood Park was a forward-looking community that was contained within a boot-shaped undulation of the river. We were both insulated and threatened by the water, which was a disturbing brown rather than the advertised red and rose dramatically each spring.

Wildwood Park was based on the Radburn Idea, an innovative 1920s development in Fair Lawn, New Jersey. The Fair Lawn development claimed to be the first in North America to separate traffic from domestic life. The plan had a large interior park and small access roads for residents to park their cars. The living space and bedrooms looked out onto the park. One of the central ideas was that children wouldn't have to cross a road to get to any neighbour or to school. It was conceived by two American town planners, H. Wright and C. S. Stein, and incorporated the ideas of social critic Lewis Mumford. It was initiated in 1928, designed to accommodate twenty-five thousand residents, but the Depression hit, bankruptcy ensued and the scale shrunk to a few thousand, roughly the same size as its imitator, Wildwood Park.

Radburn was, in part, a defence against Henry Ford's assault on the urban psyche, a community that was "safe for motor-age living." Mumford himself didn't drive and became a harsh critic of what he called the religion of the automobile. Like Le Corbusier in Paris, he understood how profound an impact the car would have on cities, how it would become a tyrant. Humphrey Carver, a Canadian planner, said, "Radburn is a landmark in man's quest for a better way of living . . . a noble fragment . . . an entirely new way of living at peace with the automobile." The Radburn Idea was a kind of Utopian blueprint that was implemented only a few times. Lewis Mumford somewhat grandly announced that, "Radburn is the first major departure in city planning since Venice." In its Wildwood incarnation, it also shared with Venice the threat of flood and the tenuous relationship with water.

Hubert Bird, a Winnipeg developer, saw Radburn from the air one day when flying out of New York and was struck by its essential logic. He decided that he would try to recreate it in Winnipeg. He built the houses from salvaged lumber taken from temporary grain bins that his construction company had built at the Lakehead during the war. An innovative assembly-line process was created, which also helped keep costs to a minimum. A bungalow cost $6,570 in 1948, a three-bedroom two-storey house was $9,300. Bird himself lived in an impressive house on South Drive, the elegant periphery road that followed the river and flanked Wildwood Park. After the park opened in 1948, he toured it regularly with his wife, Violet, chatting with the residents, taking a proprietorial interest in the neighbourhood he had conceived. Bird was born in England and was tall and patrician-looking and by local standards, rich. He had in effect recreated a version of eighteenth-century England, more or less what the original Red River settlers had come to escape from. The people in the park called him "Squire" and he offered an annual prize for Wildwood's three best gardens.

The location by the river was idyllic but it presented problems other than flooding. Mosquitoes were a plague in summer, and the community bought a converted milk truck with a fogging machine on the flatbed, which dispensed a thick cloud of DDT. We ran behind the fogger, partly for the relief from the mosquitoes and partly because it was an event, which were so few. A neighbour had an old Second World War gas mask. It didn't have a canister of air attached, simply a hole where the fog came in. We took turns putting it on and running goggle-eyed and coughing in a parody of Tommy Mainland's experience in the First World War trenches.

My school was at the open end of Wildwood Park, the only side not contained by the river. Beside it was a one-stop shopping centre, claiming to be the first in western Canada, containing a grocery store, drugstore, lunch counter, dry cleaner, post office, service station and bowling alley. It also sold hardware, shoes and children's clothes. In the back was a beauty parlour and a barbershop with two silver-haired men who had copies of the *Police Gazette* stacked beside the leather chairs and fishing cartoons tacked onto the walls. It smelled of the brisk, masculine hair tonic that I have never encountered outside a barbershop. It was where I got my hair cut. The glorious tonic was applied and the barber massaged my head like bread dough as he talked with another customer about fish or lawn mowers or the new Ford Fairlane. There was a round mirror in front of me and an identical one mounted on the wall behind me so that my reflection multiplied and disappeared into infinity. When I came home with my hair short and slicked, looking like a new recruit, my mother grabbed a towel and tried to fluff the curls back.

Outside of Wildwood Park the city was slightly abstract, like those antique maps of the world where the unknown areas are marked with drawings of sea monsters. I knew Eaton's, where I went with my grandmother to review the prices. I took my bike up to Ringer's drugstore on Pembina Highway to buy Beatle bubble gum with the cards inside. On Saturdays, I went downtown to art school, which was located near the jail where Peter Mainland had done time. The jail was no longer in use but it was still standing.

There were only four different house plans in Wildwood Park. The residents, with few exceptions, were roughly the same age, from the same economic strata and, uniformly the same colour; a study in homogeneity. There were bureaucrats, accountants and university professors. We watched *Hockey Night in Canada* and ate pork chops with a sauce made from Campbell's mushroom soup. We had one of the highest birth rates in the country. My parents were young and glowing and we looked like a model Canadian family, one that had risen out of the prairie soil like Red Fife wheat. The neighbourhood was heavily treed and in the autumn there was always the smell of burning leaves, easily the most evocative scent for me and the only loss to environmentalism that I deeply mourn. "Yes! There's a heap o' good livin' in the Wildwood" the advertisements claimed in 1948. "As new as the dawn of tomorrow." So my world was hermetic, a distillation of the early 1960s as they existed in nostalgic memory, protected from history, from the bloody past of the plains, from the city's lingering ethnic tensions, from poverty and diversity. We existed in the present, as if our neighbourhood were a destination rather than part of a continuum.

This historical moment was brief. On the one hand, Wildwood was the natural pinnacle of the white-picket-fence suburb; it was insular, uniform and safe. But it was also a precursor to the sixties with its unconscious nod to environmentalism and the commune-like set-up. There were a few nascently hip couples. An artist drew nudes. A woman had a loom in her living room. The little boxes made of ticky-tacky began to sprout skylights and asymmetrical additions, to become unique.

———————

Every mother told their children not to play near the river, knelt in front of them and held their shoulders and stared into their eyes and delivered a precise lecture about its dangers and solicited a promise. And we dawdled in the park and lingered near the dike and gravitated to the water like lemmings. I built forts by the river, Wrightian creations that used local materials and blended into the landscape. Salvaged wood combined with fallen poplar and elm branches. Leaves covered the earth floor. I retreated there during thunderstorms and counted the seconds between the lightning and thunder, calculating when it would hit the fort while reading a sports anthology with a flashlight. The Red invited solitude and contemplation and I walked its banks, searching for dead bodies like a Hardy boy.

When I was eight, a neighbouring girl invited me into her house. All the furniture in her living room was covered in plastic, the whole room a prophylactic, protecting the perfect present, which couldn't last. There was a hi-fi and half a dozen records, as if it were an obligation to own music of some kind. They were only played when company came, she said. One of the album covers had pastel tones and the words *Bossa Nova!* written in playful black script. Another was a singalong record by Mitch Miller. There were stacks of coasters made of cork, waiting for the sign of a glass. A handful of ceramic ashtrays were spread over the clean teak of the Danish Modern furniture. The living room invited a response, daring us to leave a stain on this perfect world.

We decided to go to my fort, where we began negotiations. Do you want to? Do *you?* I don't know, do *you?* We shyly discarded our clothes. There was a rush of excitement and then a sense of anticlimax. We sat on the leaves and talked finally, the summer air liberating, currents moving in unfamiliar patterns on our nakedness. She told me that the best film she had seen was *Swiss Family Robinson*, and described the plot in intricate detail. She had a gift for storytelling, a hypnotic voice and a well-developed sense of narrative. I could see the family foraging on the island, imagining that it was us. Afterwards we played cards then put on our clothes and went home. On the sidewalk, in chalk, someone had written the word SEX in block letters. Underneath it read; "Ask your parents what this means when you get home."

——— ———

When I was eleven I explored the woods by the river with two friends, Denny and Brian. We pulled crayfish from the water, grey and blind. Occasionally a rat would dart by. The dark clay stayed damp well into spring and then hardened into a dull grey that cracked into jagged disks. Denny and Brian and I regularly went to the river to smoke Alpines and review our pooled knowledge.

One day Denny drew a line with two dots in the clay with a stick. He explained that this was the female reproductive system. "One is for sex," Denny said, pointing to the top dot. "The other is for having babies. If you pick the wrong one, you'll kill her instantly." Life was risk.

One Saturday, the three of us patrolled the woods in the same brand of checked shirt in different colours. We climbed the curved trunk of a tree, cleaned the mud from our desert boots with sticks and each took a cigarette from the package Denny had brought. He took out a Zippo lighter and opened it by flicking it against his thigh; with a backwards stroke he brought it back up and lit it against his jeans. We dragged on the Alpines and discussed women. Below us, in a small clearing, Brian spotted the anthropological remains of a riverside meeting. We climbed down to investigate, cigarettes clenched tightly in our teeth.

There were several stubbed cigarettes, a mouldy blanket, an empty package of du Mauriers, and a used condom. Denny picked up the condom with a stick and bounced it lightly as we squatted like scientists. This was proof of some kind, someone had done it. We discussed possibilities; teachers, neighbours, famous actresses. Denny flicked the condom with a sneaky wrist movement and it landed, briefly, on Brian's face, before he brushed it away hysterically. Denny screamed, "Coodies," and we all ran blindly out of the woods onto the prairie scrub beside the dike road until we stopped, exhausted, bent over and panting. Brian punched Denny on the shoulder twice, the second time hard and we sat down and lit three more Alpines. Denny caught a grey locust and in a gesture of bravado or penance, bit off its head.

The lovers' hideout was a clue. There were others. They came from random, unreliable sources, from the faded colour pictures in a nudist magazine that had been passed around the school, the deep folds in the paper turned white from use. In the photographs, blonde women played volleyball, their breasts pointed outward like Irish setters sighting a bird. We stared at the pictures in huddled, breathless groups. Why wouldn't every grown-up become a nudist? As children we had revealed ourselves to one another like Victorian couples on their wedding night. It was rumoured that Janet Bing danced naked in her basement by herself, that the dolorous man who delivered milk each day was the real father of the Danton twins. There was a man in Sweden who could tie his penis in a knot. Denny said he had seen his older sister in the bath once and her breasts were like balloons filled with water. She had nipples like Lowney's Glosette Raisins and milk sprayed from their centres in a bluish-white arc. We practised handling water-filled balloons as preparation for the real thing. Outside the dike, beyond Wildwood, girls did it, guaranteed. This was certainly true of the North End, and especially of St. Boniface with its French influence. Sex moved through Wildwood, a swirl of rumour and anecdote, the way it had moved through the Scottish Highlands a century earlier, the way it has always moved. Like the river each spring, it sought openings, probed for weaknesses. It is the most natural of curiosities, the most compelling. Curiosity is what leads us to love. We need to know another. In the meantime, we struggled to know ourselves. In the summer, we stared at the mothers bent over in the gardens, their madras shorts stretched to the shape of a pear, and tried to calculate what we were missing.

Brian had a boarder who stayed at their house who spent all his time working on a Ford Falcon that was in the garage. He told us that no engine could pull the kind of duty the slant six could, never had been, never would be. He said his pubic hair grew so fast he had to trim it with scissors. Sometimes he got his girlfriend to cut it, he said with a wink. We never saw his girlfriend. This was how information came to Wildwood; from unreliable half-wits and two black-and-white television channels. Occasionally, it came from outside the park.

Denny had a distant cousin named Dave Adamanchuk who was a few years older than we were. He lived on the other side of town and sometimes came to visit. He was fat and had greased black hair and a stiletto knife with a small chrome naked woman on the handle. Dave claimed to be the youngest karate black belt in the city. Once three men in the North End had taunted him and he had chopped them into kindling, he said. He acted out all the parts, kicking and slashing clumsily in the air and staring down at the flattened thugs with a Presley sneer. Denny once told me that Dave had gotten at least two girls pregnant and they had been sent away to farms near Brandon to give birth. He used a Wilkinson Sword razor blade to remove the yellowed, nicotine-stained layer of skin on his index finger so his father wouldn't find out he was smoking and pound him.

He and Denny and I walked over to the dike road that bordered the neighbourhood and stared down at the golfers standing idly waiting for friends, dressed in checked pants and pale hats. I sometimes culled the ditches along North Drive for errant golf balls. Those that weren't creased badly or waterlogged, I sold to men on the course. I thought that anyone who golfed there was rich and was surprised at the poor deals offered me and the squabbling over balls they identified as already theirs.

The three of us walked down the dike and waited by the green, watching two men tee off. We were partly concealed by the dogwood and shrubs. The two balls landed within twenty yards of one another and the men started slowly toward us, pulling their golf carts. Dave stepped on the rough and ran onto the course, his weight swaying and his black ankle boots sliding on the grass, and scooped up both balls. He turned a slow circle, trying to get some traction on the slippery grass and ran back toward us then past us, in the direction of the river. I looked at the men who had teed off. Their movements seemed slow and deliberate but they quickly came into focus, running at a speed that surprised me. Denny quickly overtook his cousin, racing toward the river, Dave tiring already. We sprinted down the path that paralleled the river, the mud dry. We had no idea where the golfers were when we slid through a clutch of dogwood off the path and lay motionless in a thicket, our breath forced out in raw gasps despite our attempts to quiet it. We didn't speak for ten minutes. The golfers hadn't followed this far. Dave took out a package of du Mauriers and gave us all one and lit them. He took out his stiletto and flicked open the blade expertly. "They're lucky," he said, prying at a piece of dried clay in front of him. Dave came by a few more times that summer. He had the swagger of an explorer, telling us false, exotic stories. I was always glad to see him go.

Denny and I shared a paper route that included much of Wildwood Park. It also included some of the magisterial homes along South Drive, on the river. They had long driveways and several cars. One of them belonged to the Luptons, whose daughter Gloria sunned herself in a pink bikini. Denny and I split the route, lugging the awkward canvas *Free Press* bags, but we met up to deliver the Lupton paper together, resting it on the doorstep and looking into the large bay window, hoping for a glimpse. One day we delivered the paper and the door opened. Mrs. Lupton and Gloria were standing there, wearing summery two-piece outfits. They were already tanned; not a garish, oily brown but the soft, faded buttery hue of a spring vacation in the Caribbean. Their blonde hair was sprayed into short, sweeping helmets. Gloria was wearing gold sandals and a skein of blonde hairs trailed downward from her navel into her short skirt. The air inside the house was cool and rich. Mrs. Lupton told us that they were moving the following Thursday and we could stop delivery then. Gloria smiled politely and Mrs. Lupton closed the door.

"They wanted it," Denny said.

"What?"

"Couldn't you tell? They were dying for it."

That Sunday, I sat uncomfortably once more in the rear pew with my grandmother, checking the contents of my pockets and listening to Reverend Donald Ray's subtle warnings as the Red River inched upward, "The LORD saw that the wickedness of men was great in the earth, and that every imagination of the thoughts of his heart was only evil continually." And so He sent a flood to purge mankind, everyone but Noah and his family and the unthinking animals.

My family had travelled a great distance, geographically, culturally and economically in two generations. But here we were, my grandmother and I, living in a world as small as Fanagmore. Sex had slipped through the gates, as it had with her mother, Catherine, as it does everywhere. And now we were in church, waiting for the bad news.

My thoughts were continually wicked: naked in my fort, the nudist photographs from the schoolyard, inchoate sexual longings for teachers, actresses, a friend's sister. It is a preacher's great gift to make an individual feel that his soul has been glimpsed, that the preacher has uncovered a private sin and is speaking to him alone in the sermon. Donald Ray had no great gift, but sin is reliably generic. The flood was coming to deal with my continual thoughts of sex. But religion had lost much of its anger over the centuries; the water wouldn't cover the world, merely Wildwood Park.

It may have been God who brought the flood but the land had also been cursed, legend had it, by Indians. Before Lord Selkirk had come to settle, the Chippewa, Cree and Assiniboine had all used the land where Wildwood Park stood. The Cree called the river Miscousipi—red water river. Selkirk snookered them, offering an annual supply of tobacco in exchange for the land, though given the natives' view of land ownership, it's hard to say who got the better of the deal. It was one of the lowest elevations in the area and was surrounded by water on three sides. The natives understood that it was on a flood plain and none of them were silly enough to erect a permanent settlement, but the woods contained deer, moose and bear, which they hunted regularly. The curse was the result of a white man killing a native woman, perhaps a soured romance, rather than a casualty of war.

There had always been floods in the Red River Valley. The first major submersion after the land deal came in 1826 with the floodwaters rising thirty-seven feet and producing a lake seventeen miles wide. Houses were lifted from their foundations. Chimneys collapsed, stonework eroded. The ice breaking up on the river made a sound like thunder. The Scots wondered at the persistence of the plagues sent to them. The Egyptians had had ten (turning the Nile to blood, frogs, lice, flies, death of cattle, boils, hail, locusts, darkness and death of the firstborn). But the Presbyterians were closing in on the record: the Red was already the colour of dried blood, and there were floods, locusts, flies, mosquitoes, hail, snow, death of livestock, Catholics and Indian attacks. Still, the 1826 flood was the biggest setback. An observer wrote back to Scotland, "All former reverses are scarcely worthy of notice compared with the present and this I consider an extinguisher to the hope of the Red River ever retaining the name of a Settlement." Some of the settlers bailed out after the flood, moving to the United States.

Sanford Fleming, chief engineer for the Canadian Pacific Railway, understood that Winnipeg was on a flood plain and argued in 1879 against running the railway line through it. "It is futile to assume that the Red River shall never again overflow its banks. Man is utterly powerless to prevent its occurring periodically, and whenever it occurs the disastrous consequences will be intensified in proportion to the increased number of inhabitants within the submerged district." Fleming thought the railway should be routed through Selkirk rather than Winnipeg, but the political wars had already been fought over issues that had to do with money rather than common sense: Winnipeg was the site.

The Red River sits on the bed of a former glacial lake, Lake Agassiz. Below the enviable topsoil, there is a glacial till of rock and gravel. The river is 560 miles long and drains an area of forty-eight thousand square miles and takes its colour from the red clay that lines its banks. The Red is slow and unchanging and largely without guile, a comparatively shallow river. The incline is gentle, three inches per mile on the Canadian side of the border, and it has distinctive national traits; the flood years on the American side usually don't match those on the Canadian side, though there have been common floods. Since its regular movement is so stately, the Red hasn't evolved as a river; it is pretty much unchanged from what it was during prehistory, no deeper or faster or slower. It isn't on display in Winnipeg where views are either co-opted by industry or by the wealthy. Its most public presence is in late April when its normally sedate nature is replaced by a flowering psychosis.

The Red is one of the few rivers in North America that flows north, starting in North Dakota and ending at the delta of Lake Winnipeg. During flood years, it picks up bloated livestock and kitchen chairs and children's toys from Grand Forks and Emerson and Morris and spreads them like charity over the valley. I used to walk to its edge and stare into the opaque water that carried American secrets, perhaps American corpses. The Red was dangerous in the way that strangers in cars were dangerous; you could be whisked away.

The Red usually isn't prone to flash flooding. Every year presents a fresh, ontogenic drama. Water levels are noted daily, calculations made, prophecies delivered. Big floods tend to be cumulative; several years of heavy rain or snow unleashed by a late spring and quick thaw. During the extended dust-bowl years, the Red didn't flood. After the 1948 flood, a minor one comparatively, it was predicted that it wouldn't flood for a long time. But in 1950, it delivered a sucker punch.

That flood was big news, in part because television was trying to define itself and one of its strengths was news. Floods are the disaster best suited to television because they give the networks ample lead time. You can set up cameras, establish human-interest stories, pick out which of the plucky, tired workers you want on-air. The 1950 flood received international coverage, benefiting from a recent agreement with Hollywood to include more Canadian coverage in their newsreels. In return the Canadian government would relax its restrictions on imported American films. The flood was ideal. It had good visuals and a narrative line that was designed for the camera. The river developed a television personality; big and predatory and relentless. The people were brave and exhausted, united as if by war, defending their homes against a common foe. Soldiers were employed to sandbag, which gave visual guidance to the military theme. There had been other big floods: 1826, 1861 and again in 1916; and minor catastrophes in 1882, 1897, 1904 and 1948. But 1950 was the first flood ratified by film, it is the flood that settled in the city's historical consciousness.

Each spring, its name was invoked. In the 1960s, as the river began its annual threat, experts were polled to see if the year was going to be a bad one. On the evening news, photographs from the 1950 flood were shown in murky boxes behind the newscaster. I looked for our house among the identical dark, peaked roofs that seemed to be floating on the water. The 1950 flood inhabited my imagination like a bogeyman, a dark enchantment that could return at any time and take everything. It was a reminder that I could never completely relax, even in this small perfect world.

The 1950 flood began with record snowfalls in North Dakota and Minnesota. The spring was late and the rains were heavy during runoff. In late April, Emerson, at the border, was evacuated, then Altona and Rosenfeld. The Red River Valley looked like a rice paddy from the air. Farms looked like hieroglyphs; a line of shining silo domes, the roofs of barns and the linear patterns of trees planted as a windbreak all set in a Red Sea, as it came to be called. A line of boxcars faded to coloured pastels sat as if on the water, the tracks and fields submerged. Farmers sandbagged their houses and finally abandoned them, defeated. They held .22-calibre rifles to the heads of cattle that couldn't be saved and watched them fall shuddering on the damp ground. A few defiant men stood on their roofs, staring at the new lake forming around them, plucked to safety finally by rescuers in aluminum fishing boats.

In Winnipeg, men and women worked madly to build dikes. Water seeped through the city. The large, rounded late-forties cars moved carefully along roads that had six inches of water over them and offered suspense; at any minute you could fall into an unseen hole. Even as the water filled the city in patches, there remained the article of faith upon which the city had been founded; the waters would recede. But they didn't.

Wildwood Park, at one of the lowest elevations in the city, was like the canary in the coal mine. A dike had been pushed into place by a bulldozer and then packed by hand; in places it was thirty-five feet wide. At night, Wildwood residents walked along it with Coleman lanterns, looking for signs of erosion and damage. Ten feet of water lapped quietly at the dike, exploring for weaknesses, licking at the mud and sand. Three engineers who lived in the park formed an ad hoc committee to deal with the river. They worked out of a garage, their wives bringing them coffee and feeding them casseroles as they drew up plans to save their new homes. The Red moved patiently up the bank and made its first gains in darkness, seeping through weak spots and trickling over low spots after midnight on May 6. A few hours later it was clear that the dike wasn't enough. At 4:30 a.m. the sirens sounded in

Wildwood Park, the signal for evacuation. It was almost exactly two years after Wildwood had been built. People bundled their children up and drove off in the bleak pre-dawn, to neighbours or family or out-of-town motels. The water rose to the second floor of the homes and the YMCA Canoe Club sent out canoeists to help people recover totems—wedding dresses, photographs, heirlooms—from abandoned houses. Garages floated off their concrete moorings and moved clumsily along the flooded roadways.

That morning the headline in the *Tribune* read, ALL CITY DIKES BROKEN. The enemy was inside the gates, creeping up drains and flooding basements, overwhelming houses near the riverbank, entering through cracks in foundations. The insurance companies circled the wagons and declared the flood an "Act of God" that wouldn't be paid out on. On May 9, the theatres closed; the Bijou, Rialto, Roxy, Rio, Rose, Furby, Lyceum, Gaiety, Tivoli, Deluxe, Plaza, Capitol and Wonderland all shut down. The river had risen 28.4 feet, the fourth-highest recorded level. Pumps and sandbags were flown in from Minneapolis. Hip waders arrived from Saskatchewan.

The next day central heating went out in thousands of homes. There were electrical problems as water filled conduits and shorted the power. The river rose another foot. By May 11, only three of the city's eleven bridges were operating, at a reduced flow, and the city was cleaved, further isolated within itself. Most of the restaurants and taverns closed. The University of Manitoba was immersed. Hotels were filled with families. Shallow lakes pooled everywhere. The headline on that day's paper read, 40,000 QUIT FLOODED CITY IN CANADA'S BIGGEST EXODUS.

It crested on May 15, having risen 30.3 feet and produced a lake that was seventy miles long and thirty miles wide. It was rumoured that the Americans were the cause of our problems, diverting the Mississippi River. But the truth was less dramatic. The flood was a matter of inches, of unexpected rainfall, of melt rates and spring blizzards in the northern United States.

One hundred thousand people were evacuated in the 1950 flood. On May 16, Bob Hope closed his radio show with a message of Yankee optimism and a vague offer of help: "The great city of Winnipeg tonight is fighting a life to death battle to hold back the rampaging Red River. Winnipeg is going to win that battle. If Winnipeg should lose that battle then Uncle Sam would open his heart and his pocket-book, because Uncle Sam lives by the line in the good book, 'Love thy Neighbour.'"

In the aftermath, relief efforts in Holland sent over trees and shrubs to replant Wildwood Park. Princess Elizabeth and the Duke of Edinburgh came to view the damage and were taken to Wildwood because it was one of the hardest hit neighbourhoods. The pair served like curators of the disasters that regularly befell the empire, flying to each of them with renewed sympathy, observing the wreckage, comforting the homeowners, engaging the tradesmen in small talk, shaking their heads with weary rue. They stood at the Wildwood Park Shopping Centre and the Duke estimated the depth of the flood water and degree of devastation, offering his royal *gravitas* as a coda.

Part of the appeal for television and newsreel crews was the fact that the fight against the water was carried on by individuals. There was no coherent government plan to combat the flood. Families worked to save their homes, neighbours banded together to keep the community dry. It made for a marketable back story, a sense of frontiersmanship that played well in both the United States and Europe. What the provincial government had in place was something called Operation

Blackboy, which called for the evacuation of the entire city, save "75,000 fit men and women" and a state of *de facto* martial law. The public was unaware of this plan, which came within a few inches of being implemented. But after 1950, the public urged the government toward concrete action.

The city had been built on an article of faith, a trust in God's plan, but now the citizens wanted government to pick up the slack. In 1962, construction began on a floodway that would divert the river in the event of another flood on the scale of 1950. It was initiated by Premier Duff Roblin and became known as Duff's Ditch, and less kindly, as Roblin's Folly. More than 100 million cubic yards of earth were excavated, more than the St. Lawrence Seaway Project or the Panama Canal, which had stolen Winnipeg's title of Gateway to the West. The channel was 29.4 miles long, thirty feet deep and between 380 and 540 feet wide. The project employed one thousand people and cost $62 million. It was an understated prairie monument, a negative space burrowed in the ground.

Despite the floodway, the Red River threatened in 1966 and again in 1969. The homes on South Drive were exposed to the river, outside the modest but critical dikes, and volunteers from Wildwood offered to sandbag. I was fifteen in 1969 and went to the home of one of my father's business partners who lived on the river. I went because he had a popular, voluptuous seventeen-year-old daughter, and because I felt that I had helped bring the flood through my indiscretions. When I arrived, half the teenaged boys in the neighbourhood were already there, their shirts off in the cold spring air, trying to impress the daughter, who was nowhere to be seen.

I discovered the city incrementally, going outward in ever-increasing circles. I sometimes walked up to Pembina Highway to shoot pool. The Garry Cinema, where I had watched Disney films with my Aunt Jean, had been turned into a bowling alley and pool hall. The pool room was run by two Ukrainian men named Dougie and Izzy. Dougie was broad and completely hairless and in his seventies. Izzy was black-haired and wiry and maybe even older. They were both incredibly combustible and came skittering around the counter screaming incomprehensibly when one of the tough guys from across the tracks jammed the tip of his cue through the acoustic ceiling tile after a bad shot. The ceiling had hundreds of holes. The pool hall was filled mostly with kids from the wrong side of the tracks, which was what made it interesting. The actual train tracks were half a block west but Pembina Highway was the symbolic line. The houses on the other side weren't that different from our side, slightly smaller, the paint a little older, the yards browner. The difference was palpable though. The kids were wilder and tougher. The girls chewed gum and smoked Player's and looked like they'd already been divorced. These were broad generalizations but broad generalizations were what defined high school life. The final home of my great-grandfather, Peter Mainland, one-time Shetland billiard player, had been on the wrong side of the tracks.

I loved pool, the new universe that opened up with each break. I played with friends for small amounts of money. Occasionally I played the house shark, who was in his early twenties, a lean elegant man who had his own cue and drove a second-hand Cadillac with a baseball bat in the trunk. He would spot me fifty points and then take my three dollars in a dazzling exhibition of his offhand, God-given talent. He alternated between soft graceful shots that moved the cue ball like an obedient dog and full steam hammer shots that left the potted ball spinning in the pocket for thirty seconds. When he made a particularly brilliant shot, he whispered, "Oh sweetness," and moved his hips in a small samba motion.

When I got my driver's licence the city began to unfold. I drove the singular family Corvair downtown and to the Pony Corral restaurant on Pembina Highway to neck in the parking lot and to parties in River Heights that someone's cousin had heard about at Catholic school, parties where we drank beer and talked among ourselves and realized we didn't know anyone. I had been to the suburb of St. Vital and to the lounge out by the airport, which I thought was sophisticated because of its proximity to international travel. But the North End remained a separate country, even with the car. Sixty-five years after my grandparents had arrived, the divisions were still relatively intact.

The city was defined by Main Street, heroically wide and filled with faded vintage signage and small businesses and the original facades that were seen in Lewis Foote's photographs from the 1920s. In winter the spaces were bleak, the streets empty. What brought us north was the Commercial Hotel, which sold beer to minors without any fuss. Our fake ID scheme had run its course and the hotels along Pembina were careful who they sold beer to. The Commercial had that entrenched stale beer and cigarette smell of hardcore taverns, a dismal, dangerous room. Native men lingered in the parking lot, spectacularly underdressed for the cold in winter or wearing leather jackets in summer. It would be the easiest thing in the world to get your lights punched out. The wait for the beer was always dramatic, a few tables of hard-assed angry men staring at us as if we were prey. When our case of Carling Black Label was safely loaded into the trunk of someone's mother's four-door sedan, and the doors locked, we sped out of the parking lot with a sense of relief. Crossing Portage Avenue was like leaving East Germany.

We took the beer down to the dike near the Wildewood Club and drank them. We wandered the dark golf course like refugees and talked about which of our female teachers we were most likely to have sex with and which of our male teachers were Nazi war criminals. When we finished the beer, we threw the empties into the river and watched them bob toward Lake Winnipeg. That September, I left to join my family in Calgary where my father was involved in starting a new faculty at the university. I was seventeen and the city had almost ceased to be imaginary.

12

NEW

ROMANS

CALGARY LOOKED NEW and
Aryan. The sky was a pale blue dome. When I arrived from
Winnipeg, my mother picked me up at the airport and we
drove to the university where my father was. On the expansive
grounds, blond workers with tanned faces and faded jean
jackets stared into the sun. They looked like the posters of
Nordic farmers that the Manitoba government had sent out to
attract settlers seventy years earlier. Now I was the immigrant.
Calgary was booming, the oil business drawing hopeful
labourers and desperate families from Ontario and the Mari-
times. The population was 400,000, smaller than Winnipeg
but growing at a much faster pace. By the late eighties it would

be 650,000, eclipsing Winnipeg. Calgary was growing the way Winnipeg had grown sixty years earlier and it had the same sense of giddy importance, the idea that it was the new Rome.

Calgary's insistent newness made Winnipeg seem a dark place with grim prospects, the old country. Calgary was intent on keeping itself new, tearing down anything remotely dated and replacing it with something that shone. It would always be the New World, the Newest World, undergoing cosmetic surgery at a record clip. Renewal was Calgary's gift and curse.

Like Winnipeg, Calgary had been built at the confluence of two rivers, the Bow and the Elbow. But in Winnipeg, the rivers were largely out of view. The Bow, on the other hand, could be seen everywhere. You saw it while driving along Memorial Drive, or walking on Prince's Island. It came from the Rocky Mountains and was blue and clear and offered some of the best trout fishing in the country. In the evenings, canoeists and kayakers moved along in colourful flotillas. The sky seemed bigger, an optical effect that was much commented on. Its volume suggested both limitless possibility and the existence of God.

Though God left office the year I arrived. The Social Credit government, which married fiscal prudence with Christian evangelism, ruled the province from 1935 until it was defeated by Peter Lougheed's Conservatives in 1971 and God was replaced, at least politically, by oil. When my family got there, Calgary had the distinctive energy of a preacher who had woken up one day to realize that there was more money to be made in rock and roll than in the Bible. At the height of the oil boom, between $1- to 2.5-billion worth of building permits were issued annually. In one year, Calgary built more office space than New York and Chicago combined. More high-rises were being built than currently existed. It became the wealthiest province with the highest per capita income. Residents repeated these wonders as a form of communication. Less advertised was the corollary of every boom; the country's highest rates of abortion, suicide, divorce and teen pregnancy. Alberta was a party, with the same progression of intoxication, elation and regret. Subdivisions sprang up, oddly denuded, awaiting lawns and trees. The city seemed to be unpacking itself after arriving from a mail-order house.

We lived on the northwestern fringe of the city, where the growth was concentrated, a frontier that was edging daily toward the mountains. Our house was new, a large, charmless barn with a two-car garage, stucco ceilings that sparkled and a pretty much treeless yard. We were perched, briefly, on the edge of the city. Behind us was a view of the mountains. On certain days, when the light produced the purplish hue celebrated in bad paintings, the mountains appeared much closer, as if they had been moved like a film set. The sunsets were garish and alive and evanescent. Red-tailed hawks circled west of the house in the open scrubland, descending noiselessly to strike a gopher or a mouse. The glacial hummocks and gouged pastures around us were evidence of slow geological violence. Farther west, buffalo bones, some worn to the size and smoothness of stones, lined the bed of the Jumping Pound Creek, evidence of the Indian practice of running herds off a cliff, their thundering weight suspended in that brief flight. The chinook winds came through the Bow valley and hit our house with such force that it shook. The first winter we were there, a chinook wind descended and raised the temperature so quickly that people wore Bermuda shorts to shovel the melting snow from their driveways.

On my route to high school I walked past a corral filled with horses; by the time I graduated the land was lost to developers. The school itself, Sir Winston Churchill, was brand new; we were the first graduating class. It looked like it had been modelled on a British fort, with small slit windows for firing muskets. I arrived halfway through September, classes already underway, a new kid among new kids. I played football as a way of fitting in. The players had to wear a suit and tie on Fridays, game day. The team had oversized linemen and blond, earnest Mormons who prayed before each game and cheerleaders whose perky breasts leapt with enthusiasm at every touchdown, and the whole effect was like living in America, or at least what I imagined America to be.

Calgary had a pronounced American influence, mostly through its cattle and oil connections. There were more than thirty thousand Americans living in the city and its first library had been built with a Carnegie Foundation grant. Our football coach was a disciplinarian who held the American belief that football was a religion. We practised in the frosty mornings, doing push-ups on the frozen ground. You will *remove* your gloves, he told us, you *will* become warriors. You will *destroy* St. Francis. We had pep rallies where the team was introduced and a certain antiquated allegiance was pledged to the school, which had, as yet, no tradition, in football or anything else. Not every player was in the gymnasium, grinning stupidly and waving like the queen to students who had been press-ganged into attending. Some of us were outside in a Ford Econoline van sharing a joint, investigating another tradition, listening to Pink Floyd on the eight-track and remarking on the band's genius. The parking lot was filled with students' newish cars.

My impression was that there was money everywhere and everything was new. New houses and malls were being built around the school. Neighbourhoods went up like barn raisings: Dalhousie, Silver Springs, Varsity Estates. Had there been larger windows in our classrooms, we could have watched them going up, a civics lesson in itself.

———————

Calgary had a rich history of which I knew almost nothing. What little remained of the city's architectural past was in the process of being torn down to make way for new high-rises. This zeal reached an apex a decade later when six hundred old houses and buildings were destroyed in a single year. In the early years of the century, Calgary had been called the Sandstone City but few of the marvellous sandstone buildings remained. They had been built for the most part by Scottish stonemasons and had the weight and detail of castles. The past was being obliterated, as if it posed a threat.

And perhaps it did. Calgary was first fuelled by the land boom of 1910 and later by oil booms. The city's growth had proceeded with the pace of a blackout drunk; fevered development was followed by sober reflection. Each hangover was accompanied by resolutions that were later abandoned.

When creating a city and its accompanying civic persona, who do you model yourself on? Few places create themselves out of whole cloth. Their personalities are a process of theft and evolution. Calgary vacillated more than most, grappling first with its British cultural inheritance, then toying with imported European ideas, all the while flirting with an emphatically American vision of the romantic frontier.

Its most ambitious plan for reinvention was never realized. In April 1912, Thomas Mawson, a British planner and architect, came through Calgary on his way to Banff. Mawson was tall and dark-haired and had a thick moustache and the rhythm and pitch of a snake-oil salesman, and gave a speech to the Canadian Club of Calgary titled, "The City on the Plain and How to Make it Beautiful."

Mawson saw in Calgary a rare opportunity; the chance to design a great city. The conditions that allow for this are rare: money, civic ambition and political will (albeit often in the form of fascism). Baron Haussmann had done it in Paris in the 1850s under Napoleon III. Daniel Burnham had done it in Chicago and L'Enfant in Washington, D.C. These cities had been recreated on a grand scale, with a self-conscious notion of empire and history. Calgary had some of the same conditions. It was growing at a desperate pace: in 1905 there were five thousand people; in 1912 there were seventy-five thousand people and more than four hundred real estate companies. The city had money and ambition and a few nice buildings that had whetted its appetite for monument. The new sandstone city hall had a seventy-foot clock tower and a domed roof that provoked a sense of formality; citizens weren't allowed to chew tobacco while visiting. More than two hundred palm trees were planted on its grounds, a challenge to the climate itself. All but one died during the first winter and two hundred stark reminders of prairie hubris waved weakly until the next summer when they were hauled away.

Mawson invoked Paris and Vienna and the City Beautiful Movement in England in his speech. He flattered the women and spoke in poetic metaphor and appealed to the city's sense of destiny. "The eyes of the whole Dominion are upon you," he told a crowd, "and not only of the Dominion itself, but of all interested in City Planning both in the States and in Europe."

His pitch worked; early the next year, the city council voted unanimously to hire Mawson to draw up a plan. He asked for $25,000 to produce a model and drawings but settled for $6,000 in the hope that the plan would be implemented and he would take his profit there. After several months he delivered a bound book, titled *Calgary, Past, Present and Future*, and thirty detailed drawings that had been augmented by watercolours that showed Calgary reconfigured on a grand, European scale. The new Civic Centre was set on the river where a boating reach had been created. There was a grand central plaza, sculpted gardens and a series of three-storey Ecole des Beaux Arts buildings set on a grid. There were monuments that had streets radiating out from them like spokes from a hub. Miles of riverside parks were planned. The Fourth Street bridge was modelled on the Pont Alexander III in Paris and had an elaborate gateway. Both the Canadian Pacific and Canadian National railway stations were conceived on a huge scale and they faced one another down the length of a wide boulevard. Mawson felt that travellers arriving in Calgary should be immediately awed.

While his proposal was being debated, the Dingman oil well blew in at Turner Valley, and the city grew even more delirious. By the summer of 1914 there were five hundred newly incorporated oil companies though few of them had any equipment or expertise. Some had jars of sewing-machine oil in the window, labelled as "Genuine Dingman Gold!" But the Dingman well proved to be a false spring and little oil was recovered. The oil companies left town, leaving a trail of bad debt. Hotel rooms were papered with worthless stock certificates. Before the oil strike, a recession had been gaining force. Settlers weren't coming west in the same numbers and land prices stagnated. Most of the real estate companies collapsed.

Buildings were left uncompleted and tradesmen moved on or returned east. To complete the mood of despair, in August 1914, war was declared and attention and resources switched to military planning.

In the wake of this deflation, Mawson's grand urban plan was rejected. The city was more than $2 million in debt and didn't even have enough cash for his modest fee, though city council eventually found the money to pay him. Some of Mawson's suggestions were eventually implemented—the riverside parks for example—but most were forgotten. The city grew up largely in opposition to his design principles. It wouldn't be Paris or Chicago. No grand spaces were created, the streets and sidewalks remained narrow and Calgary grew on the will of developers rather than through an aesthetic vision. Copies of Mawson's book are in the library, but his drawings for the city, a portfolio of elegant, detailed water-colours, disappeared without a trace. In 1976, residents of Sunnyside, a neighbourhood north of the Bow River, found a series of drawings and watercolours behind the wallboard of a garage they were renovating. The owner suspected that the drawings might be valuable and called the University of Calgary. My father and Bill Perks, dean of the environmental design faculty, went out to the garage and recognized them as Mawson's lost world.

———————

At the same time that Mawson was imagining his European City on the Plain, Guy Weadick, an American trick roper who was married to a trick rider known as Flores LaDue, was creating the Calgary Stampede, the self-described Greatest Outdoor Show on Earth. Weadick had $100,000 in backing from four local businessmen and cattlemen and the show he proposed centred around a rodeo and featured historical exhibits, trick roping and an Indian village. Its stated mandate was to "preserve and enhance the agricultural and historical legacy of Alberta," though this wasn't entirely true. It was a commercial enterprise and history was revised to yield something with crowd appeal. The first Stampede parade took place on Labour Day, 1912, and was watched by eighty thousand people, more than the population of the city itself.

Calgary's actual history was less marketable than Weadick's romantic notions. For one thing, it was only thirty-seven years old at the time of the first Stampede. The city had been founded by Ephrem Brisbois of the North West Mounted Police in 1875 as one of a series of outposts to curb the whisky traders who were having such success with the natives. In the style of most civilizing forces, Brisbois named the new fort after himself. He was a harsh, unhinged commander and his men rebelled. Brisbois was relieved of his command after the first winter. He resigned soon after and died forgotten at the age of thirty-nine. Fort Brisbois was renamed Fort Calgary by Colonel James Macleod who took the name from a Scottish village on the Island of Mull. He argued that Calgary was a fitting name for a town at the confluence of two rivers because it meant "clear running water" in Gaelic, though what it actually means is "bay farm."

Two thousand Cree, Blackfoot, Stoney, Sarcee and Peigans marched in the inaugural Stampede parade alongside the North West Mounted Police. This public display of harmony belied a tawdry history. After the buffalo were slaughtered for fun and profit, the natives faced starvation and this was used as leverage to get them onto reservations; if they moved, they would receive government rations. But the promised food didn't always arrive and rarely in the quantity required. They had been hunters for centuries and now there was nothing to hunt. They were encouraged to become farmers, to embrace the ethic that had brought thousands of eastern European immigrants to North America. The promise of farm land to natives who had freely occupied all of the territory defined a relationship that has been misguided, often tragic, and tinged with bitter ironies. In 1880, starving Sarcees threatened Fort Calgary and their brief insurrection was quashed without bloodshed by the mounted police. Less than a generation later the two groups were the most prominent part of the Stampede parade, offering a bright, sanitized history that skirted the essential grief of colonization. Weadick needed natives for his parade because they carried an aura of authenticity and danger and because they were colourful. They were still occasionally categorized as savages in local newspapers. The local Methodist missionaries recruited them for the parade, their influence still considerable and the natives became part of the tourist culture, the story we agreed to tell when company came.

As an immigrant I first inhabited the tourist culture, the costume of the cowboy. I bought a pair of Justin cowboy boots at a store on the Eighth Avenue Mall where the salesman patiently explained why the cowboy boot was in fact more comfortable and more practical than the Wallabee, a duck-toed shoe then enjoying a perverse vogue. He drew the outline of my stocking foot on a piece of cardboard and noted the pointed shape, the exact shape, he said, of a cowboy boot. I had to ask myself, he said gravely, whether I wanted to be a man or an accountant.

The cowboy was our frontman, but the city was oil. Oil was a lubricant and an intoxicant and, finally, an aphrodisiac that shaped the city. Oil was first noticed by nineteenth-century settlers who saw it seep out of the ground and they occasionally used it to grease their wagons and as medicine for cattle. The 1914 oil strike at Turner Valley was a disappointment but it established the idea of oil, its golden promise. With the discovery of the Leduc field in 1947, a bonanza, the idea became entrenched. The city grew at a lively pace but took a huge jump in 1973, inspired, oddly, by a Holy War. On October 6, 1973, on Yom Kippur, Egyptian tanks invaded the Israeli occupied Sinai Peninsula and Syrian troops crossed the Golan Heights to launch an assault on Jerusalem. Israel, backed by the United States, rebuffed the strike and mounted a counterattack. On October 16, Arab oil producers met in Kuwait to discuss ways to use their oil resources to get the West to scale back its support of Israel. They agreed to cut oil production by twenty-five per cent initially, with a further reduction each month of five per cent, until a Middle East settlement could be reached.

Within days the price of oil soared. It had been selling for three dollars a barrel and non-Arab producers raised their prices to over fifteen, taking advantage of the shortage. It was a boon for Alberta and wealth was created overnight. In restaurants, in elevators, on buses, I overheard conversations about how someone had bought a house for $40,000 and sold it six months later for $60,000. The response was always the same: the listener knew a more dramatic case, buying for $50,000 and selling for $100,000. This was the city's litany: calling out a price and receiving a greater one. People flipped houses like flapjacks. The speculative free-for-all of 1910 was repeated and the money and visible growth gave the city a boozy confidence.

My neighbour was in oil. Everyone was in the awl binness, it seemed. After graduating from high school, I was in it myself. In late June, a friend, Rhys Jones, and I rented a white Ford Maverick from Avis and drove to Medicine Hat. We could see the derricks of drilling rigs from the highway, driving over the dry farmland, with its rolling irrigation systems, past groups of Hutterites in their black garb and Bluto beards. The women had bright spotted kerchiefs over their heads and cheeks the colour and shape of McIntosh apples. We drove toward the derricks, speeding along the gravel section roads, looking for work.

The first derrick belonged to a Commanche rig. It consumed the farmland it was on with a collection of metal huts and the noise from a dozen different engines. A man in his early twenties sat on a forty-gallon drum, his eyes out of focus. One hand was wrapped in dirty gauze and blood had soaked through onto his oily jeans. A sign on the outside of a shack said, "This Rig Has Worked 0 Days Without an Accident." There was a job opening here. The driller asked us if we had any rig experience. We said we didn't, yelling over the noise of the engines, aware that we looked like urban nancies. He said he had no use for us, none at all.

We drove past Redcliff, which had been touted in the early years of the century as "the smokeless Pittsburgh." In 1915, a tornado had come through Redcliff, taking the roof off the Ornamental Iron Works, razing the cigar and knitting factories, destroying the town's business core and its spirit. It was now an abandoned-looking suburb of Medicine Hat. We checked into the Corona Hotel and ate in a booth at the Chinese/Canadian Food restaurant. When Chinese men had settled here after the fall of the Manchu dynasty in 1912, they retained their braided pigtails, which signalled allegiance to the emperor. Local drunks cut them off with buck knives and held them up as trophies. They were discriminated against and started their own businesses; laundries, corner stores and restaurants that served a bland facsimile of Chinese food.

Medicine Hat was another one of the western towns that had envisioned itself as a vital hub sixty years earlier. In one year it sent out forty thousand pamphlets advertising its glories. The town had a peculiar booster in the form of Rudyard Kipling, who had written an article about Medicine Hat titled "The Town That Was Born Lucky," which appeared in 1908 in *Collier's* magazine. He said that Medicine Hat would be the "New Ninevah," the ancient capital of Assyria. The city boomed with the same lunatic pride seen across the Prairies and was poised to challenge Calgary and Edmonton, but its real estate boom collapsed by 1915 and the city withered. Now it had a certain antique charm at its core, and was slowly being surrounded by the same strip malls, chain restaurants and car dealerships that circled every town like a predator.

It took three days of driving out to rigs to find jobs as roughnecks. We both finally got on with Whitco, a small outfit digging gas wells. The driller's name was Joe, a man in his forties with a thin blond pompadour and pointed face. He came to pick us up at the hotel for the afternoon shift, poking his head in the door of the lobby and saying, "Pitter-patter let's get at her." His glove compartment had a beer in it and empties rolled against our unscuffed workboots as we drove down the gravel section roads. "It ain't cold but it's wet," Joe said, finishing a beer and throwing the bottle out the window, checking the rear-view mirror to see it smash on the gravel.

The temperature was in the mid-nineties, and even hotter near the engines. I wrestled with drill pipe and slid on the oily steel-mesh floor and lost my hard hat. Joe screamed curses that

were lost in the noise and the diesel smoke from two D-8 cater-
pillar engines blew back over us. The work was confusing and
exhausting and there was no lunch break, a crushing disappointment. Steel parts clanged into place, engines strained, a
chain spun violently, spitting mud. It was still light at 9 p.m.
when a dark storm front approached from the northwest. Six
antelope moved quickly through a farmer's rape crop, spring-
ing in silent, sustained leaps. The air cooled and at ten the rain
hit like an artillery attack, bouncing off the steel in sheets. I assumed we would quit and go home and I was heartbroken
when we stayed on. Medicine Hat is a semi-arid climate with
rattlesnakes and cacti and a dry heat that climbs over 100°F
in July and dips drastically at night. I had been sweltering
through the afternoon and now I was wet through and cold as
a stone.

The shift was supposed to end at midnight but the graveyard crew didn't come out to relieve us. The day-shift driller
lived in a trailer forty yards from the rig and the toolpush sent
me over to wake him. I hammered on the padded door and
a man finally opened it angrily, scratching and blinking. He
was about fifty, with rockabilly sideburns and black hair that
fell into his eyes. I told him we needed an extra hand and
he turned away, swearing. In the kitchen, a pale teenaged girl
with lank hair and thin lips leaned against a counter. She wore
a man's shirt and her bare legs were the colour of skim milk.
Her face was puffy with sleep and she blinked opaquely. There
was a bottle of Black Velvet rye whiskey on the small Formica
table and the sink was filled with dishes. I closed the door and
walked back to the rig. We worked until 2:30 a.m. and then
drove back to town in the rain. I slept for twelve hours.

Over the summer, I listened to country music on the radio
and ate in the glare of the Husky station and flirted with

waitresses. My room was airless and water stained and the bathroom was down the hall. The lobby had faded brocade furniture and old copies of *The Christian Science Monitor*. A television was on constantly. One night I came back from a four-to-midnight shift and saw that the window of the Corona bar had been broken and there was a large bloodstain on the sidewalk by the door.

When I worked the graveyard shift and slept during the day, my room was so hot I had to leave the door open for ventilation. I woke up once at noon in the still suffocating air to see a middle-aged prostitute sitting at the foot of my bed, smoking a cigarette. She was thin and missing some teeth and was wearing a cotton dress and cowboy boots. She asked me if I was looking for a date. Charlie Pride was on someone's radio down the hall. I was soaked with sweat. "I could of just taken your wallet," the woman said to me as part of her sales pitch. I gave her five dollars as a gesture of goodwill and tried to get back to sleep, without success. When the rodeo came to town, the Corona was booked and I was turfed for the duration. Every room in town was gone. I slept fitfully in a small park near the hotel and heard a drunken cowboy and his new friend coupling about thirty feet away the first night.

We moved the rig every three days, punching shallow gas wells, then packing up and driving to the next lease and re-assembling the rig. Rhys went back to Calgary after a month or so and a dozen different misfits replaced him; a British alcoholic who fell into a sump filled with drilling mud, an engineering student from Edmonton who quit partway through the first shift, a lanky outcast recently sprung from a medium-security prison where he was serving time for breaking and entering. He told me his *modus operandi*, which was to rent a large house near the Elbow River in Calgary and throw extravagant parties that played to the Hollywood-ish notions of money the recently wealthy had. While his guests were enjoying the champagne and drugs he or one of his friends broke into their homes, assured they were out. It was like stealing candy from babies, he said.

There was no union in the oilfields. People were hired without any questions asked so it was a famous repository for every kind of wingnut. The derrickman was a short, muscular, good-natured man with a pronounced dent in his forehead. A woman had thrown a pool ball at him from six feet away in a Grande Prairie bar. "Damn near knocked me off my feet," he said.

In August, we drilled a series of holes at Suffield, which had once been touted as a summer resort and was now occupied by a British army base. It was, we were told, British property and we had to go through a security check for every shift. The soldiers took artillery practice, which was a bit unnerving, the shells falling not that far away, though it was impossible to tell from the sound. The soldiers came into town each Saturday night, short lumpy men with military haircuts, all of them dressed like Elton John in short baggy pants, platform shoes and tight shirts. And this in a town where even the mayor wore snap-button cowboy shirts. Their chances of picking up local girls were about the same as their chances of winning the Nobel Prize for chemistry. They lingered in the cabaret at the hotel and got beaten up with frightening regularity by local rig workers. I used to see the soldiers sometimes, walking along the highway into town in those impossible shoes, under the hot sun. One of them had been hit by a truck, a minor diplomatic incident. But I admired their tenacity. Like spawning salmon, they kept returning upstream, battered against the rocks but ever hopeful.

We moved the rig to Saskatchewan and drilled in farmers' fields. The oil company leased an area that was larger than what we actually needed to set up the rig. When the drilling was slow, Joe would get into his pickup truck and flatten all the wheat within the confines of the lease, purely out of meanness. A farmer came out and screamed at him and then went home and came back with a rifle and took a shot at us, which was less exciting than I thought it would be. Joe's wife came out from Calgary, a small woman wearing a white-fringed, fake-leather jacket even in the heat. Her hair was permed and she looked like a whipped dog and after two days she drove away in her Ford Falcon that had one fender painted with primer.

The graveyard shift was the best because it was cool, cold almost, and the sunrise was such a hopeful and dramatic sight. It leaked through the purple strata of cloud hovering over the eastern horizon and for an hour I was grateful for the warmth. On slow drilling nights there would be forty-five minutes before I had to be back on the floor to make a connection, to attach another drill pipe. I could have catnapped but one of the other roughnecks had fallen asleep on a pile of sawdust bags and Joe had spray-painted his boots safety orange. Instead I walked as far away from the rig as possible to escape the noise and lit a cigarette and revelled in the night landscape.

On the way home from the graveyard shift we shot at rattlesnakes that sunned themselves on the road. Once Joe locked up the wheels of his truck on the tail of one and it lay pinned to the asphalt. I thought it was dead but when Joe approached it, it quickly coiled and struck, hitting his cowboy boot. It was fascinating and primitive and I was afraid of it but sickened at its plight. I suggested, conversationally, that we just drive off. Joe got a metal rod out of the back of his truck and beat the snake to death, not stopping until it was unrecognizable. We didn't speak on the drive back to town, listening to the swap meet on the country station where people advertised gently used Maytags.

Joe drank beer all day and smoked plastic-tipped cigarillos that were advertised as "wine-dipped" and had a homemade tattoo on his bicep that read "Marie you bitch." When we walked into the Husky truck stop for breakfast at 8:30 a.m., he would loudly announce to the rest of the sleepy men, "We already done our eight hours." He once told me that anyone who didn't think Merle Haggard was a genius should be whipped. His fifteen-year-old daughter had run away a year earlier and he hadn't heard anything. He slept in his truck most of the time and lived like a mullet. When I told him in mid-September that I was going to quit and go to university, he said, "I don't imagine you'll be too hard to replace."

I came back to the rigs most summers, working for Commonwealth, Hi-Tower, Big Indian, in part because the money was so seductive and in part because the rigs represented a certain view I had of the West, a place of resourcefulness and sad music and melancholy big-haired waitresses, all of which held a lot of appeal for an English major.

———

The success of a western film often resides as much in its villain as in the hero. Without Lee Marvin's swaggering menace, *The Man Who Shot Liberty Valance* would have suffered. *Shane's* prim, miniature Alan Ladd was less interesting than the dark-hearted Jack Palance. Alberta had Pierre Trudeau as the devil-worshipping, black-hatted gunslinger who had stolen the province's God-given resources. Alberta produced eighty-two per cent of the country's oil and gas and sold its oil to Ontario and Quebec at a subsidized price. A local source estimated that over the years Alberta had subsidized central Canada to the tune of $50 billion and Trudeau was the name put to this lost revenue. It helped that his hatchet face had a Mephisto-phelian cast, a smile that could chill a lawyer's blood. It also helped that he had co-opted the image of gunslinger himself. Oil became the moral equivalent of the virginal, gingham-clad schoolteacher, with Trudeau as the ravaging foreigner. A popular bumper sticker read, "This Car Doesn't Brake for Liberals." My parents had campaigned for Trudeau, a lonely job. Western separatist movements sprang up and they even-tually captured twelve per cent of the popular vote before withering. Stan Cox, the president of West-Fed, one of the brief alignments, wept openly when he publicly predicted the effect Trudeau and his policies would have on Cox's grandson.

Despite the fact that the majority of Calgarians hadn't been born in Alberta, residents sang its virtues as if they were a tradition that had been passed down through generations. It was a city of boosters. Our human capacity to attach ourselves to an idea, a place or a leader with such certainty and venom, our need to belong, was manifest. So we were a nation. Our nationalism, like most, was a response to another, larger na-tionalism. We nursed a collective wound.

We were led by Premier Peter Lougheed, a former profes-sional football player who was charismatic, telegenic and had a tough-talking style. He confidently declared, "My con-stituents are Albertans first. They will follow me, they will fol-low me wherever I lead them." He didn't lead us too far, delivering us, after a fourteen-year mandate (1971 to 1985), not to the Promised Land but to another former football playing premier, the affable Don Getty, who watched the provincial government from the golf course with the same sense of mystery a child feels when viewing a passing train. The outsized destiny that Lougheed had espoused waned but we still had an effective enemy. Bumper stickers appeared: "Let the Eastern Bastards Freeze in the Dark." Nations have been built on less.

———

In that first year after I left Winnipeg, I returned regularly, driving across the prairie for eighteen hours, stopping only for gas and take-out food, relieved to be back among old friends and familiar sights if only for a weekend. Inevitably my visits petered out. More often, old friends visited me, coming through town on their way to Banff to ski. Many of my friends moved during the seventies; to Calgary or Vancouver or Toronto where the work was. Winnipeg became the place you left and cherished in ways you didn't when you lived there. When I ran into ex-Winnipeggers we celebrated its unique energy, its sense of community and enviably affordable housing. I romanticized the winters and Jeannie's Bakery and the North End which I had no claim to. Winnipeg had culture and diversity and pastrami while Calgary, like all boom towns, was barbarous.

When I got there, Calgary boasted the youngest population in the country; thirty-seven per cent were between the ages of twenty and thirty-four. Only eleven per cent were over the age of fifty-five, a testament to energy and renewal and change. Winnipeg had made the same boast sixty years earlier and now it was one of the greyest cities in the country, rivalling Victoria, the perennial retirement haven. Winnipeg's population stagnated and the physical city, at least the parts familiar to me, remained strikingly unchanged over the years. Driving downtown from Fort Garry, I went by the same businesses that had always been there, some of them, oddly, in prefab buildings that had the temporary look of Arctic research stations, surprised to still be there. My sister lived in Winnipeg and we sometimes went to Ray & Jerry's, a steak house on Portage Avenue that had the gracious feel of the 1950s, a place where women checked their furs and drank grasshoppers and had their cigarettes lit for them. The interior was dark and modern, designed by my father when he was a young partner in a local architecture firm. It was the kind of place that Frank Sinatra would have gone to if he were in town. We had martinis, shrimp cocktail, steak and cheesecake, sampling the decade that had become, improbably, hip.

My sister still lived in Wildwood Park. The riverside was landscaped now, a pleasant place with the feel of a city park. Gone was the dense growth and prairie grass and any hope of finding a dead body.

I came out one summer and visited my Aunt Jean, still my grandmother's twin at this point, in a convalescent home. I had seen her once in Calgary when she had come to visit the family. Well into her seventies, she sat immobile for hours, smoking, staring out the window into the fir trees that surrounded my parents' house, as though imagining a different life for herself. At the convalescent home, Jean and I sat outside and she smoked my cigarettes and made faces by pulling at the corners of her mouth and wiggling her fingers, a broad parody of a lunatic. It was a sunny day near the end of summer when the heat had lost some of its edge. Jean sang, "Jeepers, creepers, where'd you get those peepers." The grounds were dotted with pairs like us, visitors staring into vacant faces, trying to glimpse something familiar. Many of the older people had a medicated gloom but Jean exuded a goofy joy. Her face was as lined as W.H. Auden's, an unrepentant smoker's face. I was struck once more at how utterly dissimilar Jean and her twin were. There wasn't anything that suggested kinship. Jean's hair was grey and short and dry and institutional. She told me that dancing was all the rage. She leapt from one subject to another; something was exquisite, someone was a dodo, someone else put on airs. There was nothing like a cigarette, she said, taking a deep, exaggerated drag on one of my Player's Lights, holding it up like a model in an advertisement.

It was pleasant in the sun, amid the trees and the manicured grounds. There is something relaxing about conversation with the mad; it takes away the burden of logic. We spoke of English dogs and my great-aunt Edith and golf and lunch meat. I remembered seeing movies with Jean at the Garry Cinema, *Pinocchio*, and mentioned this and we chatted about movies a little. She said that George Sanders was such a snob, an actor who had married two different Gabor sisters (Zsa Zsa and Magda) and was dead, a suicide. I recalled that I had come to her house one January with a goldfish in a plastic bag full of water that I had bought at the pet department in Eaton's. I had to transfer buses at Stafford and after waiting outside in minus 20° F weather for ten long minutes holding my new pet, I feared for its life. I ran the ten blocks to my grandmother's but she wasn't home so I went to the next street, to Jean. She remembered the goldfish. "How is he?" she asked. Flushed down a toilet fifteen years ago. "What was his name—Alfie something?" Jean pointed out her colleagues on the lawn around us, most of them immobile in their wheelchairs, and offered a few unkind words. Eventually, hospital attendants circulated like waiters, rounding everyone up. Jean and I waved goodbye. It was the last time I saw her.

Jim Mainland, the last surviving brother, ended up in the same home as Jean. He was still dapper in his eighties. He flirted with nurses and tried to escape, thinking he was heading home to Fort Garry, dressed like Edward, the enigmatic Prince of Wales. The hospital staff took away all of Jim's shoes finally, a mortal blow to a dandy, but he escaped once more, stepping gingerly through the March snow in his argyle socks, heading south to where he once lived, like a migrating bird. The police picked him up, wild-eyed and unconcerned, a diminutive man stunned by old age.

My grandmother, her secret now revealed, was in West Park Manor on Grant Avenue, on the way out to the zoo. Without the Eaton's white sale, the bingo games, the United Church and the annual repainting of the house, her life was quickly winnowed. She and her new friends did aerobics in wheelchairs, arms swaying like branches. When I returned to Winnipeg to visit, I noticed distinct, if incremental changes. There was a period of hallucination; reports of rabbits on the roof of the building, rabbits the size of ponies. There was a whimsical phase, where she laughed like a schoolgirl.

On a day when my sister, mother and I all visited, she complained of recent thefts. Someone was stealing her clothes, she said, though this wasn't true. A very old woman walked by the open door to my grandmother's room in a medicated shuffle. It took her fifteen seconds to negotiate the three feet and we watched politely and returned her mad smile.

"She's a detective," Georgie said.

"She's a detective?" my sister asked.

My grandmother nodded. "She's not very famous though. Too slow."

The information that came to her dwindled. There were fewer visitors; friends were dying and family members had moved to other cities. Television became an abstraction and reading too difficult. She was left with her fracturing memory, turning to herself for distraction, though she kept her benign nature through this gentle downward spiral. She became unburdened in some ways, unembarrassed when I lifted her out of the wheelchair in the bathroom.

There were several photo albums in her room and I gravitated to them when I visited her alone. They were the same ones we had looked through twenty-five years earlier at her kitchen table. Now it was our most effective means of communication; I turned the pages and she put names to the faces and identified the context.

There was a photograph of Georgie and Jean as five-year-olds, dressed in identical flowered dresses, their hair drawn up on one side with ribbon. A later photograph of them, a studio portrait taken when they were eleven, shows them still dressed identically, this time in dark tunics with lace collars and high boots. Their hair was cut and combed in the same style and their heads were framed by absurdly large bows. The family was still emphatically presenting them as twins, even as their physical differences flowered past the point of credibility. My grandmother was heavier and taller, her features less refined. In the portrait she looks defiant; neither is smiling.

It was the photographs of Detroit that Georgie lingered on. Perhaps it was in Detroit that she had been happiest, truly an immigrant, free to remake herself, away from the tangled family, her history at bay. In those photos she looks like a modern woman, the only time she could make that claim.

Meanwhile, my new country was crumbling. Nineteen eighty-two was the year when the panic quietly set in, when the statistics began to betray us. There was a surplus of oil and the price fell drastically. Unemployment in Alberta went from 3.8 per cent to 10.2 per cent within two years. Farm debt rose to crisis proportions and we led the nation in housing foreclosures. Where vacancy rates had approached zero in Calgary in 1981, two years later landlords were offering free trips to Las Vegas to anyone who would sign a lease. Of the eighty oil firms listed on the Toronto Stock Exchange in 1980, only forty-two remained in 1986. We had become used to the idea that the future would be bigger and more profitable than the present, which for more than a decade, it had. Everyone seemed to be leveraged and the collapse was particularly loud. In the classified section of the *Calgary Herald*, houses were advertised for sale with all their furniture and two cars. As it had been in ascent, the city was again defined by numbers, often delivered with the same kind of one-upmanship, a sense of gruesome pride in the sheer scale of the bust. Everyone claimed to see it coming. Certain failures became emblematic. People talked about the extraordinary rise and calamitous decline of Dome Petroleum as if it were a neighbour.

When I walked downtown from my apartment one day, there were chalk outlines drawn on the sidewalk, like police outlines at a murder scene. They were, I guessed, a graffiti artist's reference to the reported suicide rate among oil executives, although I don't know if many actually leapt to their deaths. The windows in those buildings were all sealed. Inside one of the outlines was a limerick.

A marketing man name of Hoyle
Came west to make money in oil

He mortgaged his home
Put his money in Dome
And leapt to his death like a pumpkin.

My apartment building which made the unsubstantiated claim of being the oldest in the city, was only a few blocks from where Thomas Mawson's watercolour drawings for his Paris-on-the-Prairie urban plan had been found. Ralph Klein was now mayor, an *uber* common man among common men, an ex-journalist and tavern habitué. As a reporter he had been a rumpled champion of the little guy, decrying the blockbusting tactics of the developers and lamenting the razing of neighbourhoods. As a politician, he quickly grasped that Calgary was a company town. "In our efforts to make the commercial core a more human place," Klein said in a speech to the South Calgary Rotary Club, "we must be careful to avoid the trap of putting sunlight ahead of commerce: sunlight does not turn the wheels of our factory."

That image was an interesting one. The city's downtown resembled a factory in many ways. It was functional and blunt and uninterested in aesthetics and it emptied at the end of every day. There was a dearth of sunlight and public space and an abiding philosophy that commerce is its own reward. What was less clear was what the factory now produced. By 1984, Calgary had twenty-five million square feet of vacant office space. More than any single product, it was producing a sense of existential dread. When the city was booming, its joyless core was justified. Without money and the mood of wilful optimism that had sustained its spaces, it became oppressive. The high-rises that skirted Calgary's zoning laws had looked like progress when oil was edging toward thirty-five dollars a barrel, but now they looked like the grim souvenirs that soldiers brought home from a war.

I had come to view bumper stickers as a barometer of the public mood, the graffiti of the middle class. A new one appeared: "Please, Lord, send me another oil boom and I promise not to piss this one away." There were dire predictions: that the province's oil reserves would dry up within forty years; that the price of benchmark West Texas Intermediate crude was going to crater yet again; that the multi-billion dollar Heritage Fund that Peter Lougheed had created had been raided and there wasn't enough left to buy a new Ford half-ton. For three years running there was a net out-migration, Maritimers going back east to weather this economic storm among family, Ontarians seeking work at home. The city emptied but it became more humane, more of a community, more like Winnipeg. It no longer looked to the future, which held little sustenance. It huddled against itself for comfort.

My visits to my grandmother were erratic, usually more than a year apart. So each visit found a new version of her. When I arrived she was often in the common room, sitting around a table with others, almost all of them women. Some were slack-faced and blank, a few twinkled madly. There were women who were mentally hale, and coveted my grandmother's visitor. Almost all of them were thin, their clothes pale, their hair white, giving an impression of mummification, the flesh already inching toward dust. There was the faint smell of something like baby powder. On one visit each of the women had a plastic glass filled with juice and a piece of cake in front of her, like a kindergarten class. It was someone's birthday, which can seem a mockery to a ninety-year-old woman infantalized by disease. The birthday girl seemed vaguely proud though and they sang "Happy Birthday," prompted by attendants.

In later visits, my grandmother recognized me in a generic way; she knew there was a connection, but she often didn't know what it was. She sometimes mistook me for my father. She thought her mother was alive and younger than her. Or she thought my mother was younger than me. Others were among the disappeared, gone from her memory or stored in some place she no longer had access to. I couldn't imagine what she saw, what shape her thoughts took. History might have looked like a garage sale to her, familiar items strewn around the lawn, a few treasures. Huge chunks of her life had been jettisoned, it seemed. What do we keep, that which is most precious or that which is most painful? One of the few things that was left at the end was her illegitimacy. It was what was at her core.

On my last visit to my grandmother she began a stream-of-consciousness monologue. "They're hoodlums," she said. "The Rosses. They're all fussy hoodlums." In her mind she returned to the Gladstone schoolyard and imitated those who had taunted her more than eighty years earlier. "*You're* not a Ross, *you're* not a Ross," she said in that mocking cadence familiar to every schoolchild. So the children had known. She hadn't escaped her secret by crossing an ocean. Everyone had always known and she carried this knowledge still, like a scar.

The afternoon sun came in the window of Georgie's room and it was pleasant in the warmth, hypnotic. She enacted familial slights and crimes, a cathartic sprint through the central fact of her life, her illegitimacy. Ghosts were revived and animated amid the plaid blankets and institutional furniture. Below us, in the lobby, the unfortunately named Mr. Young, who had greeted me like Jimmy Durante when I came in, was playing the piano with arthritic fingers and I could hear the optimistic bounce of a pre-war song.

I stared at my grandmother, bound by the wheelchair, a saintly smile, her rounded and spotted cheeks, the dark hairs on her lip, her lives contained within her like Russian dolls. Perhaps senility is simply the final merging of the private life we all carry inside us with the facade we present to the world. She had trouble moving, and trouble thinking, and was emptying herself gradually so that God could find a place within. As a child I had once dreamed that my grandmother was dead. It woke me up and I wept for an hour. I was unsettled for several days, a knot in my stomach, worried that it was a premonition. She used to wait around corners with a hairbrush, grabbing me and attempting to brush my hair with a hundred strokes, which she held as the optimum. When I stayed with her as a teenager, she would ask me if I knew any nice girls. I did but I was looking for the other kind.

To be human means to be able to feel at home somewhere, with your own kind. My own kind had evolved from Calvinists staring at God from their perch on the northern Scottish coast. They had left the homeland to forge a new society and in the process help obliterate the existing native culture. We had wandered away from God though not with haste or malice. We had built a family and helped build a nation as a defence against loneliness. My grandmother had left Scotland when she was six but she was still connected to the country in a visceral way.

"We had the Ford, Jim didn't, he had the other one, as big as a train," she said, lost in remembrance. "He loved that car though. The houses were huge, so grand, oh my. Don always liked a chocolate cake." My grandmother mentioned the pub she had been to in Scotland, surprised not to see the devil sitting there, playing cards and eating peas with a knife. They went to visit a relative, Mrs. MacKay, up in the Highlands and when my grandmother asked where the ladies room was, Mrs. MacKay escorted her to the front door and pointed to the hills covered in heather. "There's not a soul to see you," she said.

My grandmother recalled the 1950 flood. "The water came up the ditch, rising from the river, up toward Johnny Soviak's service station, it came to swallow the city, an inch every day, you heard it on the radio. But we stayed dry. High ground, Don said, build your house on high ground. We prayed in church. The university was gone, underwater, and those people by the river, goodness the water sneaking in." She quoted a psalm. *God is our refuge and our strength, a very present help in trouble. Therefore we will not fear though the earth should change though the mountains shake in the heart of the sea; though its waters roar and foam.*

And she remembered Jean, her twin. "I told her but she wouldn't listen. Burning up, burning in bed. Don't smoke I said. You know, but she had to, a fire that went up and up. She had to. It was always her way. Sitting up against the headboard, propped up like the Queen of England, reading a magazine, smoke so thick. She took the Midnight Special to Winnipeg Beach you know. Dancing all night in that pavilion, the boys following her like ducks. Kissing in the seat. But the fire took everything. The house burned down, what could be saved? You couldn't see for the smoke."

Perhaps Jean had been my grandmother's tormentor, holding their secret like a sword, always with the upper hand. Georgie had been bound by their common lie for almost a century while Jean seemed bound by nothing. And now she was consumed in an imaginary purging fire.

"Catherine was here, visiting," my grandmother said, referring to her mother, her sister. "I don't think she's well. Poor thing. How will she manage? The prices these days." The writer Isak Dinesen said that all sorrows can be borne if you put them into a story. Here were my grandmother's sorrows, released finally in this fractured narrative.

"And father," she asked me, finally. "Do you have any news about him. He must be getting on, he'd be, what, almost eighty now I suppose." Both her fathers had been dead for more than fifty years.

My grandmother died not long after this, on August 28, 1989. She was ninety. I was in Winnipeg at the time, on business, staying with my sister, when we got a phone call at 6 a.m. from the nursing home telling us that she had passed on peacefully, as they say, though I wasn't convinced. The service was held at the Fort Garry United Church, and she lay among the mourners, unburdened finally in that bright space.

Epilogue

ASCENSION

IN DECEMBER, I made a final visit to Scotland. I had expected the weather to be catastrophic and was pleasantly surprised. Evening came early and Glasgow was wet and cold. I drove north in another fluorescent car, alone on the road past Ullapool. The sky was clear and pale and the morning looked like the dawn of creation against the settled rock. Scourie was closed, effectively. The bed and breakfasts were shut down, the Scourie Lodge done for the season. The hotel, with its restaurant and bar, alas, was closed. Some of the residents had gone south for the season and the village was empty. Mrs. Macdonald of the Minch View Bed and Breakfast kindly agreed to take me in. In the evening, before dinner, she gave me an ounce of Scotch in a water glass to take away the chill.

The landscape seemed more spectacular in December, limned in greater relief against the winter sky and empty village. Simon Schama wrote that in dramatic landscapes we seek compensation for our mortality. Perhaps it was this quality that the Romantic painters had sought to express when they came to Scotland with their easels, spurred by Sir Walter Scott's precise and loving descriptions. The land is so extreme. I was forty-three, mortal now for three years by current standards, and the land opened up for me like the upward swirls of a Turner painting, the details blurred in favour of a larger purpose. The season and weather and mood of isolation depressed me slightly. I missed my family with a physical pang.

I went to the Sunday service at the Free Presbyterian Church in Scourie. There were nine of us in the small space; Robert Ross, his wife, his sister, his two sons and a few others. We were dressed in the same dark, simply-cut clothes that would have been worn a century ago. I sat six rows from the back and was surprised when everyone occupied the pews behind me. I felt vulnerable, caught in a crossfire between the minister's words and the silent stare of the congregation.

Robert Ross took his place in the pew with his family. There was a minister now, elevated in a slightly grand pulpit, his face business-like. Directly below him a more modest pulpit mimicked the form. A stout man sat there with a Bible in his hand. He had a full, reddened face, eighty-two years old yet robust and vital. He led the congregation in the singing of the psalms. *Behold, I was brought forth in iniquity, and in sin did my mother conceive me.* He had a startling, rich baritone and the first bar was sung by him alone. The congregation joined in and the voices found an emphatic harmony, then spun away from one another like fighters after a bitter exchange. A woman keened. Certain voices wandered from the undulations of the melody, investigating separate keys, then returned forcefully. The sound was oddly soulful, a raw sound that had the bleak insistence of mourning.

The minister prayed for the destruction of the papacy and the fall of Rome. He hoped that those who were deluded and deceived by other faiths would see their error, and called for a day when no man would have to tell his neighbour the News; the world would be Free Presbyterian. Liberation would come to those who accepted God's gift of grace. They would experience a happiness that was indescribable. Heaven would hold some surprises; people we expected to be there would be absent. Others who seemed unlikely candidates would get in. This was the closest thing to optimism he afforded.

Robert Ross and this small group were at the end of something, an impending millennial casualty. In Canada, the Winnipeg church was long gone and the only surviving member, Mrs. Steedman, attended the Dutch Reform church service with some reservations. I had visited her in Winnipeg, at her prim apartment overlooking a shopping centre. She told me that something was missing in my life and I conceded that that was possible, even likely. You haven't accepted the Lord as your saviour, she said. There is still time. She went on in that vein for a while then finally said, "I didn't mean to preach," though she did. In Vancouver, the Free Presbyterian Church still existed in theory, though the last bitter split had left it with a single member. In Chesley, Ontario, the congregation consisted of a lone Dutch family. This was the sum of Canada's remaining Free Presbyterians, maybe ten people who were embracing a previous century even as a new one was approaching.

When my grandmother was here for the last time in 1905, the church was full. She was cramped, sitting among her new brothers and sisters on the hard wooden bench, harboured by the Ross family and isolated within it, her mother in South Africa, her father a ghost.

Outside, the hills had a light dusting of snow and the wind pushed at the corrugated iron walls of the church, making a low hum against the crenellations. There is no greater evil than sin, the minister told them, for original sin is the foundation upon which all other sins are built. In the small crowded room, Georgie's sin shone like a beacon. She stared at the varnished wood that contained them and imagined that it was snowing inside the church, the flakes swirling among the dark suits, its lightness and absence of colour bleaching the air. The snowflakes settled on the rough floor and on her thick black wool skirt. Georgie's feet dangled and she became weightless in the white air, carried aloft by the soft currents, out of the iron building the colour of old coins, buoyant above the landscape that itself argued for creation, its gnarled trees and rough contours losing definition as she moved beyond the yearnings of her mother and silences that filled the house, past the razor tongues of schoolchildren, the tended garden of the neat brick Winnipeg house, bleached white sheets moving stiffly in the approach of a prairie thunderstorm the colour of a bruise, the Johnson's polish gleaming on the hardwood floor, the urgent scream of the kettle, tea sipped from the cup that was a gift, resting on the Formica in the newly painted kitchen, spotless, sitting alone with her Christian doubt and the earnest fear etched with daily use, talking with Jean, the words burdened by secrets, laughing with her husband before the arguments and the retreat to silence, her daughter arriving and finally a private perfect love, outside the reach of history, moving upward still, floating weightlessly now in the blank air that enveloped her, held her, stole her away from the stone hills and the dread weight of blood.

LIST OF ILLUSTRATIONS

Except where noted these photographs are courtesy of the Gillmor, Ross and Mainland families.

PAGE 1   Christmas dinner, 1962, author in foreground

15   The "twins," Georgina (seated) and Jean Ross

37   George Ivel, Georgina's natural father

51   Georgie on her only trip back to Scotland, at Fanagmore

67   The Free Presbyterian Church at Scourie

101   Christina Mainland, with sons (from left) James, Thomas and Donald

131   Bessie and Lachlan Ross

161   My grandfather, Donald Ross, plying his trade

175   Jean and Les Barratt on their wedding day

213   Wildwood Park at the peak of the 1950 flood

237   A detail of Thomas Mawson's grand urban plan, 1913, courtesy of the University of Alberta Archives

269   Georgina Mainland with my mother, Donna

ACKNOWLEDGEMENTS

In his book *The Labyrinth of Solitude* Octavio Paz wrote, "The question of origins is the central secret of our anxiety, and our anguish." Exploring those origins breeds another kind of anxiety but this path was smoothed by a number of people. The most valuable resource for a book that deals with family is, unsurprisingly, the family. My parents, Douglas and Donna Gillmor, acted as researchers, fact-checkers, archivists and photo editors as well as unfailing supporters. It was Doug Pepper at Random House who suggested I write this book, or at least a book something like it. My mandate was slightly vague, a comforting and frightening thing for a writer, and an act of faith on the publisher's part. I would like to thank Anne Collins, my editor and long-time guardian angel, for her doggedness and elegant touch.

Parts of this book first appeared in different form in *Saturday Night* magazine. A memoir about my grandmother titled "Georgie's Secret" (February 1996) and a piece on the oil fields titled "Working" (June 1993) were both shepherded into print by Dianna Symonds. I was first sent to Shetland in 1993 by Cathrin Bradbury, who was then editor of the *Globe and*

Mail's long departed (and lamented) *Destinations* magazine, and the chapter on Shetland owes its genesis to that piece.

My book was intended as a personal investigation rather than a work of scholarship. Still, even non-scholarly investigations rely on a staggering number of sources. Of the dozens of books, articles, journals and archives I consulted, several bear special mention. John Prebble's two standards, *Culloden* and *The Highland Clearances,* offered an invaluable Scottish overview, as did John Macleod's *Highlanders: A History of the Gaels.* Fintan O'Toole's article, "Imagining Scotland," which appeared in *Granta,* was a great help. Robert Ross's hospitality and his generous gift of the *History of the Free Presbyterian Church of Scotland* were much appreciated. I am indebted to the staff and archives at the Inverness public library, which became a haven, and to the Shetland archives in Lerwick.

In the New World, R. Douglas Francis's *Images of the West* was a constant companion. And I relied on Alan Artibise's *Winnipeg: An Illustrated History*; two of J. M. Bumstead's works, *Floods of the Centuries* and a book he edited, *The Collected Writings of Lord Selkirk*; as well as *The Best Possible Face: L. B. Foote's Winnipeg* by Doug Smith and Michael Olito. Alexander Ross's doom-laden but oddly optimistic journal, *The Red River Settlement: Rise, Progress and Present State* proved to be an indispensable document. The Provincial Archives of Manitoba were a rich source and I am grateful to the helpful staff and also to the special collections at the University of Guelph. Among the various Detroit references, Robert Conot's book *American Odyssey* stands out.

I would also like to thank the University of Calgary archives for the photographs of Thomas Mawson's paintings, Dian Freeman for her genealogical and photographic help as well as the Canada Council for their generous assistance, which made the several visits to Scotland possible. Thanks to Jan Whitford, at Westwood Creative Artists, for her support and advice. And finally, thank-you to my wife Grazyna Krupa for her patience, encouragement, and delicate reading of the manuscript.

Donald Ross MacKay Gillmor, Toronto, 1999